How to Do *Everything* with

Mac OS X Tiger™

Kirk McElhearn

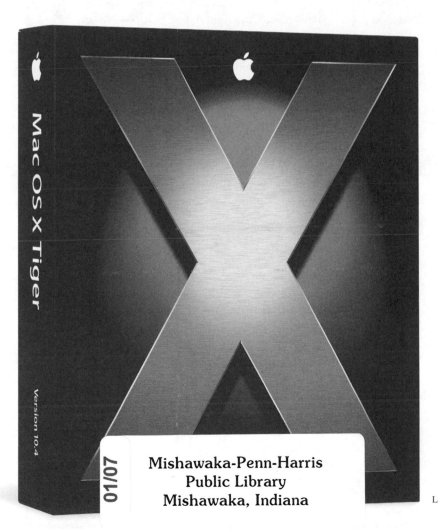

McGraw-Hill/Osborne

New York   Chicago   San Francisco   Lisbon
London   Madrid   Mexico City   Milan   New Delhi
San Juan   Seoul   Singapore   Sydney   Toronto

The McGraw·Hill Companies

McGraw-Hill/Osborne
2100 Powell Street,10th Floor
Emeryville, California 94608
U.S.A.

To arrange bulk purchase discounts for sales promotions, premiums, or fund-raisers, please contact **McGraw-Hill**/Osborne at the above address.

How to Do Everything with Mac® OS X Tiger™

1234567890 CUS CUS 0198765

ISBN 0-07-226158-7

Acquisitions Editor	Roger Stewart
Project Editor	Emily Rader
Acquisitions Coordinator	Agatha Kim
Technical Editor	James Bucanek
Copy Editors	Emily Rader, Robert Campbell
Proofreader	Andrea Fox
Indexer	Rebecca Plunkett
Composition	International Typesetting & Composition
Illustration	International Typesetting & Composition
Series Design	Michelle Galicia and Peter F. Hancik
Cover Series Design	Dodie Shoemaker

This book was composed with Adobe® InDesign®/MAC.

About the Author

Kirk McElhearn is a writer, journalist, and translator, and has written or cowritten more than a dozen books on the Macintosh, Mac OS X, the iPod, iTunes, digital music, and more. Kirk has been a Mac user since 1991, when he bought his first Mac, a PowerBook 100. As a journalist, he is a regular contributor to *Macworld* magazine, *TidBITS, iLounge*, and *Technology and Society Book Reviews*. A native New Yorker, he has lived in France for more than two decades, and currently lives in Guillestre, a village in the French Alps.

Kirk opines about Macs, the iPod, iTunes, books, music, and more on his web site, Kirkville, http://www.mcelhearn.com. You can contact him at kirk@mcelhearn.com.

About the Technical Editor

James Bucanek is a professional software engineer with a long history of developing products for Apple computers, starting with the first local area network for the original Apple][. James spends his days writing software and trying to keep the hot Arizona sun from overheating his G5. He can be contacted at james@twilightandbarking.com.

Contents

Acknowledgments

A book may only have one name on the cover, but dozens of people work behind the scenes, contributing in different ways to make it as good as possible. I'd first like to thank Todd Stauffer, who created the *How to Do Everything* series, and Roger Stewart, my editor, for keeping it so successful. Well-deserved thanks go to my agent Neil Salkind for being a matchmaker and helping get this from proposal to final book.

Many people at Osborne worked on this project, and I'd like to thank them all: Agatha Kim, the Acquisitions Coordinator, kept things flowing; Emily Rader and Bob Campbell, the copy editors, saw to it that the text reads smoothly; Andrea Fox, the proofreader, spotted the tiny lapses and made me look good; ITC handled illustrations and composition; Pattie Lee did the cover; and Lee Healy wrote the cover copy. Special thanks to Emily Rader, the project editor who oversaw the copyediting, query review, proofreading, and indexing stages of this project; Emily is the only person I worked with on this book who is in the same time zone as I am.

I'd especially like to thank James Bucanek, the book's technical editor, who checked all the technical details and shared his take on some of Tiger's features. I've worked with James on several books, and I'm very fortunate to have someone of such deep knowledge of the Mac to prop me up and point out discrepancies.

I'd like to thank Mike Shebanek of Apple Computer for his assistance during the Tiger beta campaign. Mike was a great help, answering some nitpicky questions as the operating system went through the beta testing process.

I'd also like to thank Rob Griffiths and Mark Willan for the many chats we've had over iChat, where they both helped me resolve problems and iron out details.

Finally, many thanks to Marie-France and Perceval for their help on the home front.

Introduction

Having used a Macintosh computer since 1991 and since the advent of Apple's System 7, the initial release of Mac OS X was quite a surprise. It took a while to get used to the major changes that Apple had wrought in this operating system, but the rewards were many: a more attractive, easier-to-use interface; a more stable operating system; and the solidity of Mac OS X's Unix underpinnings.

Mac OS X 10.4, code named Tiger, is a mature operating system; and many changes and refinements have been made since the first version of Mac OS X. Apple has been especially attentive to user feedback in improving the interface and adding features to the operating system (or in same cases restoring features lost since Mac OS 9).

Tiger is the fourth major upgrade of Mac OS X and by far the most satisfying version of this operating system. Tiger introduces many new features and functions that make working with your Mac even easier: Spotlight, which lets you find anything; Dashboard, which keeps useful information at your fingertips; Automator, which lets anyone become a programmer; and all the stuff that's under the hood, which makes Tiger more stable, more responsive, and more reliable than all the previous versions of Mac OS X.

In this book I'll tell you all about Mac OS X 10.4. You'll learn how to work with the Finder and customize it to fit your own style. You'll discover how to work with files, folders, and windows, and how to save time in the most common tasks. I'll show you how to surf the Web easily with Apple's Safari web browser, how to use Mail to manage your e-mail, and how to keep in touch with your friends using iChat.

You'll see how easy it is to manage your personal information with Apple's programs, such as iCal, its calendar program; Address Book, its contact manager; and iSync, which lets you synchronize your information with another Mac.

I'll tell you about printing, faxing, connecting computers on a network, and keeping your Mac in good shape. I'll also talk about computer security and tell you about adding hardware to your Mac, such as mice, keyboards, external disks, and more.

Mac OS X also shines in the area of digital music, and I'll show you how to get the most out of iTunes and how to use your iPod.

After reading this book, you'll see how easy it is to use Mac OS X and how much you can do with this powerful operating system. If you're new to the Mac, you'll find out how to do everything you need with Mac OS X. If you've just upgraded from Mac OS 9 or earlier, you'll see how easy it is to get up to speed with this new operating system. And even if you're a seasoned Mac user, you'll find lots of new features and functions that will make your computer use more efficient and more fun.

This book was created on a 933 MHz G4 iBook, with the assistance of an aging 400 MHz iMac. I used Microsoft Word for writing and reviewing, Snapz Pro X for screen shots, and Graphic Converter for touching up illustrations. I used Inspiration to create the book's outline, Mail to manage my correspondence, Circus Ponies' NoteBook to organize my tasks, and iChat to keep in touch with some of the people involved with the book. Finally, iTunes provided a soundtrack as I was working, playing The Grateful Dead, moe., Bill Evans, Bach, Handel, Schubert, Mahler, The Durutti Column, Coldplay, Brian Eno, Harold Budd, and much more.

Part I

Get Started with Mac OS X

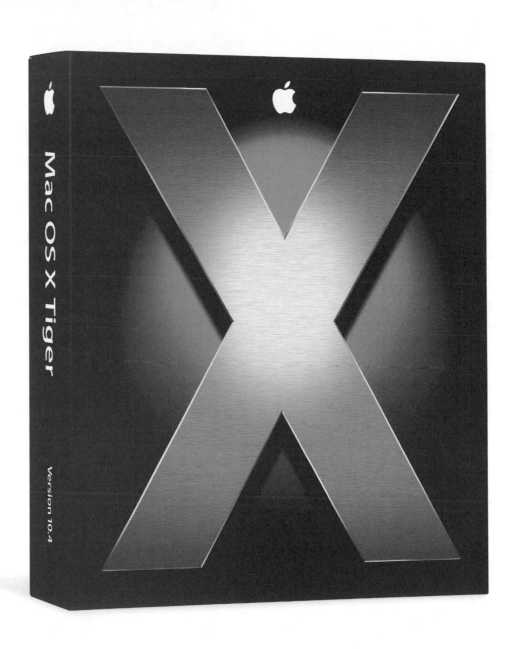

Chapter 1

What's New in Tiger

Mac OS X Tiger

Version 10.4

How to...

- Discover new features in Tiger
- Meet Spotlight, Dashboard, Safari RSS, and Automator
- Find out about enhancements to Mac OS X applications

Mac OS X 10.4, or Tiger, is the fourth major version of Apple's Mac OS X. Released in May 2004, Tiger includes "more than 200 new features," as Apple's marketing material says. But Apple didn't exaggerate—there are many differences between Panther (Mac OS X 10.3) and Tiger, and the changes Apple has wrought on its operating system are profound and will have a great effect on the way you work.

If you're upgrading from an earlier version of Mac OS X, this chapter will give you an overview of what's new in Tiger. I'll go over the main changes in Tiger and tell you how they'll make you more productive. I'll also cross-reference many of these changes to the appropriate chapters in this book.

Think of this chapter as an introduction to whet your appetite for Tiger; you'll see what awaits you in Mac OS X 10.4. If you already have upgraded, you may discover some features you hadn't noticed yet. But in both cases, this chapter will give you a glimpse of some of the compelling features that make Tiger an excellent operating system.

Find Anything with Spotlight

One of the profoundest changes in Tiger is Spotlight, the system-wide search technology that lets you find anything on your Mac. With several ways to search your Mac—the Spotlight menu, the Spotlight window, search fields in Finder windows, and search fields in Open and Save dialogs—you'll never lose a file again.

Spotlight's depth and breadth are astounding; your Mac indexes every file it holds, looking not only for filenames, but also for the contents of your files and for keywords.

When searching in the Finder, you can use smart folders to save your searches, and run a new search simply by opening a folder. Searches can be simple (all your PDF files, for example) or complex (all documents in your home folder that you've opened in the past week). Smart folders use the same indexes as Spotlight to search in every nook and cranny on your Mac.

I look at Spotlight in depth in Chapter 5, showing you how to find anything, how to create and save smart folders, and more.

Get Quick Info with Dashboard

You often need some quick information, and until now you've probably used the Web to find it: when you need a stock quote, you go to a financial web site; when you want to look up a phone number, you go to your local Yellow Pages web site; and for the weather, your local TV station or newspaper can provide that information. There are other tasks you may need to do occasionally but not want to open an application to perform: make simple calculations, convert miles to kilometers, or see this month's calendar.

Dashboard is here to help make all these simple tasks, and many others, available at your fingertips. By pressing a single key on your keyboard, you'll see a full array of *widgets*, or mini-applications, each designed to do just one thing, but to do it efficiently and attractively.

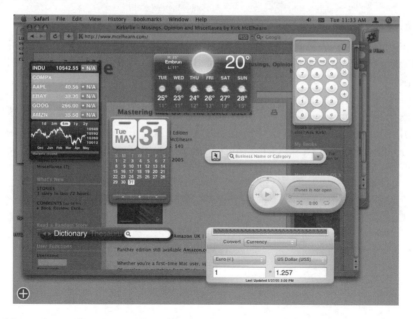

Dashboard comes with dozens of widgets to perform simple tasks, and when you're finished, just click your mouse anywhere on the background and they whisk away, letting you get back to work. In addition, you can download hundreds of other widgets to help you work—and play—efficiently. You'll find out all about Dashboard in Chapter 3.

View News Headlines with Safari RSS

The Web is a great place to get news, but it can take you a long time to check all the web sites you want to read, looking for which stories are new. Safari's new RSS (Really Simple Syndication) feature lets you get the news you want in a jiffy, viewing only headlines and story summaries so you can quickly choose which stories you want to read in full.

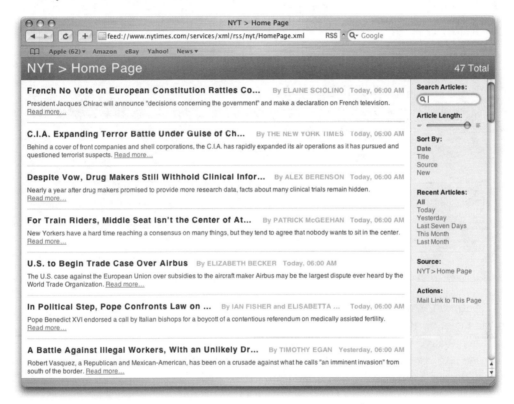

Safari comes with dozens of RSS *feeds,* or URLs, so you can get your daily news by just selecting a bookmark, and you can add RSS feeds for any other site that offers them (many web sites provide their news like this) by adding a new bookmark. Find out about Safari and RSS in Chapter 10.

Automate Actions with Automator

Not everyone wants to program computers, learning arcane languages and spending long nights trying to debug their code. But why not take advantage of the fact that computers can automate your repetitive actions, saving you lots of time? Apple has created Automator, a simple way for any user to combine common actions into *workflows* and run them with a single click. You don't need to know anything about programming; you just drag and drop preset actions into the order you want.

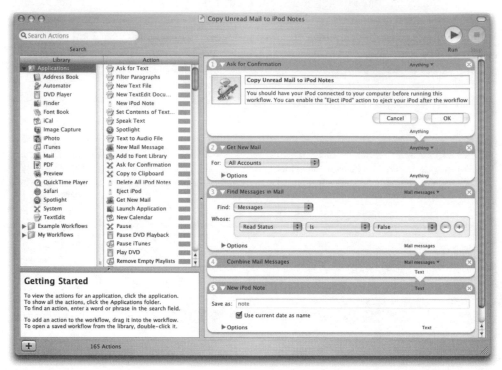

Automator workflows can be single-step actions that allow you to simplify basic tasks or multistep, complex actions that get your Mac to perform many actions to save you time. With this type of programming for nonprogrammers, anyone can create their own time-saving workflows and have more time to enjoy life. Chapter 5 tells you all about Automator.

Application Enhancements

Mac OS X has many more enhancements in the various applications included with the operating system. From the Finder to QuickTime, from AddressBook to Mail, Tiger has plenty of important new features. Here's a brief overview of some of them:

- *Mail,* the e-mail application included with Mac OS X, has a new interface, making mailboxes easier to manage, and Spotlight searches let you find mail messages in seconds. Mail's smart mailboxes help you better organize your e-mail, displaying messages from specific senders, with selected subjects, and more. (See Chapter 10.)

1

■ *iCal,* Apple's calendar and to-do application, has been streamlined and offers better management of To Do items, as well as Spotlight searching to find your appointments and tasks when you need to. You can search for events and To Do items within iCal, but also with Spotlight using its menu or window. (See Chapter 15.)

■ *Address Book* lets you search for any of your contacts using Spotlight technology, and the Address Book Dashboard widget lets you find contact info quickly. As with iCal, you can search for your Address Book information from the Spotlight menu or window, as well as from within the program. (See Chapter 15.)

■ *Preview,* Apple's tool for viewing images and PDF files, now lets you annotate PDFs, making comments you can share with others, and offers many improvements in display of graphics files. (See Chapter 13.)

■ *TextEdit,* Apple's "simple" text editor, now lets you create tables, lets you use lists with numbers, letters, or bullets, and it lets you save your documents in either Rich Text Format or a Word-compatible .doc format. (See Chapter 13.)

■ *iChat AV,* the text, audio, and video chat software included with Mac OS X, now lets you carry out multiperson audio and video chats. You can also show your buddies what you're listening to on iTunes and work with Jabber accounts. (See Chapter 10.)

■ *Safari,* Apple's web browser, now lets you view PDF files directly in its interface; if you click a PDF file link on a web page, you don't have to download the file and then open it in Preview. It's RSS features (see earlier in this chapter) give you access to all the news that you can digest. And you can save an entire web page—the text, images, and layout—in a web archive, to view offline or send to others. (See Chapter 10.)

■ *User accounts* now allow parental controls, so you can keep your children safe from many of the dangers of the Internet. You can specify which web sites they can view, who they can chat with, and who they can exchange e-mail with. You can also limit users to specific applications, to make sure they don't fiddle with programs they don't need. (See Chapter 8.)

■ *Finder,* the heart of Mac OS X, provides enhancements across the board, with better searching (using Spotlight technology), smart folders, burn folders, and more. (See Chapters 3, 4, and 5.)

Moving Ahead

As you can see, Mac OS X 10.4, or Tiger, is a feature-rich upgrade to an already powerful operating system. With the many applications Apple includes with Tiger, your Mac is more versatile than ever.

I haven't mentioned the many changes Apple has made under the hood or the many subtle interface changes that make working with Tiger a pleasure: Apple has improved graphics display and made lots of tiny changes to make the overall interface simpler and clearer. With a strong focus on improving your access to files, folders, and applications, and with plenty of security enhancements to protect you from the dangers of the Internet, Tiger is a big leap forward in many ways.

So, read on to find out more about these new features and to get the most out of Tiger.

Chapter 2

Your First Steps with Mac OS X

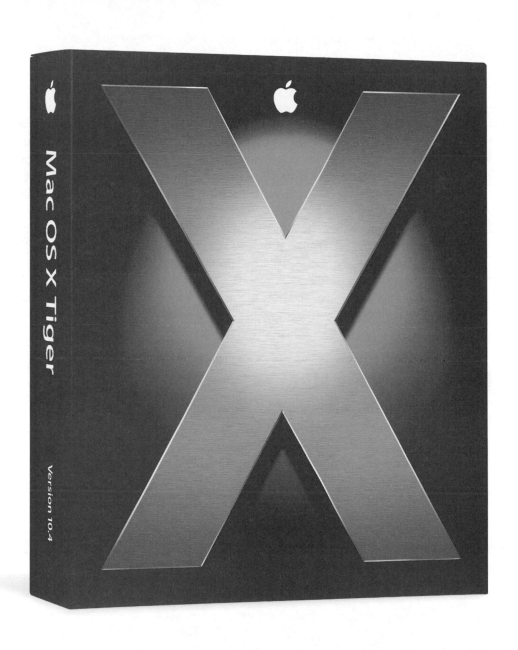

How to...

- Start up your Mac

- Install Mac OS X

- Use the Mac OS X Setup Assistant

- Put your Mac to sleep and wake it up

- Shut down your Mac

Whether you've just bought a new Mac, upgraded from an earlier version of Mac OS X, upgraded from Mac OS 9 or earlier, or switched from Windows, it's time to get acquainted with Mac OS X and take your first steps with this operating system.

In the first chapter of this book, I've given you an overview of what's new in Mac OS X 10.4, Tiger, and what's different from Mac OS 9, if you're familiar with that operating system.

Now, it's time to look at how you get your Mac up and running—whether it's a new Mac or an upgrade from a previous version of the operating system, I'll show you how to get Mac OS X 10.4 installed and set up.

I'll also show you how to perform the most basic operations with your Mac: how to start it up and shut it down, and how to put it to sleep and wake it up. After reading this chapter you'll be ready to get to work with your Mac and discover its myriad possibilities, functions, and applications that I discuss in the rest of this book.

Get to Know Your Mac

Apple sells many different types of Macs. As of press time, their product line is broken down into three major segments:

- **Portables** Apple sells two types of portable computers. Its PowerBooks, all in aluminum casings, are professional laptops, with fast processors, high memory capacities, and the widest range of features. iBooks are consumer-oriented laptops, with affordable pricing, but more limited features. At the time of this writing, the PowerBooks come in three sizes: 12-inch, 15-inch, and 17-inch screens; and iBooks come in two sizes: 12-inch and 14-inch screens.

2

■ **Desktops**   Apple currently sells three types of desktop Macs. The first is the aluminum G5, a tower model, which is full of technical innovations. The next model is the iMac G5, which, with its LCD (flat) screen and sleek lines, has been one of Apple's most popular models. Finally, the eMac, the only Mac with a CRT screen (that's a screen with a tube, like in a TV), was designed originally for the education market, and its low price and excellent feature set make it a fine Mac for home use as well.

■ **The Mac mini**   Fitting somewhere between the portable and desktop lines, the Mac mini is Apple's latest innovation. For a very low price, the Mac mini comes without a keyboard, mouse, or monitor. You can either use older hardware with a Mac mini, or buy the necessary peripherals. The Mac mini is so small that it *can* be used as a portable; you can easily shuttle it between home and office, though you can't work on it in between the two unless you carry a monitor, keyboard, and mouse with you. (And even then, you need to plug it into an AC outlet to power it.)

■ **Servers**   Apple's Xserve rounds out their product line. This enterprise server, which provides advanced features and uses Apple's Mac OS X Server software, is a high-capacity server for companies that need to share and serve files and provide other network services. I won't talk about servers or Apple's Mac OS X Server in this book.

What You Need to Run Tiger

Mac OS X 10.4 Tiger is compatible with a Macintosh computer with a PowerPC G3, G4, or G5 processor, a built-in FireWire, a DVD drive, and 256MB of physical RAM. The built-in FireWire requirement is important: any G3 Mac without FireWire cannot run Tiger.

However, the 256MB minimum for RAM is really a minimum; I can't see anyone being very productive with so little RAM. Buying additional RAM is the best investment you can make for your Mac. I'd strongly recommend you buy as much as you can afford, upgrading your Mac to at least 512MB, if not more.

If you use demanding programs, such as graphics and layout software, you'll want to put even more RAM in your Mac, and, in many cases, as much as you can (well, maybe not for the G5 Macs, which can accept up to 8GB RAM).

While Tiger requires a DVD drive (since it ships on a DVD), you can obtain CDs from Apple if you have an older Mac that is compatible with Tiger but doesn't have a DVD drive. Check the upgrade page on Apple's web site (www.apple.com/macosx/upgrade/) for information about its Media Exchange Program.

Tiger also requires at least 3GB of available hard disk space. It would be difficult to run Tiger with so little disk space, especially once you start adding files to your Mac. If you have an old Mac with a small hard disk that nevertheless is compatible with Tiger, I'd recommend upgrading the hard disk to give you breathing room—you wouldn't want to run out of space to hold your photos, music files, and videos.

Set Up Your Mac

Whatever Mac model you have, it comes with very limited instructions showing you how to connect its cables and turn it on. (See your Mac's documentation for a picture showing its different connectors and what they are for.) You'll need to connect the following cables:

- **Power cable** If you have a desktop model, you'll need to plug a power cable into your Mac and plug it into an AC outlet. If you have a portable, you may need to connect its adapter cable right away; your battery may or may not be charged.

- **Keyboard and mouse** If you have a desktop model, plug one end of the USB cable included with your Mac into the keyboard, and the other end into one of your Mac's USB ports. You can plug your mouse into the other USB port on the keyboard or another USB port on your Mac. If you have a Mac mini, plug in your keyboard and mouse. If you have a portable, you won't have a keyboard and mouse, though you can add one; if you want to use a keyboard and mouse, just plug them into your iBook's or PowerBook's USB ports.

- **Your monitor** Connect your monitor to your Mac's video port. There are different types of video ports, and some screens require adapters. If you have a portable, you can use its adapter to connect an external monitor as well; depending on your model, this monitor will either display the same thing as your portable or it will give you an extended display.

- **Speakers**   If your Mac has external speakers, plug them into its speaker jack.

- **Modem cable**   If you want to connect to the Internet using your Mac's built-in modem, or if you want to send faxes from your Mac, connect its modem cable to your Mac and then to your telephone jack.

- **Ethernet cable**   If you are going to connect to a local network, or to certain cable or DSL modems, you'll need an Ethernet cable (not included with your Mac). Plug this into your Mac's Ethernet port and then into your cable or DSL modem, or your network's hub, switch, or router.

- **Other peripherals**   If you have any other peripherals that connect either via USB or FireWire, you can plug them in now, or you can wait until after you've got your Mac up and running. It's often better to wait and connect these devices after you've installed your operating system and any drivers these devices require. See Chapter 18 for more on using peripherals.

Next, turn on your Mac by pressing its Power button; this button looks like a circle with a line protruding from it. On desktop Macs, this button is usually on the front, though on Apple's flat-panel iMac G5, it's on the back—on the right side below all the plugs and sockets. On portables, this button is between the keyboard and the screen.

Install Your Mac's Software

If you have a new Mac, when you first turn it on, you'll see the Mac OS X Setup Assistant. See the section "The Mac OS X Setup Assistant," later in this chapter, for the next step.

But depending on the country you live in, this might be different. In some countries, you'll be greeted by a screen telling you to insert your Software Restore CDs or DVD. This installs Mac OS X, as included with your Mac, and also copies any software that is bundled with your Mac. Depending on the model you purchase, you may have additional software included, such as productivity software or games. After this has completed, you'll be prompted to restart your Mac, and when you restart you'll see the Mac OS X Setup Assistant.

Install Mac OS X

If you're installing Mac OS X on an existing Mac, you'll be doing so from the Tiger DVD you purchased, and you'll run the Mac OS X installer to do so. (If you don't have a DVD drive, see the previous "Did You Know" section for information about obtaining Tiger on CDs.) Your Mac will be in one of the following situations:

- **It has no operating system on it.** If you have erased your hard disk, after backing up your data, it will be empty and ready for you to install.

- **It has a previous version of Mac OS X on it.** If you have Mac OS X 10.0, 10.1, 10.2, or 10.3, you'll have a few different installation options.

 If you're not sure which version you have, select the Apple Menu | About This Mac to see the version number. If you already have Mac OS X 10.4 or later, you don't need to install anything.

- **It has Mac OS 9 or earlier.** You probably won't have anything earlier than Mac OS 9, since Macs originally designed to run on older versions of Mac OS won't run Mac OS X. If this is the case, you'll be making a new installation, but retaining your old files.

Always back up all your personal files—anything you can't reinstall— before updating your operating system. Copy these files to a CD, DVD, or an external disk. While Mac OS X installations generally go smoothly, any number of problems, such as disk corruption, power outages, hardware failures, and so on, could interrupt your installation and cause you to lose data.

The following three sections walk you through the Mac OS X installation process, giving you step-by-step instructions on how to install the operating system.

Start Installing Mac OS X

1. To start installing Mac OS X, insert the installation disc in your Mac's drive. The DVD mounts, and its window opens. You'll see an icon called Install Mac OS X. Double-click this icon. If you are upgrading from Mac OS X, you'll have to click the Restart button on

Install Mac OS X

the next screen and then enter your administrator's password to proceed. If you're upgrading from Mac OS 9, you'll just click the Restart button.

NOTE *To install Mac OS X on an empty hard drive, insert the DVD and start up your Mac while holding down the c key on your keyboard; this tells your Mac to start up from the DVD instead of from its hard disk. If for any reason your Mac won't start up as described in step 1, double-click the Mac OS X Install icon, and then click Restart, which starts up the installation disc.*

2. After the Mac OS X installer starts up, you'll see a first screen telling you to select the main language; this is the language used by the installer, and also the main language set for Mac OS X after installation. Select your language and then click the arrow button to continue.

3. The next screen is a Welcome screen that tells you about which Mac models can run Mac OS X and gives you some information on installing the operating system, especially on older Mac models. Read this, and then click Continue to go to the next screen.

NOTE *If you see a message saying you must update your computer's firmware (this is special software that's loaded onto a chip inside your Mac), you'll need to quit the installer and restart using your current startup disk. Go to the Apple Software Updates web site (www.apple.com/support/downloads) and download a firmware updater for your Mac. Follow the instructions provided with this file, and then relaunch the Mac OS X installer. You'll probably only need to do this if your Mac is a few years old; this is generally only the case for Macs originally designed to run Mac OS 9.*

4. The installer now displays its Software License Agreement. Read this (really) and click Continue. Then click Agree if you agree with it. If you don't, you'll have to quit the installer.

5. The next screen, Select a Destination, lets you choose on which volume, or partition, you'll be installing Mac OS X. If you haven't partitioned your hard disk, you'll only have one choice here. If you have, choose which partition you want to install Mac OS X on and click it to select it.

 **Partition Your Hard Disk**

This is a good time to talk about partitioning your hard disk. Partitioning means cutting your hard disk into two or more slices, each of which acts like an individual disk.

Partitioning is a good thing to do for several reasons: it gives you a second disk to use for backups, it lets you store files outside of users' home folders (see Chapter 7 for more on these folders), and it can even be a way to install a new version of your operating system while maintaining the previous installation, just in case.

I partition the hard disks on all my Macs. In fact, it's the first thing I do when I get a new Mac. I usually have two partitions: one for running Mac OS X and another for backups and big files, like digital music files and photos.

The first thing you must do, however, is back up all your data—when you partition your hard disk, it erases the disk and all your files.

To partition your hard disk, select Utilities | Disk Utility at any point in the installation process before you select your destination. Select your hard disk in the column at the left, and then click the Partition tab. Select the number of partitions you want from the Volume Scheme pop-up menu, and set their sizes by either dragging the dividers in the Volume Scheme map or by selecting the partitions and entering a size in the Size field. Enter a name for each partition, and select Mac OS Extended (Journaled) for each partition's format. If you have a Mac that can start up in Mac OS 9 and you want to be able to do so, check Install Mac OS 9 Disk Drivers. (In fact, it's a good idea to do this anyway, just in case you need to use your Mac in target mode to connect it to another Mac running Mac OS 9 via a FireWire cable. (See Chapter 18 for a discussion of target mode.)

Did I tell you to back up your data? Because if you didn't, you're about to lose it. So, back up your data.

Click Partition to tell Disk Utility to erase your disk and create your partitions. When this is finished, quit Disk Utility (select Disk Utility | Quit) to return to the installer.

Select Installation Options

6. At this point, you can see an Options button on the bottom of the screen. Click this to see installation options:

■ **Install Mac OS X**   This installs Mac OS X for the first time, on a blank hard disk or partition. If your hard disk is blank, or if you have partitioned your hard disk, choose this option. (If you don't have a blank disk or partition, you won't see this option.)

■ **Upgrade Mac OS X**   If you have a previous version of Mac OS X on your Mac, this option displays instead of Install Mac OS X. This only installs files that have changed since the version you have installed. This is probably the best way to upgrade your Mac; it's certainly the easiest, since you don't have to worry about reinstalling any drivers or other programs.

■ **Archive and Install**   If you already have a previous version of Mac OS X on your hard disk, this moves your existing system files to a folder called Previous System and installs a new copy of Mac OS X. If you check Preserve Users And Network Settings, this copies your existing user accounts and network settings into the new system. You won't need to go through the Setup Assistant with this option, and all existing files that were in your and other users' home folders will be automatically placed in these folders.

■ **Erase and Install**   This erases your hard disk and installs a new copy of Mac OS X. If you choose this, select the disk format; in most cases, you'll select Mac OS Extended (Journaled).

7. When you've selected your installation method, click OK, and then click Continue to go on to the next screen.

Customize Your Installation

8. The Installation Type screen lets you choose to perform an "Easy Install" or to customize your installation. Customizing is a good idea, because you can choose to *not* install things you don't need, saving as much as a couple of gigabytes on your hard disk. Click Customize to choose among different software files that are installed. Here's a list of your choices, and an explanation of what you may or may not want to install:

■ **Essential System Software**   You have no choice, and must install this.

- **Printer Drivers** Mac OS X can install drivers for many popular printers. This section lets you choose Brother, Canon, EPSON, Hewlett-Packard, Lexmark, and other printer drivers. The Gimp-Print package is a group of open-source printer drivers for older printers; see Chapter 14 for more on Gimp-Print.

- **Additional Fonts** This installs fonts for nonwestern languages. This includes extra fonts for Chinese, Korean, Arabic, Hebrew, Thai, Cyrillic, and other languages.

- **Language Translations** These are text files that allow you to use Mac OS X in different languages. These files contain texts for menus, alerts, and dialogs. If you only work with one language (the language you selected on the first screen of the installer), you can uncheck this category. If you work with other languages and want to be able to run Mac OS X and its applications with their interfaces in these languages, select the packages you want to install. By not installing any of them, you save more than 1GB.

- **X11** This is a special program for running Unix programs in Mac OS X.

As you check and uncheck the different categories and packages, you'll see how much space is required for your installation. This can range from 4.8GB, if you install everything, to as little as 1.9GB if you only install the operating system. When you've made your choices, click Install.

9. The installer now checks your installation disk, making sure there are no problems. If it finds minor problems, it will repair them, but if there are major problems with your disk, it will tell you so and stop the installation procedure.

10. Now it's time to go make a cup of coffee, or tea, and to take a break while the Mac OS X installer does its work. This can take from about 20 minutes to more than a half hour, depending on the speed of your Mac and what you've selected to install.

NOTE *If you are a software developer, you'll want to install the Apple Developer Tools, which are in the Xcode Tools folder on the installation DVD. Just insert the DVD and double-click the file named XcodeTools.mpkg. This launches the installer and guides you through the installation of the Developer Tools.*

The Mac OS X Setup Assistant

After the installation process has finished, the Mac OS X Setup Assistant displays. This begins with an animation and music, and continues through a series of screens that help you create your first user account and set up your Mac to use the Internet.

1. The first screen, the Welcome screen, asks you to select the country or region you're in. Select this from the list, or check Show All if your country or region isn't listed, and then click Continue. If you need to hear instructions to set up your Mac, press the ESCAPE key. Mac OS X includes VoiceOver, an assistive technology that helps visually disabled people work with their computers.

2. The next screen, Do You Already Own A Mac, helps you transfer data and files from another partition on your computer or from a different Mac. You have several options:

   ■ **Transfer My Information from Another Mac**   If you check this and then click Continue, the Setup Assistant tells you how to connect your Mac to another Mac with a FireWire cable. The next screen tells you how to restart the old Mac, and the following screen lets you choose what to transfer. You can choose to transfer user accounts (either all existing accounts or only selected accounts), network and other settings, the contents of your previous Applications folder (though this does not overwrite newer versions of Apple programs that have been installed), and other files and folders. Check the items you want to transfer, and then click Transfer; the Setup Assistant will copy all these files. This may take several minutes, especially if you have a lot of files on the old Mac.

   ■ **Transfer My Information from Another Partition on This Mac**   If you check this and then click Continue, the Setup Assistant finds the older system installation on another partition on your Mac. It then lets you choose which items to transfer. Follow the procedure described in the previous bullet point.

   ■ **Do Not Transfer My Information**   Choose this if you want to set up a new account or if you don't have any previous data or files to transfer.

3. The next screen, Select Your Keyboard, asks you to choose your keyboard layout. Again, if the one you want isn't listed, check Show All. Keyboard layouts are listed by country and/or language, and you'll also find variants of some keyboard layouts here. Select yours and then click Continue.

4. If your Mac is already connected to a network, the Setup Assistant will skip the next screen. If not, you'll see a How Do You Connect? screen, asking you to choose your method of connection. You can choose from AirPort Wireless, Telephone Modem, Cable Modem, DSL Modem, Local Network (Ethernet), or My Computer Does Not Connect To The Internet. According to your choice, the screens that follow will differ. You'll need to enter your connection information. You must have either information from your ISP, such as a user name, password, and a telephone number for dialup access, or information from your administrator regarding the way you connect to a local network. After you've filled in the necessary information, click Continue. If you're not sure what to enter, select My Computer Does Not Connect To The Internet; you'll be able to set up network access later, as I discuss this in Chapter 10.

5. The next screen, Enter Your Apple ID, asks you to enter an Apple ID. You'll have one if you already have a .Mac account (see Chapter 11) or if you have already registered to use any of Apple's web sites. If you do have one, enter it in the User Name and Password fields. If not, click Continue.

6. The Registration Information screen asks you to enter your name, address, e-mail address, and more so you can register with Apple. Enter this information and click Continue.

7. The next screen, A Few More Questions, asks you how and where you'll be using your Mac, and whether you want Apple to send you Apple news about new software, products, and other information. Select your options, and then click Continue.

8. You now come to the Create Your Account screen. This is where you create your first user account. (I discuss user accounts in Chapter 8.) You'll see that your name has already been entered in the Name field and that Mac OS X has suggested a short name. But this short name is usually just your first and last name in lowercase and in one word; it's not really short. You can (and probably should) change this to something shorter, since you can use this to log in to your Mac, and a shorter name means less typing. Enter a password, retype your password in the Verify field, and then enter a hint that can help you remember your password if you forget it.

(Don't forget your password; you'll need it for many things, such as logging in to your Mac, installing software, and more.) Click Continue when you've entered all the necessary information.

9. Mac OS X creates your account, and then tells you about .Mac. If you have an account, check I'm Already A .Mac Member, and then click Continue and enter your .Mac user name and password. If you have purchased a .Mac box, you can check that option to enter an activation key and start using the account. If not, you can either purchase .Mac online, or you can simply skip this step. You can always purchase this later; see Chapter 11 for more on .Mac. Click Continue after you've made your choice.

10. If you said you didn't want to purchase .Mac, Apple touts it again on the next screen, offering you a free 60-day trial of the service. You can set this up now, or do it from the .Mac preferences later. Click Continue after you've made your choice.

NOTE   *Apple tries to convince you to create a .Mac trial account, but you don't have to renew it after the trial period if you don't want to.*

Your First Updates

Once you start up your Mac and connect to the Internet, it's likely that Software Update will open and display updates that have become available since your Mac OS X software CDs were prepared. It's a good idea to download those updates right away, before getting to work on your Mac, since they may contain bug fixes that make Mac OS X and its applications run more smoothly. See Chapter 19 for more on updating software.

Upgrading from Mac OS 9

If you upgraded from Mac OS 9, you'll find that Mac OS X has installed its software on your hard disk and left all your existing files and folders where they were. Click the icon for your hard disk in the Finder window sidebar and you'll see your previous data. You can copy your personal files to your home folder (see Chapter 7), and if you're planning to use the Classic Environment (see Chapter 13) to run Mac OS 9 applications, leave your System folder where it is. You'll select this System folder later in the Classic preferences.

Put Your Mac to Sleep and Wake It Up

Macintosh computers are designed so that when you've finished working with them temporarily, you can put them to sleep. This puts your Mac into a low-power consumption mode rather than shutting it down completely. There are several advantages to this:

1. You don't need to quit your applications, though you should save your files in case you have a problem such as a power cut.

2. You don't need to restart your computer and relaunch your applications the next time you want to use it.

3. Your Mac starts up very quickly when you reawaken it; this takes just seconds.

So, if you have finished working but plan to come back to your Mac soon, click the Apple menu and select Sleep.

Your Mac will go to sleep immediately. Some Mac models have a light on their power button (it's on the front of some portables) that fades on and off, looking like your Mac is breathing peacefully.

You can also put your Mac to sleep by pressing its Power button. On some models, such as iMacs, this puts the Mac to sleep immediately; on others you must click Sleep in the dialog that displays or press the s key on your keyboard.

To wake your Mac, just press any key on the keyboard. It takes a few seconds, and you'll see your screen light up as your Mac awakens, exactly in the same state as it was when you put it to sleep.

Shut Down and Restart Your Mac

When you've finished working on your Mac and want to shut it down for the day, select the Apple menu, and then choose Shut Down. This displays a dialog asking you to confirm that you really want to shut it down. If you don't reply in 120 seconds, it will shut down anyway.

When you shut down your Mac, you don't need to quit your applications. If you haven't saved your open documents, your applications will ask you to do so, but it's always a good idea to save them first.

CAUTION *Your Mac won't restart or shut down until you have saved all your open documents. Don't shut down your Mac and walk away unless you're sure everything has been saved, or it will wait for you to save your documents and never shut down until you do so.*

Another way to shut down your Mac is to press its Power button and then press RETURN or ENTER.

You can also restart your Mac by selecting the Apple Menu | Restart. This shuts down your Mac and starts it up again right away. The only time you'll want to do this is after installing software, which sometimes tells you to restart, or if you're having problems with the operating system. Restarting can clear up some problems because it fully clears your Mac's memory. Sometimes, after your Mac has been running for a long time—especially if you put it to sleep and don't restart it often—it can get sluggish, as its virtual memory files increase in size.

I'd recommend that you put your Mac to sleep during the day, when you're away from your desk or not working on it, and that you shut it down at night to prevent such problems.

Part II

It's All about the Finder

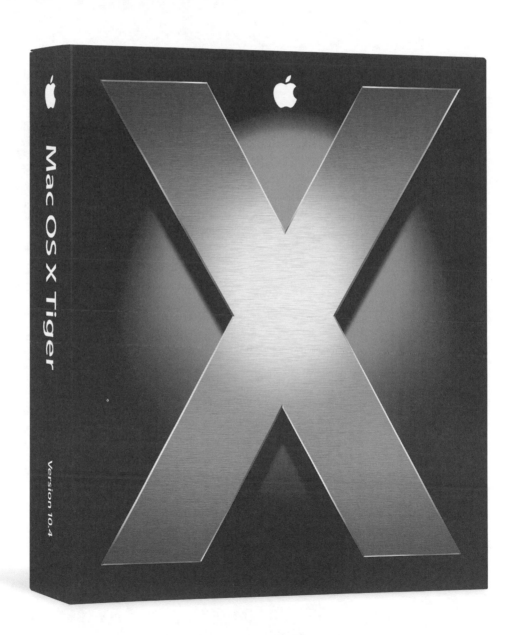

Chapter 3

Get to Know the Finder

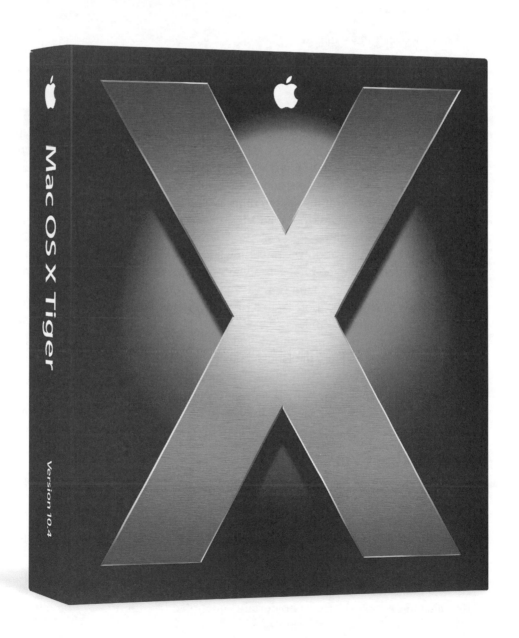

How to...

- Work with Finder basics
- Customize the Finder
- Use the Dock
- Discover Finder menus
- Find out about Dashboard
- Master the Trash

When you turn your Mac on, it goes through its startup process, displaying a screen with a few messages as it progresses; it displays the login screen (if you haven't turned on automatic login); and then, after you log in, it displays the interface of the Finder. This program is the heart of Mac OS X, the conductor that leads the rest of the operating system in its symphony of operations. The Finder manages windows, the Desktop, your files, the Dock, and everything you do that isn't in a specific program.

Whenever you use windows containing files, folders, or applications, you're using the Finder. While the Finder is always running, it's only active when you're working in it. The Finder's icon is always visible in the Dock.

No matter what application you're working in, you can click this icon to come back to the Finder.

In this chapter, you learn about the Finder and the many elements that are a part of it: the Desktop, the Dock, its menu bar, and the Trash. This chapter shows you how to work with the Finder, how to use its menus, how to work with the Trash, how to use Dashboard, and how to set Finder preferences and customize its display. (See Chapter 6 to learn about working with Finder windows.)

A Look at the Mac OS X Desktop

When you first start up your Mac, the Finder displays, showing four items (see Figure 3-1):

At the top of the screen is the menu bar; attached to the top of the screen, and visible at all times, it contains menus and commands for the Finder, and these menus change when you switch to another application—each application has its own set of menus (though they all share the Apple menu, which I explain later in this chapter). The menu bar also contains *menu extras,* icons or text displays that give you information or provide access to certain functions. In Figure 3-1, you can see

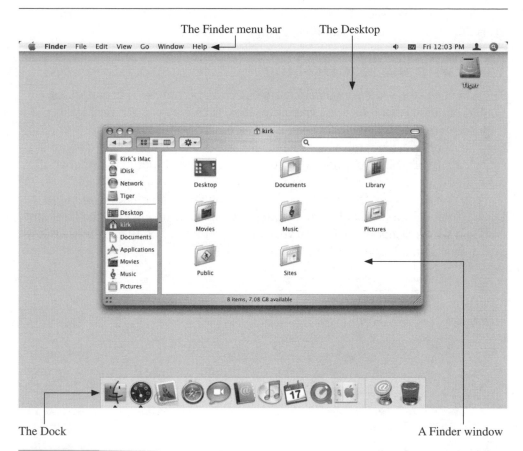

FIGURE 3-1   The Finder, showing the menu bar, the Dock, the Desktop, and a Finder
window

a handful of menu extras at the right of the menu bar: a volume menu, where
you can change your Mac's volume; the input menu, showing the active keyboard
layout; the clock, showing the day of the week and the time; the user menu, where
you can switch users; and the Spotlight icon. The user menu, which displays if you
turn on Fast User Switching (see Chapter 8) lets you choose a different user and
open a new session for that user. You'll learn about Spotlight, which lets you find
anything on your Mac, in Chapter 5.

At the bottom of the screen is the Dock, a combination launcher, application
switcher, and control center that you use to work with applications and windows.

The background of the screen is called the Desktop. You're probably familiar
with how this works if you already use a computer. (If you're new to computers,
don't fret; I'll explain it in the next section.)

Finally, you can see a Finder window open above the desktop. You learn everything about working with Finder windows in Chapter 6.

Work with the Mac Desktop

The Mac Desktop—the actual background seen in Figure 3-1—is part of the Finder, but it's also a folder you can use to store files. You can see the Desktop folder icon in the Finder window displayed in Figure 3-1. But you don't want to keep all your files here; this is why Apple has provided a home folder, containing subfolders to organize your files. (You can see the home folder in the sidebar of the window in Figure 3-1; for more on the home folder, see Chapter 7.)

You can access the Desktop easily, either by clicking the Finder icon in the Dock (if the Desktop is not hidden by other windows) or by clicking the Desktop icon in a Finder window sidebar. As you can see in Figure 3-2, files on the Desktop also appear in the Desktop folder.

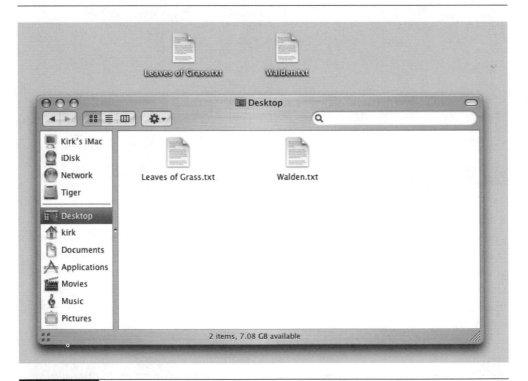

FIGURE 3-2   Files on the Desktop are both on the Desktop and in the Desktop folder.

Did you know?

Is the Desktop Really the Desktop?

If files on the Desktop are both on the Desktop and in the Desktop folder, where are they really? Well, it doesn't make a difference; it's not just a question of semantics, but the Desktop, which is just an abstraction for the Desktop folder, is a clever illusion on Apple's part. Because many users put files on the Desktop as they work with them, Apple made the Desktop folder accessible so you have another way to get to the files you leave on the Desktop. If you used a previous version of Mac OS, such as Mac OS 9 or earlier, you'll remember that you didn't have a Desktop folder; one did exist, actually, but it was an invisible folder, so you had only one way to get to files on the Desktop.

While many users find it easy to place files on the Desktop for quick access, you'll probably find storing your files in your home folder and its subfolders more practical (even though one of these subfolders is the Desktop folder), but you can choose any place you like. Your Desktop will quickly get cluttered if you put all your files there.

Customize Your Desktop

Mac OS X gives you many options for customizing your computer and your working environment. One element you can customize is your Desktop: you can change its picture, or background, the way it displays icons, and what information it displays with icons.

To change the Desktop's presentation, select Show View Options from the Finder's View menu (or press ⌘-J). The contents of the View Options window that displays (Figure 3-3) depend on which window is active. When the Desktop is active, its title bar shows "Desktop"; if another window is active, it shows both the name of that window and different view options. (See Chapter 6 for more on view options in Finder windows.)

This window lets you choose exactly how you want icons to display on the Desktop:

- ■ **Icon Size**   Move this slider to increase or decrease the size of icons on the Desktop.

- ■ **Text Size**   Choose the size you want for Desktop labels, text that displays the names of your icons.

FIGURE 3-3 The View Options window shows Desktop display options.

- **Label Position** Icon names can either be below icons (bottom) or to the right, as shown in Figure 3-4.

- **Snap to Grid** This keeps icons aligned on an invisible grid, making them look more organized.

- **Show Item Info** This displays information about the icon and is especially useful when you display your hard disk icon on the Desktop.

- **Show Icon Preview** This option, when checked, shows a thumbnail image of graphics or movies instead of normal icons.

- **Keep Arranged By** This arranges icons by Name, Date Modified, Date Created, Size, or Kind. Select your choice from the pop-up menu.

NOTE *You can also choose what types of items you want to display on your Desktop: whether you want to display icons for hard disks, removable media, or network volumes. You learn about this and other Finder preferences in the section "Customize the Finder."*

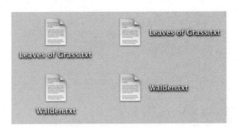

FIGURE 3-4   You can choose from two label positions: either below or to the right of icons. This choice is global for each window.

Change Your Desktop Picture

Your Mac displays a standard Desktop picture, or background, when you first start working with it, but you can change this to one of the many Desktop pictures Apple includes, or even use your own picture. To change this, hold down the CONTROL key (CTRL) and click anywhere on the Desktop. (If you have a two-button mouse, right-click on the Desktop.) Select Change Desktop Background from the contextual menu. This opens the Desktop & Screen Saver preference pane (Figure 3-5.)

This preference pane lets you choose which picture you want on your Desktop. Choose a collection from the list at the left, and then click one of the pictures in the preview section at the right to apply it. If you want to use a picture that's in your Pictures folder, choose Pictures Folder from the list, and then select one. If you want to use a picture in another folder, select Choose Folder from the list and navigate to the folder containing your picture. And if you have a picture file on the Desktop or in another window, you can just drag it into the Desktop Picture zone to use it, as shown in Figure 3-6.

TIP   *If you get tired of the same picture, check Change Picture at the bottom of the Desktop & Screen Saver preference pane, and then choose a frequency from the pop-up menu. This changes the Desktop picture at the selected frequency, choosing each time from the folder selected in the Collection pop-up menu. And check Random Order to have the pictures change randomly. Your Desktop need never be boring again!*

Customize the Finder

The Finder offers a number of options that affect how certain items are displayed and how other items react. Some of these affect the Desktop, others change the way Finder windows display, and others control certain Finder operations, such as

FIGURE 3-5 The Desktop & Screen Saver preference pane is where you can change your Desktop picture.

FIGURE 3-6 Dragging a picture to the Desktop Picture zone changes the picture immediately.

emptying the Trash. To access the Finder preferences, choose Preferences from the Finder menu. The Finder preferences window (see Figure 3-7) displays.

The Finder preferences window has four panes, each of which is accessed by clicking one of the icons in the preferences window toolbar:

- **General**   These preferences affect the display of items on the Desktop, new windows, and spring-loaded folders.

- **Labels**   This section lets you change the names for colored labels.

- **Sidebar**   This section allows you to choose which items display in Finder window sidebars.

- **Advanced**   This section contains settings regarding file extension display and emptying the Trash.

FIGURE 3-7   The Finder preferences window lets you customize some aspects of the Finder's display and operations.

General Preferences

The General pane of the Finder preferences lets you choose among several ways of displaying items and Finder behavior:

- **Show These Items on the Desktop**   Check any of these three items: Hard Disks (which includes both internal and external hard disks), CDs, DVDs, And iPods (which also includes removable media such as Zip disks and other USB devices), and Connected Servers (network volumes).

- **New Finder Windows Open**   This sets the contents of new Finder windows, when you press ⌘-N, or select File | New Finder Window. Choose from Home (your home folder), Documents (your Documents folder), Computer (the Computer window, which displays your hard disk and other volumes), your startup disk, your iDisk, or, if you want to use a custom folder for new windows, select Other and browse to select a folder.

- **Always Open Folders in a New Window**   If you check this, double-clicking a folder opens a new window. If you leave this unchecked, the folder's contents display in the same window.

- **Open New Windows in Column View**   If you check this, new windows open in column view. See Chapter 6 for more on window views.

- **Spring-Loaded Folders and Windows**   This lets you turn this function on or off, and set the delay for using spring-loaded folders and windows. See Chapter 6 for information on using spring-loaded windows.

> NOTE   *Because the Finder sidebar offers options for displaying items such as hard disks and removable media, using only one of the two (the Finder window sidebar or the Desktop) to display these items is something to consider. You may find the Finder window sidebar a useful way to deal with these volumes because it centralizes all your volumes in a small area. If you're used to using the Desktop for these items, however, you might want to keep on doing so. There's nothing to stop you from using both, of course.*

Apply Labels

Labels, like those shown in Figure 3-8, let you highlight icons with a colored background behind their names so you can spot them more easily. You can,

3

FIGURE 3-8   You can't see it well here, but these three files have different colored labels: from left to right, the labels are red, yellow, and blue.

for example, apply red labels to all pending files, allowing you to see at a glance the red-labeled files in a window. You can also use labels to search for files (see Chapter 5), to sort files in Finder windows (see Chapter 6), or simply to make them stand out.

To set a label for an icon, click the icon while holding down the CONTROL key (or click the right mouse button of a multibutton mouse) and select a label color from the contextual menu that displays.

As you can see in this illustration, the label name displays when you move your cursor over a label color. To remove a label, click the **x** at the beginning of the line of labels.

> **TIP**   *You can also select the file and then click the Action button in the Finder window toolbar to display the same contextual menu. The functions in this contextual menu are also accessible in the File, Edit, and View menus.*

Labels Preferences

You can change label names in the Labels pane of the Finder preferences. Just select one of the names and type a new name.

By default, the labels are named according to their colors. You could change them to names such as Personal, Urgent, Pending, or anything you want.

How to ... Work with Contextual Menus

Mac OS X offers contextual menus for many common operations. As you learned in the previous section, "Apply Labels," you display contextual menus by holding down the CONTROL key and clicking the mouse on a selected item. These menus are called *contextual* because what they display depends on the context, or when they're invoked.

If you have a mouse with more than one button, press the right mouse button to display the contextual menu. Some input devices, with their own driver software, let you assign a different button to display contextual menus; if you have installed special software for a mouse or trackball, see that software to find out how to assign a button to this task.

In the Finder, contextual menus offer a number of menu items that are available in other Finder menus: Open, Copy, Paste, Duplicate, and more. The contextual menus merely provide shortcuts, giving access to these commands with a single click (you can click an icon, rather than click it to select it and then click a menu).

The same commands are available in the Finder's Action menu, which is available by clicking the Action button in a Finder window toolbar.

No matter how you invoke them, contextual menus can save time because they show only what you can do with the current item, and they group the most common commands in a single menu.

Sidebar Preferences

This pane lets you choose which items display in Finder window sidebars. Your choices apply to all Finder windows, and also apply to Open and Save dialogs (see Chapter 13 for more on these dialogs).

As you can see in the illustration, this pane is separated in two parts, corresponding to the separation of the sidebar. At the top, you see volumes: Hard Disks, iDisk, and Removable Media, and your Computer and Network icons. At the bottom, you see the Desktop, Home, and Applications.

By default, all these items are checked, but you can uncheck any of them if you want to display fewer items in your Finder window sidebars. If you find you'd rather have them back, just return to this preference pane and recheck the items.

Advanced Preferences

This pane offers only two options:

- **Show All File Extensions**   This tells the Finder to always display file extensions, such as .txt, .doc, and so on. You don't usually need to know these on the Mac, but if you want to see them, check this option.

- **Show Warning Before Emptying the Trash**   If you check this, the Finder displays a warning when you empty the Trash.

Work with the Dock

The Dock is the Finder's control center and one of the most important parts of the Mac OS X interface. You use it to open and switch applications, to manage files and windows, and to see what's running on your Mac.

The Dock contains icons of things you want to access quickly: by default, the Dock only contains application icons and the Trash (Figure 3-9), along with an

FIGURE 3-9   The Dock. From left to right: the Finder, Dashboard, Mail, Safari, iChat, Address Book, iTunes, iCal, QuickTime Player, System Preferences, and, in the right-hand section of the Dock, an Internet shortcut to Apple's web site and the Trash.

Internet shortcut icon that takes you to Apple's web site, but it can also contain icons for other open applications, files, and folders. (I'll show you how to add icons to the Dock in the upcoming section "Add Icons to the Dock.")

The Dock sits at the bottom of the screen and is slightly translucent. Figure 3-9 shows the Dock as it probably appeared when you first started up your Mac—Apple includes a number of icons in the Dock for the programs you use most.

In Figure 3-9, you can see small black triangles beneath two applications: the Finder and Dashboard. These triangles indicate applications that are running. The others are merely application shortcuts waiting for you to use them. To launch one of these applications, click its icon once. As you move the cursor over the icon, you'll see the program's name appear above the Dock, and after you click, the icon will bounce a few times to show that it's opening (see Figure 3-10).

The Dock's icons are more than just pretty pictures; you can control certain actions through them. For example, click an icon for an active application in the Dock and hold the mouse button down; a contextual menu displays above the icon. You can quit an application by selecting Quit from this menu (see Figure 3-11); and for some applications, this menu offers other functions, such as allowing you to switch windows in an application (see the next section).

Switch Applications and Windows Using the Dock

While the Dock gives you a visual reminder of which applications are running, it's also an application switcher. The simplest way to switch applications is to click the icon of the application you want to switch to.

If you hold down the OPTION key while clicking a Dock application icon, this hides all the other visible applications. This is especially practical if you want to switch to the Finder and you want all your other windows out of the way, so you can see all the Finder's windows and the Desktop.

FIGURE 3-10   The iCal icon bouncing in the Dock as the application opens

FIGURE 3-11   You can use an application's Dock menu to quit the application, switch windows, and, in some applications, such as iTunes, to control the application's functions.

The Dock can also contain windows from active applications: if you minimize a window, by clicking its yellow Minimize button or by pressing ⌘-M, a miniature window with a small icon appears in the right side of the Dock. Figure 3-12 shows this part of the Dock with three windows.

As you can see in Figure 3-12, each of these three windows is a miniature of the actual window, with an icon in the lower-right corner to show you which application it belongs to. The cursor is over one of the windows, and this displays its name above the Dock—in this case, it's the Apple web site in a Safari window. To show one of these windows and bring its application to the front, click the window icon.

FIGURE 3-12   Three miniaturized windows in the Dock, with icons showing their applications

The Dock has some hidden information that can be useful as well. If you click and hold the cursor on an open application's icon, a small menu displays, showing the windows open in that application, even if the application is hidden. In Figure 3-13, a check mark indicates the currently visible window.

To bring one of these windows to the front, just select its name in the menu, as in Figure 3-13.

Add Icons to the Dock

In addition to its role as a control center, the Dock also serves as a repository for icons you use often or want to access quickly. You can add icons for applications, files, or folders to the Dock. Even though the Finder window sidebar is designed to hold folder icons, there are good reasons to put folder icons in the Dock.

When you open an application whose icon isn't in the Dock, it displays at the far-right end of the Dock, next to the separator. If you want to keep that application's icon in the Dock, click and hold the mouse button until the application's Dock menu displays. (See Figure 3-14.)

Select Keep In Dock, and the application's icon will remain in the Dock even after you quit it. You can then open the application from the Dock with a single click.

You can also add icons to the Dock by dragging them from their windows and placing them anywhere you want in the Dock. Drag an icon to the Dock, and the other icons move aside to make room for it. Release the mouse button and the icon remains in the Dock.

If you decide you want to move the icon to a different location, click it and drag it to another place in the Dock; the surrounding icons move to make room. Release the mouse button to leave it where you want.

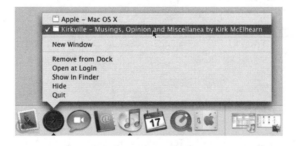

FIGURE 3-13   An application's window menu in the Dock lets you switch to any of the program's windows.

FIGURE 3-14   To keep an application icon in the Dock, select Keep In Dock from its
Dock menu.

If you want to remove an icon from the Dock, click and drag it from
the Dock onto the Desktop. This removes the icon from the Dock, in
a puff of smoke, but does nothing to the original item—only its Dock
icon is deleted.

You can add more than just application icons to the Dock; you can also add
icons for files or folders. To do this, drag a file icon onto the right section of the
Dock. (You can only put file or folder icons on the right side of the Dock, next to
the Trash.)

Two folder icons that are useful to have in the Dock are
your home folder and the Applications folder. Drag these icons
from a Finder window to the right side of the Dock.

After you place these folder icons in the Dock, you have easy access to all the
contents of your home folder. You can launch applications or open files from these
folders. As you can see in Figure 3-15, when you click and hold the cursor on one
of these folders, a menu displays its contents. This menu is hierarchical, and it lets
you dig deep within the folder and its subfolders.

Select any file, folder, or application, and then release the mouse button to open it.

   *Hold down the CONTROL key when you click the Dock icon and you won't
need to keep holding your mouse button; the menu remains visible. You
can navigate through its folder hierarchy by moving the cursor, and then
when you want to open a file, click the file's name in the menu.*

You can use the Applications folder as a launcher for all your applications. As
you can see in Figure 3-16, when you click and hold the Applications folder icon,
a menu shows its contents.

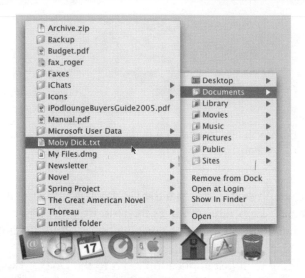

FIGURE 3-15   Opening a file in the Documents folder from the Dock

FIGURE 3-16   The contents of the Applications folder display in the Dock menu.

Select one of these applications to launch it, or move into one of the subfolders, such as Utilities, to launch the applications it contains.

> NOTE   *With the Finder window sidebar providing quick access to your home folder and your Applications folder, it might seem superfluous to add these icons to the Dock. This is only a suggestion, but doing so could help you access certain files, folders, and applications more easily. To access items in the Finder, you must first switch to the Finder and then click the sidebar icons; you can access items in the Dock without changing the frontmost application. Say you're working in your word processor and want to open a file. Just navigate in your home folder and select it; the file will open in the word processor immediately, without your having to switch out of this application.*

Customize the Dock

Just like the Finder, the Dock offers its share of customization options. You can change its size, its location, how it reacts when you move the mouse over it, and whether it hides and shows automatically.

To access Dock preferences, click the System Preferences icon in the Dock, or select the Apple Menu | System Preferences, and then click the Dock icon. The Dock preference pane displays.

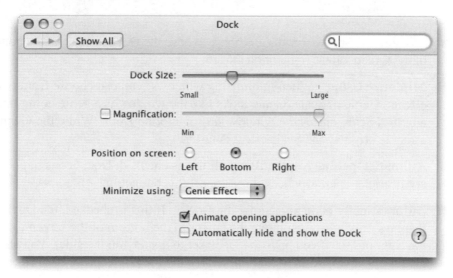

Another way to access preferences for the Dock is from the Dock itself. Click on the Dock, near the separator, while holding down the CONTROL key, to display the Dock menu. This gives you quick access to most of the Dock's settings and to the Dock's preference pane as well.

As you can see here, one of the items on this menu is Dock Preferences. This opens the System Preferences to the Dock pane, where you can set some additional preferences.

You can change the following Dock preferences in the preference pane:

- **Dock Size**   Move the slider to change the size of the Dock. When you do this, you change the height and width of the Dock proportionally. But when the Dock contains more icons than it can display at this size, it shrinks automatically to fit the screen.

- **Magnification**   If Dock magnification is on, the Dock increases in size as you move the cursor over it. (See the following illustration.) You can adjust the amount of magnification by moving the slider.

- **Position on Screen**   You can choose to have the Dock display on the bottom of the screen, on the right, or on the left.

- **Minimize Using**   When minimizing windows, you can choose from two effects: Genie or Scale. Genie looks like the window is a genie going into a bottle; Scale makes the window shrink into the Dock. While the Genie effect is original, the Scale effect is faster.

- **Animate Opening Applications**   If this is checked, Dock icons bounce as applications open. Uncheck it to turn off this bouncing.

- **Automatically Hide and Show the Dock**   If this is checked, the Dock displays only when you move the cursor to the bottom of the screen (or to the right or left, if you have the Dock set to display on the side). You can also use a keyboard shortcut to hide or show the Dock: press ⌘-OPTION-D.

TIP   *You can change the size of the Dock from the Dock itself. To do this, move the cursor over the separator, as shown in the illustration. The cursor changes to a bar with two arrows. Click and hold the mouse, and then drag up to increase the Dock size, or drag down to decrease it. Adjust the Dock size until it seems right. You can always change it later.*

Switch Applications Using the Keyboard

While you can switch applications by clicking their icons in the Dock, you can also do this without taking your hands off the keyboard. To do this, press ⌘-TAB; this displays the icons for all your open applications in the middle of your screen, with the current application highlighted. (See Figure 3-17.) Keep holding the ⌘ key and press TAB again; this switches to the next application, and you can see its icon become highlighted.

Press the TAB key until the application you want to activate is highlighted, and then release the keys; that application comes to the front.

TIP   *The icons that display in the middle of your screen are arranged from left to right according to their usage; the last application you used is at the left, followed by the next-to-last application, and so on. This means that to toggle between two applications—even if you have ten applications running—you merely need to switch from the first to the second application for it to come to the head of the list. The next time you press ⌘-TAB, you switch back to the previous application, which is now at the left. Each time you press ⌘-TAB after that, you'll switch between these two applications.*

⌘-TAB cycles through applications from left to right, and ⌘-SHIFT-TAB moves from right to left among these icons. In addition, if you press ⌘-TAB and then keep

FIGURE 3-17   As you press ⌘-TAB to switch applications, huge icons display in the middle of your screen.

holding down the ⌘ key, you can use the mouse cursor to click any of the icons to switch applications. Just move the cursor over one of the icons and click.

Switch Applications with Exposé

If you're like most users, you'll probably have a few applications open at a time and have windows all over your screen. Switching applications using the Dock or the keyboard, as previously shown, is a good way to work among these programs, but you still end up with a disorganized screen. There has to be a better way to make sense of all these windows.

Well, Apple came up with a great way to do this; it's called Exposé. This feature lets you get a view of all your application's windows, or all the windows of a given application, when you press a keyboard shortcut or mouse button, or move your cursor to a hot corner of your screen. You can then switch to the window you want with a single click.

Exposé is easier to demonstrate than to explain, though. Look at the following:

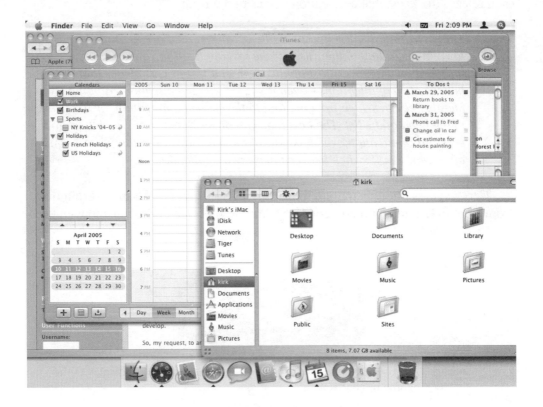

This screen is typical of what many users see as they work. Three applications are open—iTunes, Safari, and iCal—as well as the Finder. It's pretty hard to make sense of which window is which, and it's even harder to see at a glance what these windows contain. But if you press the Exposé All Windows shortcut (the F9 key), you see all your open windows in smaller versions across your screen, and if you move your cursor over the windows, you see the names of their applications (or the name of a document, web page, or other unique information about the window), as shown next.

To switch to one of these windows—and its application—just click it. This window comes to the front, and all your other windows return to their previous positions.

Exposé works not only for switching applications, as in the previous illustration, but also for switching windows within an application. Say you have four Finder windows open and you want to switch quickly to one of them. Instead of clicking on parts of the different windows, moving some of them out of the way to see where the others are, press the Exposé Application Windows shortcut (F10).

You'll see all the windows of that application spread across the screen, and when you move your cursor over them, you'll see their names. Click one of these windows to activate it. No matter how many windows you have open, Exposé shrinks them all to fit your screen, so you can see miniatures of them.

Finally, you may have files scattered across your Desktop, or you may want to access removable media or network volumes mounted on the Desktop. Press the Exposé Desktop keyboard shortcut (F11). All your windows move off to the side of your screen, showing the Desktop, and allowing you to work there, moving or copying files, and opening folders or volumes.

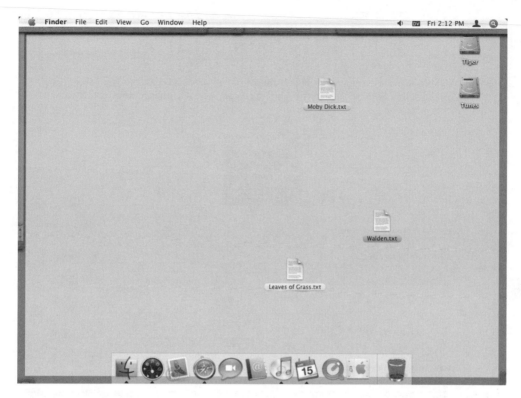

To return to the previous view, with all your windows visible, press the F11 key again.

Set Exposé Preferences

While I explained how to use Exposé's preset keyboard shortcuts previously, you can change these to shortcuts that you find easier to remember and use. You can also set hot corners to invoke Exposé, or you can set mouse buttons or a combination of modifier keys and mouse buttons to invoke Exposé.

To do this, open the System Preferences, either by clicking its Dock icon or by choosing the Apple Menu | System Preferences and then click the Exposé button to display the Dashboard & Exposé preference pane.

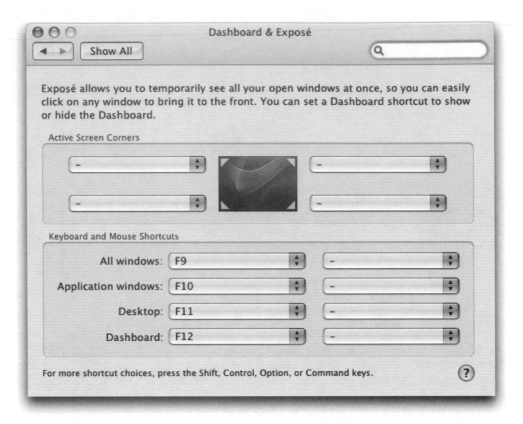

As you can see here, this preference pane has two sections: Active Screen Corners, and Keyboard and Mouse Shortcuts. You can set both of or either of these to activate Exposé (and Dashboard, which I'll look at later in this chapter).

- **Active Screen Corners** If you want to invoke Exposé from a hot corner—meaning that its actions are activated when you move your cursor into a corner of the screen—choose which corner you want to use, and then click that corner's pop-up menu. You have three choices: All Windows, Application Windows, and Desktop, which correspond to the three Exposé actions I explained previously. (There's also a Dashboard menu item, allowing you to set a hot corner to activate Dashboard.) You can choose to use two corners, or more, for any of these Exposé actions, but you'll notice that the pop-up menus also contain Start Screen Saver and Disable Screen Saver; this is because you must share these corners with the screen saver controls. You can use hot corners for both screen savers and Exposé, but you cannot use the same corner for both.

3

■ **Keyboard**   The left column of the Keyboard and Mouse Shortcuts section lets you choose keyboard shortcuts for Exposé and Dashboard. By default, Exposé uses the F9, F10, and F11 keyboard shortcuts, as I explained previously. But you can change these shortcuts to any other F keys, to any modifier keys, or to any combination of these. For example, click one of the pop-up menus in this section and you'll see the keyboard shortcuts available. If you hold down a modifier key (such as ⌘, SHIFT, OPTION, or CONTROL), you'll see the shortcuts in the pop-up menu change accordingly.

TIP   *You'll notice in the Exposé keyboard shortcut pop-up menus that a distinction exists between the right and left modifier keys, such as the right and left CONTROL keys. You can choose to invoke Exposé with only the right CONTROL key and still be able to use the left CONTROL key for other keyboard shortcuts. If you choose such a key, Exposé activates when you press that key alone, but you won't be able to use that key in other shortcuts. So, if you have a CONTROL-A shortcut in an application, and you set the right CONTROL key to one of Exposé's functions, you'll have to use the left CONTROL-A combination to activate the other shortcut.*

■ **Mouse**   The right column of the Keyboard and Mouse Shortcuts section lets you set mouse buttons to invoke Exposé's functions or display Dashboard widgets. Click the pop-up menu and choose which button you want to use. Depending on how many buttons your mouse has, you'll see a corresponding number of choices, minus one; you can't use the left mouse button for Exposé because it must be used for standard clicks. If you only have a one-button mouse, you won't see these additional choices.

NOTE   *If you have a mouse or other input device (such as a trackball) with a lot of buttons, you'll find a long list in these pop-up menus. It may take some experimentation to figure out exactly which button in the menu corresponds to each button on your input device.*

Dashboard

One of the most visually attractive new features in Mac OS X 10.4 is Dashboard. Combining colorful interfaces and simple, practical applications, Dashboard presents *widgets,* or mini-applications, that provide information or let you access data. Dashboard's widgets are one-trick ponies; each one does a simple task, but does it quickly and efficiently.

A glimpse at the widgets included with Tiger shows you the type of task that Dashboard is designed for: there is a stock quote widget, a weather widget, an iTunes controller, a dictionary/thesaurus lookup widget, a unit converter, a calculator, and more. To display these widgets, just press the F12 key.

TIP *You can also invoke Dashboard by clicking the Dashboard icon in the Dock; but you don't need to keep that icon in the Dock, if you don't use it. If you want to remove it, just drag it from the Dock. Dashboard will still work without it being in the Dock.*

As you can see in the previous illustration, Dashboard widgets display in front of all your windows. You can then view their data, or access their functions, without having to move windows out of the way. When you're finished, just press F12 again or click anywhere other than on a widget to return to your normal display.

NOTE *As you saw earlier, in the section on setting Exposé preferences, you can change the default hotkey for Dashboard from the Exposé & Dashboard preference pane. You can also set hot corners or mouse buttons to invoke Dashboard.*

In the previous illustration, you can see a + sign in a circle at the bottom left of the window. If you click this, you'll display the *widget bar,* which contains all the widgets available on your Mac. This metallic bar (reminiscent of the perforated aluminum of Apple's G5 computers) rises up from the bottom of the screen, nudging the rest of your display upward.

To open a widget that's in the widget bar, just click it. You'll notice that you can open several instances of any of the widgets; this is practical if you want to keep your eye on the weather in several cities, for example, or if you have a large stock portfolio and want to check your shares.

You can click one of the arrows at the end of the widget bar to see more widgets, and if you click the More Widgets button above the right end of the widget bar, you'll go to an Apple web page where you can download additional widgets.

Some widgets are simple, such as the Dictionary widget: just type a word and press RETURN to display its definition or synonyms. To use the Calculator widget, click anywhere on the widget, and then start typing numbers; you can click the buttons on the calculator keypad, or you can use the number keys on your Mac's keyboard. Other widgets need to be set up to provide the data you want. If this is the case, you'll see a small *i* icon at the bottom right of the widget when you move your pointer over it.

For instance, with the Weather widget, click this icon and then enter a city, state, or ZIP code to get weather for that location. You'll see other options as well, such as a choice between Fahrenheit and Centigrade temperatures, and an option to display low temperatures in the six-day forecast.

Check out all the widgets to see if they'll be useful to you—I'm sure they will be. Then check out additional widgets by clicking the More Widgets button. You'll find Dashboard to be a great source of data, information, and features.

The Mac OS X Menu Bar

If you've used Macs before, you're used to seeing a single menu bar at the top of your screen. But if you've been a Windows user, this might throw you because Windows attaches its menus to individual windows. The Mac menu bar is present all the time (except for when you use full-screen applications, such as games, or for display of DVDs or QuickTime movies) and is contextual; it changes according to the frontmost application. The menu bar contains all the menus for the current application, as well as the Apple menu, which is always present. It also contains one or several *menu extras,* small icons or text displays at the right of the menu bar, which give you information about certain functions of your Mac or provide quick access to configuration changes.

The Apple Menu

The Apple menu is always visible in the menu bar, no matter which application is active. It gives you access to some essential system functions, such as putting your Mac to sleep or shutting it down. Figure 3-18 shows the Apple menu.

The Apple menu gives you access to the following:

- **About This Mac**   This displays a window showing the version of your Mac OS X software, which Mac you have, which processor, and how much RAM is installed. You can click the Software Update button in this window to open the Software Update application (see Chapter 20) or the More Info button to open the System Profiler application, which gives you information about your computer.

- **Software Update**   Like the Software Update button in the About screen, mentioned previously, this opens the Software Update application. (See Chapter 19 for more on Software Update.)

- **Mac OS X Software**   This takes you to a page on Apple's web site where you can get more software for Mac OS X.

- **System Preferences**   This opens the System Preferences application, discussed in Chapter 9.

FIGURE 3-18   The Apple menu is always accessible, no matter which application is active.

- **Dock**   This has several submenus and gives you access to Dock preferences. For more on the Dock, see the section "Work with the Dock," earlier in this chapter.

- **Location**   This lets you change your network location. See Chapter 12 for more on the network preferences and locations.

- **Recent Items**   This gives you quick access to the most recently used applications, documents, and servers.

- **Force Quit**   This lets you force quit an application that isn't responding. See Chapter 13 for more on force quitting applications.

- **Sleep**   Select this to put your Mac to sleep.

- **Restart**   Select this to restart your Mac.

- **Shutdown**   Select this to shut down your Mac.

- **Log Out [*user name*]**   Select this to log out of your session. For more on working with users and sessions, see Chapter 8.

At the right of the named menus in the menu bar is a Help menu. Every application, including the Finder, has this Help menu. The Help menu gives you quick access to online help and, in some cases, to help on the Internet. Chapter 20 looks at getting help.

Menu Extras

At the right end of the menu bar are several icons for menu extras (Figure 3-19). These icons give you access to configuration choices or show you information (such as network status, the date and time, and so forth).

The menu extras shown in Figure 3-19 are as follows: iChat, Classic status, Airport (wireless networking) status, volume, input menu, date and time, user menu, and Spotlight. Other menu extras are available, such as a battery indicator for PowerBooks and iBooks. Some third-party applications add their own menu extras.

FIGURE 3-19   Menu extras in the menu bar

To access one of these menu extras and its functions, click and hold the mouse on one until its menu displays. The following illustration shows the volume menu extra, which lets you quickly change your computer's volume.

You can investigate each of the menu extras to see what it does. Most menu extras can be turned on or off from the System Preferences.

Another way to remove any menu extra is to hold down the ⌘ key, click the menu extra, and drag it off the menu bar.

> **TIP** *If you want to change the position of your menu extras, hold down the ⌘ key, click the menu extra you want to move, and drag it to a new location on the menu bar. You can't move the Spotlight icon, however.*

All About Finder Menus

Each element of the menu bar mentioned previously is present all the time, but the rest of the menu bar changes according to the active application. The Finder menu bar gives you access to many essential functions, including file management commands, view options, and access to specific locations on your Mac.

The Finder menu bar has six menus, plus the Apple menu, discussed earlier in this chapter, and the Help menu, discussed in Chapter 20. I won't examine every menu item on every menu here because most of these menus are discussed elsewhere in the book.

The Finder Menu

The *Finder menu* gives access to Finder preferences (discussed earlier in this chapter) and lets you empty the Trash (see the section "The Mac OS X Trash," later in this chapter, for more on the Trash), as well as show and hide the Finder. (See Chapter 13 for more on showing and hiding applications.) This menu contains certain commands that other applications have as well: the Hide and Show commands, for example. Each application has a menu in this location with the name of the application in bold type.

The File Menu

The *File menu* lets you manage files and folders, and work with windows. As you can see in the following illustration, some of the menu items are dimmed. This means they're not accessible in the current context. Others show the name of an item currently selected in the Finder.

- **New Finder Window (⌘-N on the keyboard)**   This creates a new window in the Finder.

- **New Folder (⌘-SHIFT-N)**   This creates a new folder in the current window, or on the Desktop, if you are working on the Desktop.

3

■ **New Smart Folder (⌘-OPTION-N)** This creates a new smart folder in the current window, or on the Desktop, if you are working on the Desktop. I'll look at smart folders in Chapter 5.

■ **New Burn Folder** This creates a new burn folder, a special folder used to burn CDs and DVDS, in the current window, or on the Desktop, if you are working on the Desktop. I'll look at burning CDs and DVDs in Chapter 4.

■ **Open (⌘-O)** This lets you open a file, folder, or application; double-clicking an icon does the same thing. If you select File | Open With, you can choose a recommended application from the submenu, or choose Other to open a dialog and choose another application.

■ **Print** This opens the selected document (or documents) and tells its application to print it. You'll see a standard Print dialog before the documents start printing.

■ **Close Window (⌘-W)** This closes the current window.

■ **Get Info (⌘-I)** This opens a window that shows information about a selected file, folder, or application.

■ **Duplicate (⌘-D)** This makes a copy of a selected file, folder, or application. To make an alias, select File | Make Alias, or press ⌘-L. To show the original of an alias, select File | Show Original, or press ⌘-R.

■ **Add to Sidebar (⌘-T)** This adds a selected file, folder, or application to the Finder window sidebar.

■ **Move to Trash (⌘-BACKSPACE)** This moves a selected item to the Trash, though it's much quicker to press ⌘-BACKSPACE.

■ **Eject (⌘-E)** This ejects a CD, removable disc, or other ejectable medium. On most new Macs, you can press the F12 key to do the same thing.

■ **Burn Disc** This lets you burn a data CD or DVD. This menu item is only available if you have a blank CD or DVD mounted in the Finder and you have copied files to it.

■ **Find (⌘-F)** This opens the Finder's Find window, where you can search for files, folders, or applications. (See Chapter 5.)

■ **Color Label** This selects a color to apply a label to a file, folder, or application.

The Edit Menu

The *Edit menu* is similar to the Edit menu in most other applications: you use it to cut, copy, and paste items, to select all, or to show the Clipboard. It also lets you undo or redo the last Finder action you carried out, such as returning a file to its original location after it was moved. And the Finder Edit menu lets you display the Special Character palette to insert special characters (such as accented characters, symbols, and so forth) in your documents.

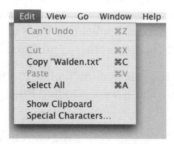

The View Menu

The *View menu* enables you to choose which window view you want to use. It also lets you arrange files and folders by name, date, and so forth, as well as clean up files and folders, aligning them to an invisible grid.

The Toolbar options—Hide Toolbar, Customize Toolbar, and Hide Status Bar— are presented in Chapter 6.

Show View Options lets you customize the way icons are displayed in a window. This is presented in Chapter 6.

The Go Menu

The *Go menu* gives you quick access to some of the most important places on your Mac. The Back and Forward menu items, which work the same as the Back and Forward buttons in the Finder toolbar (see Chapter 6 for more on the Finder toolbar), let you navigate to the previous or next window, similar to the way you go back and forward among pages in a web browser. Enclosing Folder takes you to the parent folder of the current folder in a Finder window—the folder that holds the current folder.

The six menu items with icons give you shortcuts to go to some of the most common locations on your Mac. These are the following:

- **Computer**   This is where your hard disk and any external or removable disks are shown.

- **Home**   Your home folder. See Chapter 7 for a presentation of the home folder and its contents.

- **Network**   This displays your Network folder, showing any available network servers. See Chapter 12 for more on using the network.

- **iDisk**   This leads to a submenu that mounts your iDisk in the Finder if you have a .Mac subscription; see Chapter 11 for more on .Mac. You can also access another user's iDisk or iDisk Public folder from this submenu.

- **Applications**   This takes you to your Applications folder.

- **Utilities**   This takes you to your Utilities folder, which is inside your Applications folder. This folder contains some useful tools and utilities. See Chapter 19 for more on Mac OS X utilities.

Keyboard shortcuts for the locations listed here are shown in the menu and are easy to remember: they are each ⌘-SHIFT-[*LETTER*], where *LETTER* is the first letter of the word that names the location. (The only exception is the iDisk menu item; this has a submenu, which lets you access other users' iDisks.)

The Recent Folders menu item opens a submenu showing recent folders.

The Go To Folder menu item lets you enter the path of a folder you want to open.

The Connect To Server menu item opens a dialog that lets you connect to another computer on a network. For more on networks, see Chapter 12.

The Window Menu

The *Window menu* lets you zoom or minimize windows, or bring a specific window to the front. In the following illustration, two Finder windows are open. The window with the check mark next to it is the currently active window. To switch to another window, select it from the Window menu.

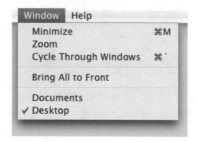

The Mac OS X Trash

If you've used a computer before, you're familiar with the idea of the Trash—you put files in the Trash when you don't need them anymore, and then empty the Trash when you're *sure* you won't ever need them again. (If you've been a Windows user, you know this as the Recycle Bin.) It's a kind of buffer between being and nothingness, but once you empty the Trash, there's little hope of getting your files back. (There are third-party software utilities that can sometimes recover deleted files. See Chapter 19 for more on disk utility software.)

Remember, when you put files in the Trash, they aren't deleted yet; the actual deletion occurs when you empty the Trash. But moving files there isn't a good idea unless you're positive you want to get rid of them. It's too easy to empty the Trash and then discover that an important file went away with the garbage collector.

Use the Trash

The *Trash* folder is just like any other folder, but it's a special one. You can drag files and folders onto the Trash icon, which is in the Dock (see Figure 3-20), or you can move them there by selecting them and pressing ⌘-DELETE.

One way you can empty the Trash is by selecting Empty Trash from the Finder menu; you can also press ⌘-SHIFT-BACKSPACE, or you can click and hold down the mouse button when the cursor is over the Trash icon in the Dock and select Empty Trash from the contextual menu. In all cases, unless you have turned off the warning in the Finder preferences, the Finder will display an alert, asking you to confirm that you want to empty the Trash. Think twice! If you have any doubts, click Cancel, because you cannot undo this action.

> **TIP**
>
> *If you want to delete your files forever, so no one—not even you—can ever get them back, select Finder | Secure Empty Trash. This not only deletes the files, it overwrites them with zeros several times so even disk utilities cannot recover them. But make sure you really want to delete these files—there's no way to get them back.*

Remove Files from the Trash

As I mentioned previously, the Trash is a folder, though a very special kind. If you put files in the Trash and later realize that you want to keep them, just click the Trash icon in the Dock to open the Trash window, move the files where you want, and then close the Trash window.

FIGURE 3-20   Here's what the Trash icon looks like when it's empty, on the left, and when it contains files, on the right.

Chapter 4

Everything about Files, Folders, and Icons

How to...

- Understand different types of icons
- Open files in several ways
- Copy and move files and folders
- Work with compressed files
- Burn your files to a CD or DVD

The objects you move around on your computer screen are called *icons*: some represent files, some represent folders, and others are used for applications or programs. If you've used a computer before, there is nothing unfamiliar about these basic objects of the Mac OS X interface. Apple was the first to adopt these objects as a metaphor for the items stored on your computer, and whether you've used earlier versions of Mac OS or Microsoft Windows, these objects work pretty much the same. But there are some differences between Mac OS X 10.4 and other operating systems, and if you're new to computers, this chapter will help you understand what all these icons on your screen represent.

In this chapter, I'll show you the different types of icons you'll see in Mac OS X, and I'll explain how to copy and move files and folders. I'll tell you how Mac OS X works with files, folders, and their icons, and I'll show you how to work with aliases. I'll also show you how to find anything on your Mac, in two different ways, and I'll tell you how you can burn your files onto a CD-ROM, if you have a CD writer either built into your Mac or connected externally.

The Different Types of Icons in Mac OS X

Mac OS X uses a variety of icons for its files and folders. In Chapter 7, you'll see how your home folder contains eight subfolders that use special icons to help you quickly see what they are meant to contain. You'll also see the other special icons on the folders at the top level of your hard disk. These icons make it easy to distinguish these special folders from the many other folders on your Mac.

Most Mac files have meaningful icons to show what kind of file they are or which application created them. Figure 4-1 shows some common files and their icons.

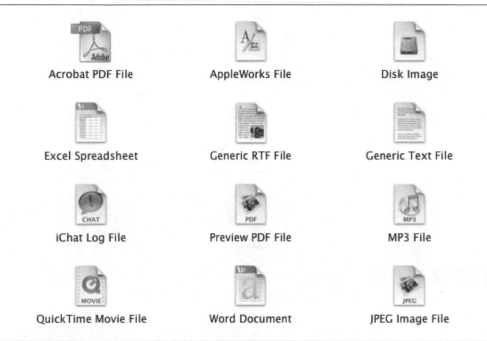

Acrobat PDF File	AppleWorks File	Disk Image
Excel Spreadsheet	Generic RTF File	Generic Text File
iChat Log File	Preview PDF File	MP3 File
QuickTime Movie File	Word Document	JPEG Image File

FIGURE 4-1   Some common file icons, with names describing their file types. Most of these icons tell you visually which application created them or which type of file they are.

Almost every Mac application uses its own special icon for its files, and you'll get used to them easily.

In addition to the icons shown in Figure 4-1, there are variations on all of these icons. As Figure 4-2 shows, icons for *aliases,* which are shortcuts to files, contain small arrows at their lower-left corners. (I'll tell you how to use aliases later in this chapter.)

Find Out Everything about Files

Every icon on your Mac represents something—a file, a folder, or an application. Each of these items has a life story: they have locations, creation and modification dates, sizes, and more. To find out everything about one of your files, hold down the CONTROL key and click your mouse on an icon. Figure 4-3 shows the contextual menu that displays when you do this.

Acrobat PDF File   **AppleWorks File**   **Excel Spreadsheet**

iCal   **iPhoto**   **Mail**

Movies   **Music**   **Pictures**

FIGURE 4-2   Some alias icons. The top three icons are file aliases; the next three, application aliases; and at the bottom are folder aliases.

FIGURE 4-3   The contextual menu displays when you click the mouse while holding down the CONTROL key on your keyboard.

SHORTCUT *If you have a two- or three-button mouse, just place the cursor over the icon and click the right mouse button.*

Select Get Info from this contextual menu to display the Info window for the selected file. The Info window tells you everything about your file.

SHORTCUT *You can also select File | Get Info from the Finder's menu bar, or press ⌘-I on your keyboard to display the Info window.*

The Info window tells you the following (if you don't see the General section of the Info window, as in the preceding illustration, click the disclosure triangle next to General to display it):

■ **Spotlight Comments**   By default, this field is blank, but you can add comments to it so Spotlight can search for custom keywords. See Chapter 5 for more on Spotlight.

■ **Kind**   This is the type of file. Here, it is a Rich Text Format (RTF) document. This line tells you if it is a folder, an application, or an alias. It also tells you, if possible, which application created the file.

■ **Size**   Files have two sizes: because of the way your hard disk stores files, they nearly always take up more space on disk than the actual amount of data they contain. The first number represents how much disk space the file uses, while the second tells you its actual size in bytes.

■ **Where**   This tells you the location of the file. In the preceding illustration, this file is in /Users/kirk/Desktop, which is my Desktop folder.

■ **Created**   This is the date and time the file was created.

■ **Modified**   This is the date and time the file was last modified.

■ **Color Label**   This shows if a color label has been applied to the file. In this case, the x is selected, showing that there is none.

■ **Stationery Pad**   If this is checked, the file is a stationery pad file. See Chapter 13 for more on Stationery Pad files.

■ **Locked**   If this is checked, the file is locked and cannot be deleted.

The bottom part of this window has more advanced information in five sections. To view each of these sections, click their disclosure triangle. Figure 4-4 shows you two of these sections.

You can change the name of an item in the Name & Extension section and decide whether or not to show its file extension. If you're used to working with Microsoft Windows and seeing file extensions, you might want to display them; otherwise, you probably won't need to see them. The Open With section lets you choose an application to open a file. It usually gives you a choice between a default application and any others on your Mac that can open it.

FIGURE 4-4   The Name & Extension and Open With sections of this window give you additional information about the file.

The other sections of this window are the following:

- **More Info**   This displays additional information about your file, such as keywords that Spotlight uses for searching, special file attributes, and more. See Chapter 5 for more on this section and Spotlight.

- **Preview**   This displays a preview of the file. You can find out about previews in Chapter 6.

- **Ownership & Permissions**   This section lets you change the owner and access rights to files, folders, or applications.

Select Icons

Whenever you want to do something with an icon, whether it's a file, folder, or application, you must first select it. You do this by clicking an icon once. The icon highlights, showing that it's selected, and you can then do whatever you want to it.

If you want to move or copy an icon, just click it and start dragging it to another location. See the sections "Move Files and Folders" and "Copy Files and Folders," later in this chapter, for more on moving and copying files and folders.

While selecting a single icon is simple, there are several ways to select multiple icons in Mac OS X, which allow you to choose which files you want to move, copy, delete, or open, and perform these operations—and others—on many files simultaneously.

Select Multiple Icons

While you often select a single icon to open a file, folder, or application, you sometimes want to select several icons at once. For instance, you may want to copy a group of files to another location, or you may want to open several files at the same time. The simplest way to select multiple icons is to click the mouse near one icon and then drag the cursor to cover all the icons you want to select.

As you can see in Figure 4-5, the Finder displays visual feedback of the selection area as you drag. You can see which icons are selected: they are highlighted. Notice that the two icons at the left are selected, even though the selection area does not cover them. As long as the selection area touches names, they become selected.

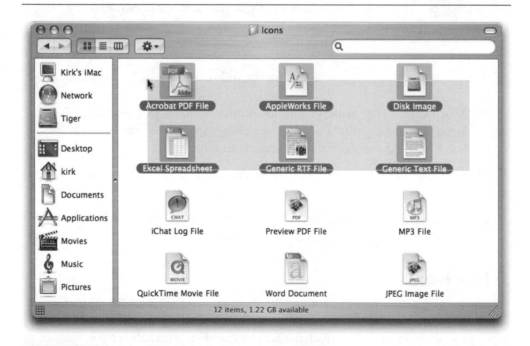

FIGURE 4-5   You can select icons by clicking and dragging. Here, I started at the bottom right and then dragged up to the top left.

But you may not need to select all the icons covered by the selection area. Say you don't want to select the AppleWorks file in Figure 4-5. After selecting the six icons in that figure, hold down the COMMAND key and click the AppleWorks file to deselect it. Figure 4-6 shows the results of that operation.

If you want to select several icons, but they don't all fit in a square or rectangle, as in Figure 4-5, you can select the first icon and then hold down the SHIFT key and click others to select them. This does not force a square or rectangular selection. You can select any icons you want, no matter where they are in a window.

In Figure 4-7, I first clicked an icon and then held down the SHIFT key and selected the others. I can now copy these files together to another location.

If you want to select all the icons in a window, you don't even need to use the mouse. Just press ⌘-A and every icon is selected.

NOTE   *⌘-A is a keyboard shortcut for Select All, which is available in the Finder's Edit menu. It's much quicker to use the keyboard for common menu item actions. This shortcut is also frequently used in other applications, such as word processors, spreadsheets, and others.*

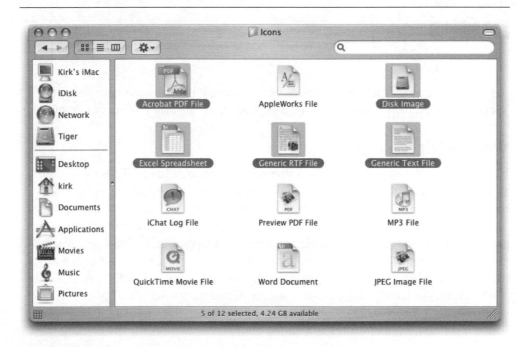

FIGURE 4-6   After selecting a group of icons, you can deselect any of them by holding down the COMMAND key and clicking them.

FIGURE 4-7 These icons were selected by holding down the SHIFT key and clicking each one.

All the previous methods of selecting icons work in all window views: Icon View, List View, or Column View. (I'll explain these different views in Chapter 6.)

Work with Aliases

Earlier in this chapter, I showed you that some icons are aliases. These icons are shortcuts—pointers to files, folders, or applications—and are practical because they let you organize different items in one location without moving the originals.

Aliases are exactly the same as normal icons, except for one thing: the small arrow at the bottom left. (See earlier Figure 4-2.) Depending on how you create aliases, their names may contain the word "alias." You can create aliases for any item on your Mac, and you can put them anywhere you are allowed to put files.

To create an alias, click an icon to select it, and then select File | Make Alias (or press ⌘-L). The Finder creates an alias of the file in the same window, as the following illustration shows. The Outline alias file is an alias for the Outline file.

Another way to create aliases is to click an icon, hold down the ⌘ and OPTION keys, and then drag the icon. This creates an alias in the same window if you drag the icon in that window, or in another location, if you drag outside that window. As you do this, the cursor changes to an arrow, to show that you are creating an alias.

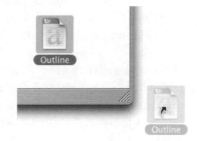

One thing you can see in this illustration is that, when you create an alias in another location by dragging the icon, the Finder does not change its name: it does not add the word "alias" at the end. It does, however, add the word "alias" to the alias' name if you create an alias in this manner in the same folder.

 *Folders with special icons, such as the Documents folder (see Figure 4-8), don't keep these icons when you make aliases from them; they look just like normal folders.*

Since you can put aliases anywhere, you might want to put some on the Desktop. You can put the aliases of any items on the Desktop, as in Figure 4-8.

FIGURE 4-8   Some aliases on the Desktop: the first two are folders, followed by two applications, and then a file.

While this gives you quick access to these items, other elements of the Finder, such as the Dock or the Finder sidebar or toolbar, can be more efficient for accessing files, folders, or applications.

Open Files, Folders, and Applications

There are several ways to open files in Mac OS X. Some of them involve working with icons in Finder windows or on the Desktop, others use the Dock, and yet others can use the Finder window toolbar. I'll discuss opening icons here; Chapter 3 talks about the Dock, and Chapter 6 tells you how to add icons to the Finder toolbar.

The simplest way to open a file—or a folder or application—is to double-click it. You can also open any item by selecting it and pressing ⌘-o, and there are other useful ways to open files on the Mac.

Since you can often open files with a variety of applications—you can open many types of text files with different word processors, and graphics files with different graphics programs—you may want to open a file with a specific application. In Figure 4-9, I opened a plain text file with Microsoft Word by dragging the file icon onto the application icon in the Dock.

If I double-clicked the file in the Finder, the Walden.txt file would open with Apple's TextEdit, which is the default application for text files. By opening the file with Word, I can apply complex formatting and, especially, save it as a Word file to send to others. Depending on the format of the original file and the application

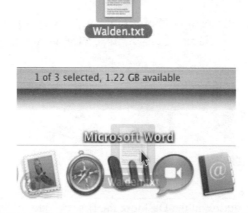

| FIGURE 4-9 | Dragging a file onto an application icon opens the file, if the application can read the file's data. |

you choose, you may see the file open immediately, or you may see a dialog asking you to choose the file's format or a message showing that the file is being converted. If you don't have Microsoft Word, for example, AppleWorks, included with many new Macs, can open its files, as well as many other file formats. And the Tiger version of TextEdit, Apple's simple text editor, can open basic Word documents, though if they contain graphics or any special formatting (such as notes, tables, and text boxes), TextEdit won't display these items.

Another way to open files with different applications is to hold down the CONTROL key and click an icon (or several icons). The contextual menu that displays contains an Open With menu item, whose submenu lets you choose an application. Whenever your Mac knows that a file can be opened by several applications, this menu shows the choices. Select the application you want to use from this submenu.

SHORTCUT   *Remember, if you have a multiple-button mouse, just click the file icon with the right mouse button to display the contextual menu.*

Earlier in this chapter, I explained how to select multiple icons. Once you have selected these icons, you can double-click any of them to open all the files at once. If all the files were saved by the same application, they would all open in that application. If they were saved by different applications, each file would open in its respective application. This saves time when you need to work on several files. Thus, you don't have to open each one individually, either from the Finder or from the application's Open command.

Move Files and Folders

Moving items is easy. For a single item, just click it and drag it to a new location. For multiple items, simply select them and drag them to their new location. I explained earlier how to select items: select what you want to move—this can be one or several items—and drag them. You can move files and folders into folders or into open windows.

As you can see in Figure 4-10, the Finder shows you "ghosts" of the files you are moving so you can be sure to place them in the correct location. The same is true when you move files into a folder in the same window or another open window. As you drag the cursor over the folder, it appears to "open" (see Figure 4-11), and you can place your files there.

FIGURE 4-10   Drag files and folders to another window to move them.

FIGURE 4-11   When moving files to a folder, the folder "opens" to show you that your files can be placed there.

 NOTE   *You never "move" files to another volume—say, a different hard disk, a removable disk such as a Zip disk, or another computer on a network. When dragging files to another volume, the Finder copies the files, retaining the originals in their initial location and creating duplicates on the other volume. See the following section for more on copying.*

Copy Files and Folders

Copying files and folders is similar to moving them (see the preceding section). You select one or more icons and drag them to another location. The only difference is that the files are duplicated in the process. After copying files, your originals remain in their initial location, and duplicates, with the same names, are created in the target location. When you drag files to another location, such as another volume, to copy them, the Finder gives you a visual clue that you are, indeed, making copies by displaying the cursor as a plus symbol (+), as shown in Figure 4-12.

You can also copy files using the Finder's contextual menu. Select one or more icons, press the CONTROL key, and click the selected item(s). The contextual menu contains a Copy item at the bottom. In Figure 4-13, this says Copy 4 Items, because four files are selected in the window.

TIP   *There are two other ways to copy items: select Edit | Copy, or press ⌘-C.*

NOTE   *If you have a multiple-button mouse, click the right button to display the contextual menu.*

FIGURE 4-12   The Finder shows you that you are copying files by changing the cursor to a plus symbol (+) on a green background.

FIGURE 4-13   The contextual menu is another way to copy items in the Finder.

Open another folder, press the CONTROL key, and click: the contextual menu is different this time and includes Paste Item at the bottom. (This doesn't tell you how many items you are pasting.) Select Paste Item, and the files or folders are copied to the new location.

> **TIP** *You can also copy items to a new location on the same volume without using the contextual menu. As I explained earlier in this chapter, if you drag files to another folder on the same volume, they are moved, not copied. But there's a trick that lets you copy files instead of moving them: while dragging the item(s) you want to copy, hold down the OPTION key. You'll see the cursor change to include the green plus symbol (+) that indicates a copy. Move the cursor over the location where you want to copy the files, and then release it; the files will be copied.*

Duplicate Files

If you need to make a copy of one or several items in the same location, select the item(s), and then select File | Duplicate or press ⌘-D. This duplicates the selected item(s), adding the word "copy" after their names. You can accomplish the same thing using the OPTION key trick explained earlier. Just hold down the OPTION key and drag the file to another place in the same folder. (See Figure 4-14.)

When OPTION-dragging a file, as shown in Figure 4-14, the Finder adds "copy" to the file's name. You can change it later to whatever you want.

FIGURE 4-14   If you hold down the OPTION key and drag a file, a duplicate is made in the same window.

Walden copy.txt

FIGURE 4-15   The text of a filename is highlighted and ready to be changed.

Change the Names of Files or Folders

As I explained earlier, when duplicating an item, the Finder adds "copy" to the item's name. You may want to change this name, or you may want to change the names of other files and folders. Changing names is easy—just click an icon and then press RETURN: the text of the item's name is highlighted. (See Figure 4-15.) Start typing to delete this name and type a new one, or click again in the name and use the arrow keys to move around if you just want to change one or several characters.

When you have entered your new name, press RETURN again. The Finder displays the icon with the new name.

TIP   *You can also change the names of files or folders from the Info window. Select an item, press the CONTROL key, select Get Info (or press ⌘-I), and then click the disclosure triangle next to Name & Extension. You'll be able to change or edit the item's name in a text field.*

Spring-Loaded Folders

One of the more interesting Finder features in Mac OS X is *spring-loaded folders*. This feature lets you copy files into folders deep in your file system without having to open lots of windows. When you drag files onto a folder and wait for a second, the folder "springs" open, revealing its contents (see Figure 4-16). You can then move your files onto another folder, which in turn springs open, while the previous window closes. You can spring into folders at any level of your Mac's hierarchy, moving files easily without navigating windows.

You can use spring-loaded folders with any folder or volume icon, whether it is in a window or in the Finder sidebar. You can keep springing open subfolders until you get to the last one. You'll need to turn this feature on in the Finder preferences—select Finder | Preferences, and then click the General icon and check Spring-Loaded Folders And Windows.

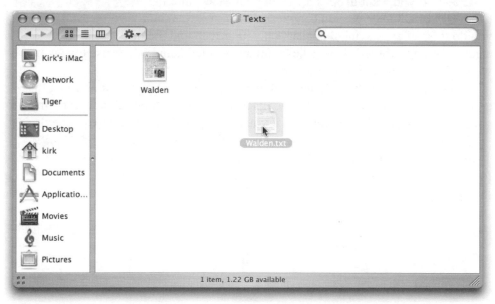

FIGURE 4-16 Using spring-loaded folders. Top: Dragging a file on the Texts folder opens this folder in the same window. Bottom: When this new window opens, you can either drop the file in that window or drag it onto another folder that will spring open as well.

Eject or Unmount Disks

When you insert a CD or DVD, or connect to an external hard disk or removable media device like a Zip drive, these items appear on the Desktop and in the top section of the Finder sidebar. When you connect to another computer on a network, the volumes you mount, or connect to, appear on the Desktop as well. (See Chapter 3 for more on the Finder preferences, which enable you to select which items to display on the Desktop.) Figure 4-17 shows some of the different volumes you can mount on your Mac.

These same volumes display in the top part of the Finder sidebar, according to your choices in the Finder preferences (see Chapter 3).

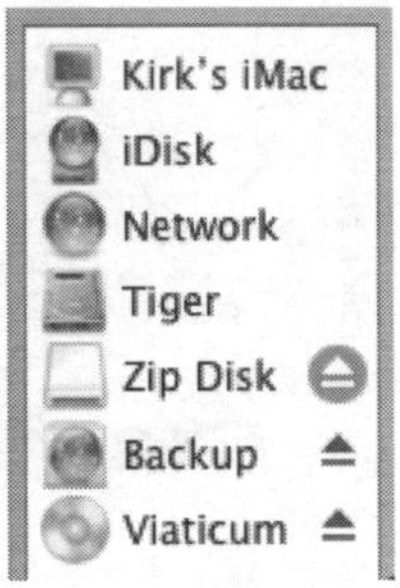
Kirk's iMac
iDisk
Network
Tiger
Zip Disk
Backup
Viaticum

When you are finished working with a CD, DVD, or other volume, you must eject it. There are several ways to do this. The easiest is to click the eject button next to the volume in the Finder window sidebar as shown in the image to the right.

Another way to do this, if you don't have these volumes displayed in your Finder window sidebar, is to click the volume's icon on the Desktop to select it, and then select File | Eject or press ⌘-E. If you want to eject a disc in your Mac's internal CD-ROM or DVD drive, you can press the EJECT key. When you do this, an eject symbol appears on your screen and the disc ejects. (Some keyboards have a key with an eject icon, and others use the F12 key, which you must hold down for more than a second.)

Another way to eject volumes is to use the contextual menu: hold down the CONTROL key and click the volume to display this menu; then select Eject. Or press your right button and click the item if you have a multibutton mouse.

Eject

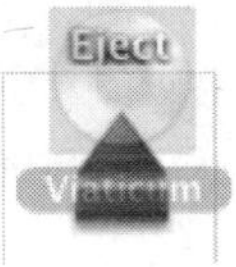

Finally, you can eject any volume by dragging its icon to the Trash. While this may seem strange, the Mac has worked this way for many years. As you do this, the Trash icon changes to an eject

Tiger
Tunes
Backup
Zip Disk
Viaticum

FIGURE 4-17 Different types of volumes mounted on the Desktop. From left to right: an internal hard disk, an external FireWire hard disk, a network volume, a Zip cartridge, and an audio CD.

symbol and shows a label saying "Eject" (for CDs, removable media, and so on) or "Disconnect" (for network volumes).

CAUTION   *You should always eject or unmount external volumes when you are finished working with them. Some volumes, such as external hard drives, may become damaged if you turn them off or unplug them while they are mounted. Don't worry, though, if you shut down your Mac; the shutdown routine correctly unmounts and ejects all mounted volumes. And putting your Mac to sleep is fine as well; your volumes will remain mounted when you wake up your Mac.*

4

Work with Compressed Files

In addition to the different types of files I have discussed in this chapter, there is a special type of file that you'll probably encounter: compressed files. These are files containing other files that have been compressed to take up less disk space. The file compression standard on the Mac has long been *Stuffit,* named after the most common compression program used for the Mac.

Since Mac OS X 10.3, Panther, Apple has included Zip compression in the Finder, and this has quickly become the more prevalent compression format for Mac OS X. Other compression formats have become common as well: tar and gzip, which come from the Unix world, are now often used by software developers to distribute files over the Internet.

Work with Zip Archives

Compressed archives can contain hundreds or even thousands of files, or they may contain just one. The advantage to using archives is that they save disk space. While some types of files cannot be compressed much (MP3 files are already compressed, as are JPEG images), compression can shrink files as much as 80 percent or more, depending on the file type. Mac OS X includes built-in Zip compression, so you can compress your own files to save space on your computer or to send to other users over the Internet. The advantage to using Zip compression is that you can send compressed files to Windows users, who can expand them easily.

To compress a file or folder, just click the item you want to compress, holding down the CONTROL key (or click the Action menu in the Finder toolbar, or the right mouse button), and select Create Archive Of [*file or folder name*].

This creates a Zip archive in the same folder as the original item.

Walden.txt   Walden.txt.zip

To expand a Zip archive you've made in this way, simply double-click it and the Finder will expand it in its current folder.

Compressed files are most useful when sending attachments with e-mail messages. Some e-mail programs, such as Entourage, which is part of Microsoft Office v. X, can compress attachments automatically without needing any additional software. When adding attachments to e-mail messages in this program, click the encoding button at the bottom of the attachment pane of the message window.

Work with Stuffit Files

Stuffit files are another common kind of compressed files you'll come across on the Mac for now. You can spot them by their file extensions, .sit or .sitx, and their icon.

Walden.sitx

NOTE   *Stuffit Expander, which was included with earlier versions of Mac OS X, is no longer provided with the operating system. I'd recommend that you download a copy of it—it's a free program—from www.stuffit.com. You'll find it useful, since it can decompress many types of archives, such as Stuffit and Zip archives, as well as dozens of other, less common compressed files. If you ever receive or download a compressed file, try using Stuffit Expander to expand it; there's a good chance it will work.*

Expand Stuffit Archives

To expand a compressed Stuffit archive, just double-click the file. Stuffit Expander opens and expands the file, placing the uncompressed version of the file in the same folder as the original. As Stuffit Expander expands the file, it displays a window showing its progress:

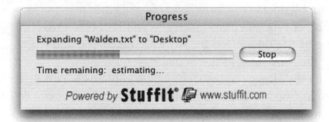

If you find you use Stuffit Expander often, you can place its icon in the Dock (see Chapter 3 for more on putting icons in the Dock) and drag your files on this icon. Or if you open the Stuffit Expander application by double-clicking it, a window displays onto which you can drag your files to unstuff them.

Stuffit Expander offers many options for working with compressed files. It can automatically use your antivirus program (if you have one) to scan files for viruses at it expands them; it can watch a special folder and expand files as they are added; and you can choose a different location to save expanded files. All these options are available from the Stuffit Expander Preferences window, which you can open by selecting Stuffit Expander | Preferences.

Work with Other Types of Compressed Files

Since you can expand Zip files in the Finder, and since Stuffit Expander can expand just about any type of compressed file, you should never run into any problems with other types of compressed files. In addition to .sit files, you may need to expand other compression types, such as .gz, .tgz, and .tar, which are Unix compression formats. As long as these files have either the Mac OS X zipper icon or a Stuffit icon, you can decompress them by double-clicking, as explained earlier.

There is another type of compressed file you'll come across: *disk images*. This is a special type of file often used for software installers, and Apple uses it for all of the software they provide for download.

You can tell a disk image by its icon, which contains a hard disk icon against a white background, and its file extension: .dmg. Disk images can be compressed, and they often are when they are used for software installers. To access the contents of a disk image, double-click the .dmg file; you'll see a dialog as the file is processed, and then it will appear on the Desktop and in the Finder window sidebar, with the same icon as for removable media such as Zip drives.

Backup_2.0.2.dmg   Backup 2

NOTE *You may come across disk images with an .img extension as well. Just double-click them to mount them in the Finder.*

In the preceding illustration, the disk image file is on the left, and the mounted disk image is on the right. When you double-click the mounted disk image, a Finder window displays. You'll usually find an installer package file in this window.

When you have finished working with a disk image, click the eject button next to its icon in the Finder window sidebar, or drag the mounted disk image icon to the Trash to eject it. You can then store the .dmg file wherever you want to, or delete it if you no longer need it.

Burn a Data CD or DVD

If your Mac has a built-in CD or DVD writer, or burner, or if you have an external device, you can burn data discs containing your files. (You can also burn music CDs; see Chapter 16.) This is a good way to transfer large files to other users, and to back up your files.

Burning a data CD on a Mac is very simple (the following instructions also apply to DVDs if your Mac has a super drive that can write to DVD-R or DVD-RW discs):

1. Insert a blank CD-R or CD-RW in your CD writer. When you do so, the Finder displays a dialog asking what you want to do.

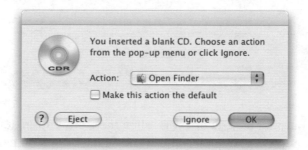

2. Choose what you want to do from the Action menu. To create a data CD, select Open Finder. Select Open iTunes to create a music CD with iTunes, or Disk Utility to create a CD from a disk image. You can also choose Open Other Application and find that application, if you want to use a third-party program to create your data CD.

3. The CD mounts on the Desktop and displays at the bottom of the Finder window sidebar.

4. If you want to change its name, click the CD on the Desktop, press RETURN, then type a new name. Press RETURN to save the change.

5. Drag the files and folders you want to put on the CD onto the CD icon, either on the Desktop or in the Finder window sidebar. You can click the CD icon in the Finder window sidebar if you want to display the CD's contents in a window. As you drag files or folders, you'll see that they are copied as aliases. You'll also notice at the bottom of this window that the total amount of disk space needed displays; make sure you don't add more files than your blank disc can hold.

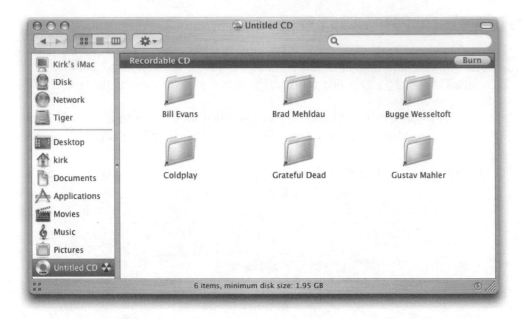

6. To start burning the CD or DVD, click the Burn button at the top right of the window, or click the yellow-and-black burn icon next to the blank disc in the Finder window sidebar. A dialog displays where you can change the disc name (if you haven't already done so), choose the burn speed (according to your burner and media), and save a burn folder if you wish.

7. A dialog displays asking you to confirm that you want to burn this CD. Choose a speed, if this option is available in the Burn Speed menu, and click Burn to write your files to the CD. (If you decide you don't want to burn this CD, click Eject.) If you want to save this as a burn folder to burn the same files again, check Save Burn Folder To and name the burn folder. (See the following section, "Use Burn Folders," for more on burn folders.) If there are too many files in the disc, you'll see a warning that this is the case; you'll have to remove some files and try burning again.

8. After the CD has finished writing, it mounts on the Desktop and you can access its files, or you can eject it and give it to another user or put it in safekeeping if it contains backed up files.

CAUTION *When you copy files and folders to a blank CD or DVD or to a burn folder, the Finder merely copies an alias. If you find you need to remove files from the disc to be able to burn it, you can simply delete aliases for files or folders. However, if you want to remove files from a folder, which appears as an alias, don't double-click the folder and move files to the Trash; you'll be deleting the* original *files, since opening the alias takes you to its target folder. If you need to remove files from a folder, delete the folder alias, and then add the folder's contents until you have reached the maximum amount of files you can put on your disc. And, just in case, if you ever do delete files from a blank CD or DVD in this manner, check the Trash before emptying it to make sure you didn't accidentally put important files there.*

Use Burn Folders

Tiger introduces *"burn folders,"* a new type of folder that you can use to store files in for burning optical discs (CDs and DVDs). What makes burn folders special is that you can save them and "reuse" them. Say you back up certain files or folders

How to ...   **Erase a Rewritable CD or DVD**

One advantage to using rewritable CDs or DVDs is the fact that you can erase them and burn new data on them. However, you cannot do this from the Finder; you must open the Disk Utility application, which is found in the Utilities folder in the Applications folder on your Mac.

Open Disk Utility and find the icon in its left column that corresponds to your CD or DVD writer. Click this icon and then click the Erase tab in the right-hand section of the Disk Utility window. If you want to quickly erase the disk, check Quick Erase. (*Quick Erase* erases the disk's catalog, but not its actual files. If you do a Quick Erase, it is possible to recover files on the disk.) If you want to fully erase the disk, don't check this option.

Click the Erase button. If you chose the Quick Erase option, your disk will be erased in a couple of minutes; if not, this can take much longer, depending on whether it is a CD or DVD.

Your disk is now ready to be used again.

every day, or every week; you can create a burn folder containing these files, and instead of manually adding the files each time you want to burn a disc, you can simply insert a blank disc and click the Burn button.

To create a burn folder, select File | New Burn Folder. A folder displays in the current window, or on the Desktop if that is active, with the name Burn Folder; change this name to whatever name you want.

Burn Folder

Double-click the burn folder to open it; you'll see that it looks exactly like the Finder window for a blank CD, as you saw earlier. Drag your files to this folder, as described in the earlier section "Burn a Data CD or DVD," and then, when you're ready to burn the folder's contents to a disc, insert a blank disc and follow the instructions in that section.

When you're finished, you can save the burn folder wherever you want, and use it to make another copy of the same files on an optical disc at any time.

Mac OS X Tiger

Version 10.4

How to...

- Find anything on your Mac
- Use Spotlight to find files by content
- Work with Smart Folders
- Automate actions with Automator

When you work with a computer, you want it to work *for* you; you want it to do the hard stuff so that you can focus on the content: what you write, the pictures you retouch, the music you listen to, the games you play. You don't want to bend your habits to match the computer; you want the computer to adapt to you, to provide you with the tools that let you work efficiently. The ideal computer would be one that you forget about, one that doesn't get in your way.

This is part of why you bought a Mac, isn't it? You wanted a computer that just works, one that feels easier to use, that lets you express yourself without worrying about what happens under the hood.

Well, Tiger has some new features designed to do just that: Spotlight, the system-wide search technology that lets you find anything on your Mac, and Automator, a program that lets you create *workflows,* which are scripted actions that you can use and reuse, allowing you to perform common actions with a single click. While these two features are quite different, both in function and use, they fit together in one way: the empower you to work more efficiently, and let you do the real work you want to do.

In this chapter, I'll tell you about Spotlight, the new search technology, that lets you search for files, folders, and applications in many ways. I'll tell you about the Spotlight menu, about the Spotlight window, and about Smart Folders, which use a similar method of searching for files. I'll also look at Automator, a new application included with Mac OS X that gives you outstanding power to make little programs that will simplify some of the tasks you do often.

Find Files and Folders on Your Mac

In Chapter 7, I explain how the folders on your Mac are organized. Your home folder has several subfolders designed to hold documents, pictures, music, and other files. Even if you stick closely to this organizational structure and sort your files and folders according to these themes, you will eventually forget where you put a file. That's where Spotlight comes in.

Spotlight creates an index of all your files; that's right, every single one of them (well, except for system files that you don't need to search). When you first install Tiger, Spotlight begins indexing your Mac, reading each file's name, contents, and additional *metadata,* or information about the files. This can take several hours the first time, if you have a large hard disk and lots of files, but after that, Mac OS X notices every time you create, copy, or modify a file, and reads it again, adding information about it to its index; it also removes file information every time you delete a file. Think of the index as a huge database, similar to what Google uses to store information about web pages. Spotlight can read that database much faster than it can read your files, so searching for anything is quick and efficient.

There are several ways to search with Spotlight: you can use the Spotlight menu, browse the Spotlight window, or search in Finder windows. (This third method is not exactly using Spotlight, but searches like this use the same index and search methods.) Let's look at all three of these search methods.

Find Files with the Spotlight Menu

The Spotlight menu, which you invoke by pressing ⌘-SPACE, is the gateway to searching for files in Tiger. Press this keyboard combination to display the Spotlight menu, which appears at the top right of your screen.

As you can see in this illustration, there is a text entry cursor in the menu's text field; start typing a few letters of the name of a file you want to find, and instantly, the Spotlight menu grows as your Mac finds files that match what you type.

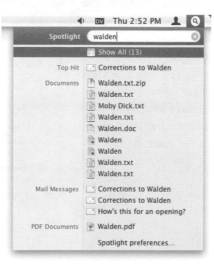

The preceding illustration gives you an example of the type of results that Spotlight can find: you see Documents, Mail Messages, and PDF Documents, and you see a Top Hit, which is the file that Spotlight thinks is closest to what you were looking for. If you press the ⌘ key, the Top Hit is selected; press RETURN to open it. You can use the UP ARROW or DOWN ARROW key to navigate this menu; when a file is highlighted, press RETURN to open it. If you highlight any file other than the Top Hit and then press ⌘-RETURN, a Finder window opens showing you the file.

You can search for much more than filenames with Spotlight. One of the most useful things to search for is the content of your files. Say you know you created a word processing document containing the words "nimble" and "dromedary"; just type those two words into the Spotlight menu, and you'll find that file. Spotlight searches are AND searches; this means that when you type more than one word, Spotlight searches for files that contain the first word and the second word. So if you're sure that a file contains two words, typing both narrows down your results considerably.

NOTE *Do you want to see how fast Spotlight indexes your files? Create a file in any program containing the words "nimble" and "dromedary," or any other words that you know are not in any of your files. Save the file, immediately press ⌘-SPACE, and type those two words. You'll find the file you just created.*

You can also search for *metadata,* or data that describes your files or their content. One example of this is digital music files, which, in addition to the music itself, contain information such as the name of the song, the artist, the composer, the album, the genre, and much more. But Spotlight goes further than that. You can search for files where the author's name is listed (Word and Excel files often have this), you can search for the e-mail address of someone who sent you an attachment by e-mail (when you download attachments, this information is saved), or you can search for your contacts using the Spotlight menu. The illustration on the right shows the kind of files I see when I search for my first name with Spotlight.

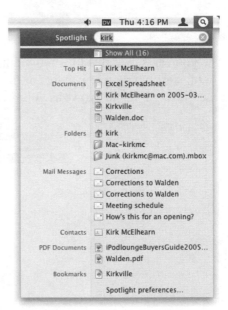

You can see that there are documents—including an Excel spreadsheet, where I am listed as author, an iChat log file, and a web shortcut to my web site, Kirkville. There are a few folders, several e-mail messages, a contact (my own Address Book card), a couple of PDF documents, and a Safari bookmark.

Setting Spotlight Preferences

You can choose the type of files that Spotlight displays, as well as the order in which they display: from the Spotlight menu, select Spotlight Preferences (it's at the very bottom of the menu), or open the System Preferences and click the Spotlight icon. Figure 5-1 shows the Search Results tab of this preference pane.

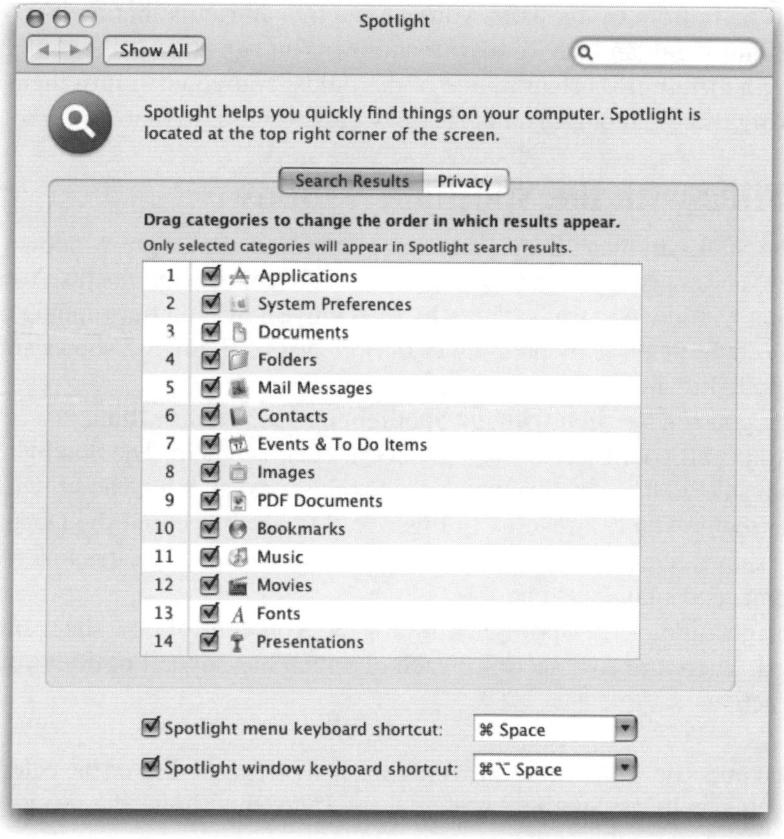

5

FIGURE 5-1   The Spotlight preferences let you change the search result order and turn off certain categories.

You can see in Figure 5-1 that you can uncheck any of the search results categories. Say you don't work with presentations, or you think you'll never want to search for fonts or movies; uncheck them. But if you think you'll often want your e-mail messages, contacts, and iCal events and to-do items to display at the top, drag these categories to the top of the list.

TIP *The Privacy tab of the Spotlight preferences lets you choose certain folders that Spotlight does not search. If you have a special folder for backups, or an external disk, or perhaps other folders you don't want to search in, add them to this tab by dragging them to the list, or by clicking the + button and selecting them.*

You can also change the keyboard shortcuts that Spotlight uses in this preference pane. At the bottom of the pane, you can see the shortcuts that are set for both the Spotlight menu and the Spotlight window. You can change them, if you want, by typing a different shortcut in one of the fields, and you can turn them off by unchecking them—though you probably won't want to do that.

Find Files with the Spotlight Window

While the Spotlight menu is quick and easy to use, the Spotlight window remains on screen, and it gives you additional ways to sort your search results. You can access this window two ways: either by selecting Show All after running a search in the Spotlight menu or by pressing ⌘-OPTION-SPACE. Figure 5-2 shows an example of the Spotlight window after running a search.

When you run a search with the Spotlight menu, you may think that Spotlight has not found all your files; it has, but it doesn't display them. The Spotlight window displays results in the same manner as the Spotlight menu, but it shows when there are more than just a few results. In Figure 5-2 you can see that the Documents category shows five results but has a "link" for "60 more." Click this link to see all the documents containing "report."

The right side of the Spotlight window lets you control how the results are displayed. There are four sections, each of which has several options you can click to activate:

- **Group By** Choose from Kind (this is the type of file, or the category, as you saw in the Spotlight preferences), Date (this shows the results by last-opened date), People (by name), or Flat List (this is a plain list, sorted by date only).

- **Sort Within Group By** By default, each group is sorted by Date. You can also select Name, Kind, or People.

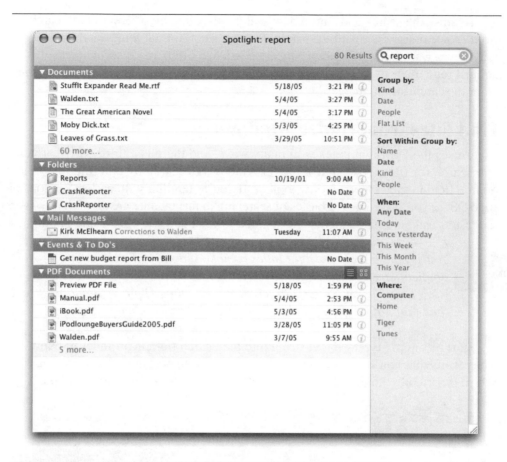

FIGURE 5-2   A search for "report" turns up many results.

- **When**   You can leave the default, Any Date, or narrow down your search, clicking Today, Since Yesterday, This Week, and so on.

- **Where**   The default choice is Computer, or your entire Mac. You can also select your Home folder, or if you have more than one disk or volume, a specific volume. In Figure 5-2, you can see that two volumes are available: Tiger and Tunes. Clicking either of these limits the search to the selected volume.

To open a file, just double-click it. To get more information about a file, click the *i* icon. This displays such information as the file's size, its creation date, its location, a preview (for some files), and more.

To erase the search and start a new search, just click the *x* icon in the Search field. You can use the Spotlight window, if you want, for all your searches; you may never want to use the menu, since the window offers more sort choices. If so, just remember its keyboard shortcut and press that combination whenever you want to search for anything.

Find Files from Finder Windows

Tiger uses the Spotlight indexes in many ways, and there is a third way that you can search for files: you can use Finder windows to search by entering text in the Search field in the Finder window toolbar. If you're familiar with earlier versions of Mac OS X, you'll see that the basics of searching in this manner are similar; however, the results can be much more detailed, similar to what you see when using Spotlight.

NOTE *You'll notice that Spotlight indexes make searching faster in many applications, since they are used across the system. Mail, Address Book, iCal, Help Viewer, System Preferences, and other Apple applications use the Spotlight indexes, providing fast search results in many places.*

Start by simply typing a text string into the Search field in a Finder window. The results that you'll see are similar to those in the Spotlight window; you can see files sorted by kind, and you'll see links to more files to expand each kind.

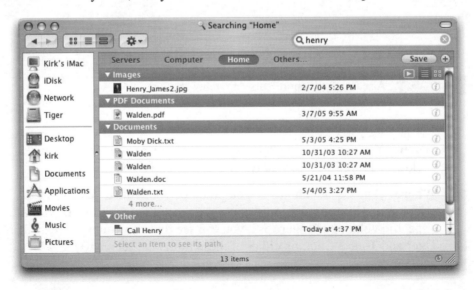

As with the Spotlight window, you can double-click a file, get more information about a file, or change the search area. In the preceding illustration, you saw that the Home folder was selected; you can click Servers, to broaden the search to network volumes (if any), Computer, to search your entire Mac, or Others, in which case you can select specific folders by adding them to a list.

 *If you click Servers, your search will take a while. Spotlight does not index network volumes, so when you search on servers, this is a live search that looks through all the files on the server volumes.*

Another way to search from the Finder is to press ⌘-F, which opens an empty New Search window and moves the text cursor into the Search field. In this case, you'll see that certain criteria are selected in the window.

5

The criteria that are selected are Kind: Any and Last Opened: Any Date. These are provided more as a hint than anything else, since they cover all files. But they show you that these menus are available, and that you can change them to narrow down your search. Each of the choices in the first menu leads to different choices in the second and, sometimes, third menus.

- **Kind**   This is the type of item. You can choose from Images, Text, PDF, Movies, Music, Documents, Presentations, Folders, Applications, and Others. If you select Others, you'll see a field display to the right of the Others menu, where you can click an arrow to choose from dozens of kinds of files. Look through this list to see the scope of data that Spotlight can look for.

- **Last Opened**   This is the latest date a file has been opened. You have several choices, some of which display an additional pop-up menu to let you refine your choice.

■ **Last Modified** This is the latest date that a file has been changed. The choices are similar to those for Last Opened.

■ **Created** This is the date a file was created. The choices are similar to those for Last Opened.

■ **Keywords** This is any keywords that Spotlight may have indexed, such as the author of a document, the sender of an e-mail message, the artist of a song, or Spotlight comments.

■ **Color Label** This is a colored label that you can apply to your files.

■ **Name** This is the name of a file, and you can choose Contains, Begins With, Ends With, or Is.

■ **Contents** This lets you enter any words that you are looking for in a file's content.

■ **Size** This is the size of the item. You can choose less than or greater than the size you enter.

To add criteria, click the + icon to the right of one of the existing criteria; to remove criteria, click the – icon. You can add as many criteria as you want, or use only one. Here's an example of a simple multicriteria search. In this example, I've searched for music files that have been opened in the past week:

You can double-click any of these files to open them in their associated application, or you can click the *i* icon to display more information, including a preview.

Clicking the More Info button displays a Finder info window, where you can see such information as the album name, the song title, the genre, the authors and composers, and more.

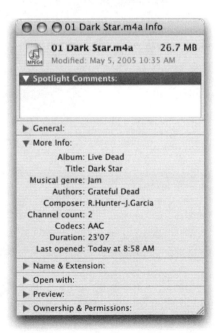

This window also shows you something useful that can help you find specific files: the Spotlight Comments field. You can enter any text you want in that field, and Spotlight indexes this text, allowing you to search for it. You can add, for example, special keywords for your projects, such as Report2005 or NDProposal, that you can later search for. Try to use text that does not appear in any files— abbreviations, combined words, or acronyms—so that searching for the keywords will return only the files to which you have added comments.

If you want to add comments to multiple files, you can do so easily using an Automator action; I explain how to create this Automator action later in this chapter, in the section "Create a Simple Automator Workflow."

Work with Smart Folders

So far in this chapter you've seen how Spotlight can find anything on your Mac. And you've seen how to search in Finder windows. You may have noticed in the previous illustrations that, when you search in Finder windows, there is a Save button. This button lets you create *Smart Folders,* which are saved searches that you can call up at any time. Using the preceding search example, if you click the Save button, a sheet displays asking you to name the Smart Folder, choose a location for it, and specify whether you want to add it to the sidebar.

If you save the Smart Folder, you can either double-click it to open it or, if it is in the Finder window sidebar, just click it once. It displays the results of the search you saved; this is the exact same search, but it is updated. If you had chosen, for example, to look for files opened in the past week, opening this folder displays files that you opened in the week prior to when you opened the Smart Folder, not those that had been opened in the week before you saved the search. It also adds new files that were not on your computer when you ran the initial search.

The Smart Folder displays differently than the original search folder:

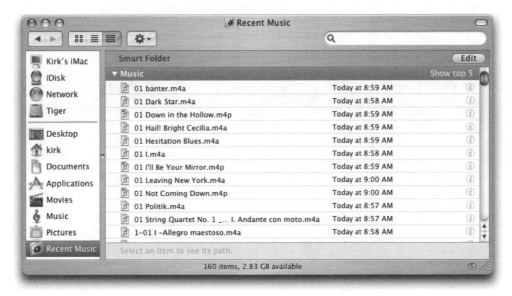

Here you can see that the search criteria are no longer visible; you can see more results in the window. However, if you want to change the search criteria, just click the Edit button at the top of the window, and you'll be able to make any changes you want. Click Save, and the Smart Folder's search criteria are updated.

Smart Folders are a great way to look for certain types of files, or to view the files that you've worked on in the past week, or simply new files that you've added to your computer recently. Combining the power of Spotlight searches and the flexibility of Smart Folders, you'll be in full control of all the files on your Mac.

Automate Actions with Automator

Automator is a new application in Tiger that is designed to let you create *workflows,* or series of *actions,* so that you can perform repetitive tasks more easily. You can use Automator to create workflows for anything that you do often, so you don't have to go through all the windows, buttons, or other choices each time. You can also use workflows to perform actions on multiple files, saving yourself lots of time and effort.

The Automator application is found in your Applications folder.

Automator

When you open Automator, you see the program's main display, which shows its library and its workspace.

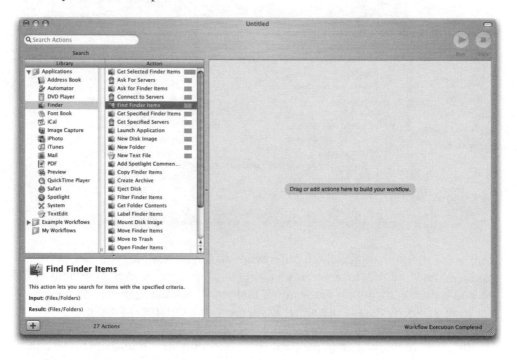

Automator's window contains the following sections. At the left, you see the Library list and the Action list. The Library is a list of all the applications for which actions are available; the actions display when you select an application, or when you click the Applications folder in the Library list (in which case all actions for all applications display). When you select an application in the Library and then select an action, a bottom pane shows the name of the action and describes what the action does, what type of input it requires, and what type of result it provides.

The workspace to the right, the large section of the Automator window, is an area where you drag actions to combine them into workflows. A *workflow* can be a single action or a long series of actions, where each action does something to its input and then passes its results on to the next action.

Create a Simple Automator Workflow

A simple example will help you understand how Automator works and will also provide you with an easy-to-make Automator application that you'll be able to use every day. Earlier in this chapter, I mentioned that you can create an Automator application to add Spotlight comments to several files at once. Let's do that now:

1. In the Library list, click Spotlight. This displays a number of actions in the Action list.

2. From the Action list, select Add Spotlight Comments To Finder Items. You'll see a description of the action in the info pane.

3. Drag the Add Spotlight Comments To Finder Items action to the workspace.

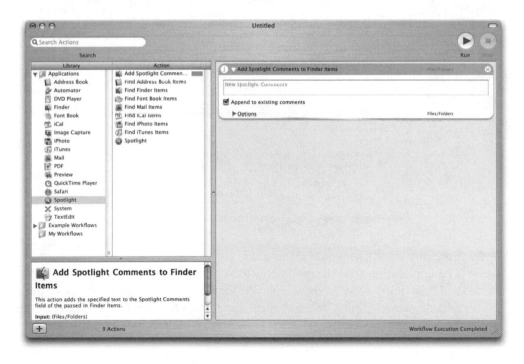

4. As you can see from this action, the input is Files/Folders and the output is Files/Folders. There is an empty text field, which says "New Spotlight Comments," and a check box in front of an option labeled Append To Existing Comments. Let's leave all this as it is.

5. Click the disclosure triangle next to Options, and then check Show Action When Run. If you don't, the workflow will run without presenting a window for you to add comments.

6. Select File | Save. A sheet displays allowing you to choose a location to save this workflow, and a File Format menu lets you choose from Workflow or Application. Choose Application, and save it on your Desktop. Name it **Spotlight Comments**.

7. Now, go to the Desktop and find the application you created. Its icon looks like this:

Spotlight Comments

8. Find a file and drag it onto the Spotlight Comments icon. This opens a simple dialog like this:

9. Enter the comments you want to add in the window, and then click Continue. The application adds the comments to your file (though you don't see this) and then quits. You can check your file to make sure the comments have been added correctly: press ⌘-I and check the Spotlight Comments section of the

Info window. As you saw in the preceding illustration, you can leave Append To Existing Comments checked, in which case your comments are added to any comments the file already contains, or you can uncheck it, in which case the comments you enter replace existing comments. To erase all existing comments, uncheck this and leave the input field blank.

You can use the preceding workflow to add comments to individual files, or to groups of files; just drag as many files as you want onto its icon. You can therefore add any special keywords you want to use to find your files or to mark them for projects so that Spotlight can find them quickly.

Create a Multistep Automator Workflow

Let's look at another example, to help you understand how to combine actions into a multistep workflow. This example will help you send digital pictures to friends or family by e-mail. Since digital photos can be large files, it helps to reduce their size so that you can more easily send them by e-mail. This workflow will ask you to select files, will then scale them to a width of 480 pixels, and will open a new e-mail message that you can address, add text to, and send. There are only three steps—which is nothing compared to some of the complex workflows you can create with Automator—but the resulting application can save you a lot of time.

1. Make sure the Automator workspace is empty. If you still have the Add Spotlight Comments To Finder Items action in the workspace, click the *x* icon to remove it.

2. In the Library column, select Finder.

3. Look for the Ask For Finder Items action, and then drag it to the workspace. Check Allow Multiple Selection, leaving the other options as they are.

4. Let's use the Search field to find the next action we want. First, click the Applications folder, so your search looks at all applications, then type the word **scale** in the Search field. You'll find a few results. Drag the Scale Images action to the workspace, below the Ask For Finder Items action. This displays a warning that the action will change the files passed into it, and asks if you want to add a Copy Finder Items action. It's a good idea to do so, in order to keep your original photos as they are. Click Add.

5. Your workspace should now have three actions and look like this:

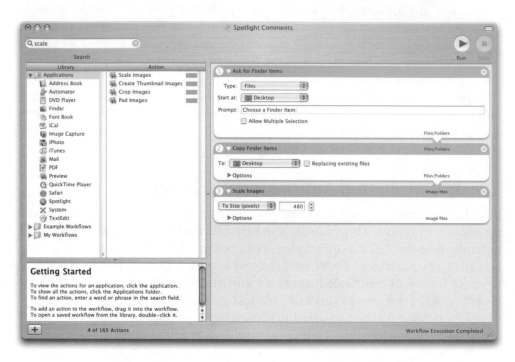

6. The third action, Scale Images, is set to scale the images to 480 pixels. This is a good size for sending photos by e-mail, but you can change it if you want.

7. In the Library column, click Mail and then find the New Mail Message action. Drag this action to the bottom of the workspace. You'll see that this displays a full interface for an e-mail message, but we won't worry about this; you'll fill in this information in Mail when the new message opens. (You can create a workflow to send a prewritten message to a chosen address, if you want.) Click the disclosure triangle next to the name of the action to hide this part of the action.

8. Now, we're going to try out the workflow to see if everything works correctly. At the top right of the Automator window is a Run button. Click this button to run the workflow; you can do this at any time to test your workflow and make sure all the actions run as you want. If you've followed all the preceding instructions, you'll be prompted to select an image (or multiple images), and then you'll see a new mail message containing that image. All you need to do is enter an address, a subject, and a message body, and then send the image.

9. Save the workflow as an application; follow the instructions presented for the first example earlier in this chapter. Name the application as you want and store it in a location where you can access it easily. The next time you want to send pictures to a friend, just double-click this application, and your Mac will do all the hard work for you.

These two examples only give a hint of what Automator can do. The best way to learn more is to examine the Example Workflows included, which you'll find at the bottom of the Library list, or look at some of the actions available for different programs. Since this is programming by drag-and-drop, you don't need to learn any special language. With a little experimentation, you may find that your Mac can save you a great deal of time.

5

How to...

- Work with Finder windows

- Work with the sidebar

- Customize Finder window views

- Use the Finder window toolbar

The Mac OS was the first consumer operating system to provide what is sometimes called the WIMP (window, icon, mouse, pointer) interface. If you haven't been using computers for more than a couple of decades, you may not realize just what a quantum leap in usability this was. Gone was the need to type arcane commands in a Spartan terminal emulator. No longer did you need a computer guru to answer your questions all the time. Apple may not have invented windows, but they tamed them and brought them to the masses.

Computer windows are simply metaphors—they are visual containers for files, folders, and applications that spring open when you double-click folders or disk icons, or when you click certain other icons. This metaphor is so ingrained into the minds of most computer users that it's hard to imagine any other way of navigating a computer. We move from folder to folder, from window to window, looking at, moving, copying, and deleting files. Understanding the way your computer's windows work is the first step toward feeling at home with it.

I'm going to tell you everything about Mac OS X windows in this chapter—how they work, how to open and close them, how to minimize and resize them, and how to customize the display of Finder windows. I'll also tell you all about Finder windows, since they have some unique features, such as the sidebar and the toolbar. Although I focus on Finder windows in this chapter, most of the information applies to application windows as well, since you close, resize, and minimize them in the same way.

Get a Handle on Finder Windows

As I pointed out in Chapter 3, the Finder is the part of Mac OS X that controls and manages windows, and that displays your files and folders. The Finder is your control center for working with your data.

Figure 6-1 shows a Finder window open in my home folder. Each of the elements indicated in the figure has special functions and uses. We'll look at all of these and more in the coming sections.

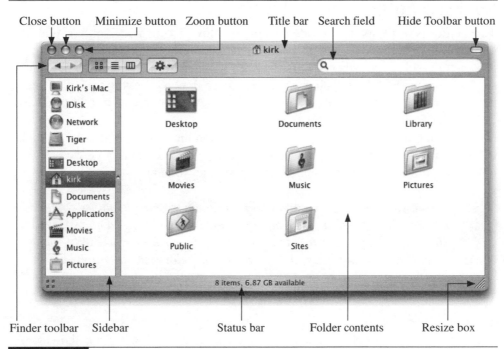

Close button   Minimize button   Zoom button   Title bar   Search field   Hide Toolbar button

Finder toolbar   Sidebar   Status bar   Folder contents   Resize box

FIGURE 6-1   A Finder window showing the contents of a user's home folder

If you don't have a Finder window open on your Mac, press ⌘-N, or select File |
New Finder Window to display one.

TIP *The preceding commands, used to open a new window, work in many
applications. In programs such as word processors, spreadsheets, or graphics
programs, these commands generally open a new file in a window. In other
programs, they generally either open a new file or create something new
(such as a new playlist in iTunes, a new event in iCal, or a new e-mail
message in Mail or other e-mail programs.)*

Finder windows are different than most other windows you'll see in Mac OS X.
Not only do they contain files and folders—some application windows may also
display these items—but Finder windows have a sidebar at the left. This special part
of the window lets you group your most commonly used places and folders so you
can access them easily.

Navigate Folders in the Finder

The Finder is designed to provide a visual display of your files, folders, and applications. Each window displays the contents of a folder, which may contain files, applications, and other folders. To open a folder from a Finder window and see its contents, just double-click it. You can keep double-clicking folders to see the contents of other subfolders. If you want to view the contents of a folder that's in the sidebar, just click it once to display it.

You can click the Back and Forward buttons in the Finder toolbar to go back to the previous folder, or to go ahead to a folder you have already viewed (if you have clicked the Back button while viewing another folder).

 *If you want to go to the parent folder of the currently displayed folder (the folder that contains the current folder), you can use a quick keyboard shortcut: ⌘-UP ARROW takes you up through your folder hierarchy, one level each time you press it. You can go back down the hierarchy by pressing ⌘-DOWN ARROW if a folder is selected.*

The Sidebar

 The sidebar contains two sections separated by a horizontal divider (see Figure 6-1). At the top, you'll find your Computer (with the name of your computer, which you can set in the Sharing preference pane; see Chapter 12); then you'll see an icon for your iDisk (if you have a .Mac account; see Chapter 11); next comes the Network icon, which gives you quick access to other computers on your network (see Chapter 12); and, finally, your hard disk. If you have any removable media mounted on your Mac, any additional hard disks or partitions, or any audio CDs, you'll see them below your hard disk. To their right are arrow icons that you can click to eject these items.

You can add files or folders to the sidebar by dragging them from any window. Just move an item over the sidebar, until you see a line between two other items, and release it. (You can also add an item to the sidebar by selecting it and pressing ⌘-T.) The sidebar will add this item—this is actually an alias of the item; the original remains where it was—and resize the contents of the sidebar to fit the space available. If you have a lot of items in the sidebar, you'll see a scroll bar, but the sidebar resizes its contents dynamically so you can fit many items in it.

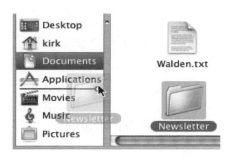

 *Be careful when you drag items into the sidebar. If you don't see a line between two existing items, and one of the sidebar's folders is highlighted, you may end up dropping the item you're dragging into a folder, moving or copying it to that folder instead of placing it in the sidebar.*

6

You can remove items from the sidebar by simply dragging them out of any Finder window. As you do, you'll see them disappear with a puff of smoke. This won't delete the original, only the alias in the sidebar.

What to Put in the Sidebar

While you can put files, folders, or applications in the sidebar, it's mostly designed for folders. This lets you navigate to a commonly used folder by clicking its icon in the sidebar; when you do, the Finder window changes to show the contents of that folder, using the view you have set for that folder. (I'll tell you about Finder window views in the "Customize View Options" section later in this chapter.)

If you put files or applications in the sidebar, you can open them with a single click (not a double-click as you do in Finder windows). But this means you may accidentally click one of these items and open it when you didn't mean to. If you want to have shortcuts to files or applications, use the Finder toolbar (see the "The Finder Window Toolbar" section later in this chapter) or create a folder for such favorites and place it in the sidebar.

Remember, whatever you put in the sidebar displays in every Finder window, so add items that you really need to access often. As you'll see in Chapter 13, these items in the sidebar also display in Open and Save dialogs, so you can access them from these dialogs as well.

If you put items in the sidebar whose names are too long, they'll get cut off, and the ends of the names will be replaced with ellipses (...). If you have a lot of items like this, you may want to change the width of the sidebar. Just move your cursor over the metal bar that separates the sidebar from the main window contents and drag in either direction. You can enlarge the column to accommodate long names, or you can shrink it to take up less space. If you'd prefer to only see icons, you can shrink the column so only icons display. And, if you don't like the sidebar, drag the separator all the way to the left, or double-click it, to remove it entirely. (You can move it back to the right by clicking and dragging the left border of the window to the right.)

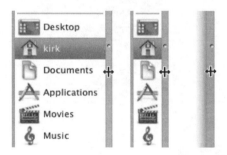

If you move the sidebar separator to show only icons, the Finder displays a tooltip when you move your cursor over any of the sidebar icons, telling you its name.

Control Your Windows

You won't want to just leave every window where it is when it opens; your screen would get very cluttered. You can move windows around, minimize them, close them, and zoom them, all with simple operations using the mouse or the keyboard.

Each Mac OS X window has three control buttons in the top-left corner. Clicking these buttons closes, minimizes, or zooms the window. When you move your cursor over these buttons, they display an ×, a −, and a +, to give you visual clues as to their function.

The three buttons, colored red, yellow, and green, do the following:

- **Red**   This is the Close button. Click this button and you'll close the window. When you close a Finder window, nothing special happens, but when you close an application window, you may see a Save dialog if you haven't yet saved a new file or if you've made changes to an existing file. (See Chapter 13 for more on the Save dialog.)

- **Yellow**   This is the Minimize button. Clicking this sends your window to the Dock, where a small version of it displays like an icon. You can bring the window back to its previous size by clicking its icon in the Dock. (See Chapter 3 to find out how to work with the Dock.)

- **Green**   This is the Zoom button. When you click this button, the size of the window changes—in some cases it gets smaller, to fit perfectly around the window's contents, and in other cases it gets bigger, to show you more. Some applications have different behaviors associated with the Zoom button. In iTunes, for example, clicking the Zoom button turns the iTunes window into a small control window; clicking it again returns the window to its previous size.

NOTE   *If you're used to working with Mac OS 9 or earlier, or if you've moved to the Mac from Microsoft Windows, you'll find it takes a while to get used to these window controls. In both Mac OS 9 and Microsoft Windows, controls are split in the two top corners of windows. It really does make more sense to group them, as in Mac OS X, so you always know which corner to go to for any of these operations.*

You'll also want to move windows around your screen to see other things. Just click your cursor anywhere on the metal part of a Finder window and move it where you want. (Well, almost anywhere—you can't move a window by clicking the sidebar separator or by clicking the button names in the toolbar, but anywhere else works fine.)

6

For other windows, those of applications that don't have a brushed metal interface, click anywhere in the title bar and drag the window to move it. Aside from the colors, these windows work the same as the Finder windows you saw previously.

You'll also want to resize your windows from time to time. While the Zoom button can help you do this quickly, you don't get to choose the final size of the window. If you want to make a window larger or smaller, just click and drag the resize box at the bottom-right corner of any window.

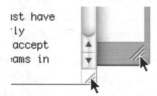

You can resize windows to make them as small or as large as you want. Moving and resizing windows in this manner is the same for the Finder and most other applications, though some applications use static windows that you cannot resize.

 *Like many operations in Mac OS X, there are keyboard shortcuts to close and minimize windows. To close a window, just press ⌘-W; to minimize a window, press ⌘-M.*

Use Different Finder Window Views

Mac OS X gives you several options for viewing the contents of Finder windows. The View button in the Finder window toolbar lets you choose from three different views: Icon View, List View, and Column View. Each of these views has its advantages, and while you may choose to always use the same view for all your windows, it is practical to use views that best meet your needs at a given time.

 To change views in a Finder window, click one section of the View button. If you click on the left section, the active window changes to Icon View; the middle section changes it to List View; and the right-hand section changes it to Column View.

6

SHORTCUT *You can change views from the keyboard as well: press ⌘-1 for Icon View, ⌘-2 for List View, and ⌘-3 for Column View.*

The view you select applies only to the window for which you select it. You can have several windows open with different views, and the Finder offers view options for each of these views so you can further customize the way your windows display.

Icon View

Icon View, which you select by clicking the left section of the View button or by pressing ⌘-1, is the default view for new Finder windows, unless you choose Open New Windows In Column View in the Finder preferences (see Chapter 3). This view, as shown in Figure 6-2, presents all your files, folders, and applications as icons with their names either beneath them or next to them.

Icon View is most practical for folders like your home folder, with a small number of subfolders.

FIGURE 6-2   A Finder window in Icon View shows the contents of the window as icons spread out across the window.

List View

List View, which you select by clicking the middle section of the View button or by pressing ⌘-2, arranges your files and folders in a list. By default, the contents of the window are sorted by name—this is indicated by the highlighting of the Name column header (see Figure 6-3).

You can change the way the window's contents are sorted in List View by clicking one of the column headers. (In Figure 6-3, you could sort the contents by Date Modified or by Kind, instead of by Name.) See the section "List View Options," later in this chapter, where you can choose which columns are displayed in this view.

To reverse the sort order, click the sort header; the sort triangle shows you which way it is sorted. In Figure 6-4, clicking the Name header changes the sort order, and the folders are sorted in reverse alphabetical order.

You can move the window columns (except for the Name column) if you want to change the display. Just click and hold the cursor on one of the window headers and drag it to a new position.

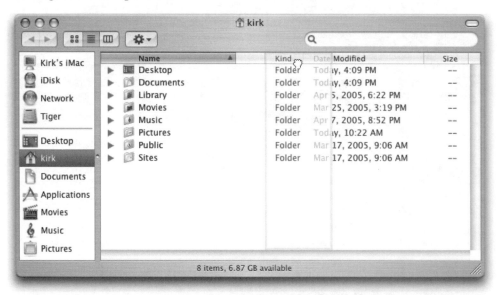

There are two ways to navigate windows in List View. The first is to open folders by double-clicking. This displays the contents of the folders in Icon View. The second, which is more practical, is to click the disclosure triangle next to

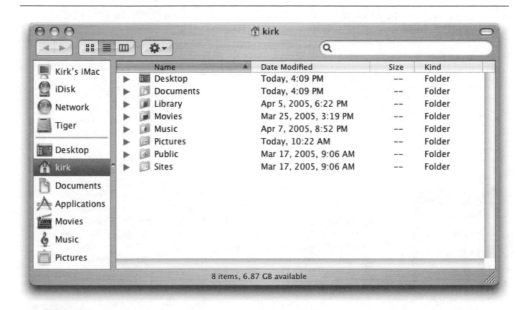

FIGURE 6-3   A Finder window in List View shows the contents of the window in a list, sorted by one of the window's headers.

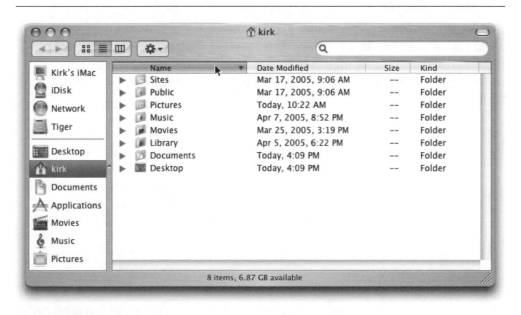

FIGURE 6-4   Clicking a window header changes the sort order.

6

a folder to display its contents. The advantage to using List View in this manner is that you always see the hierarchy of your files and folders.

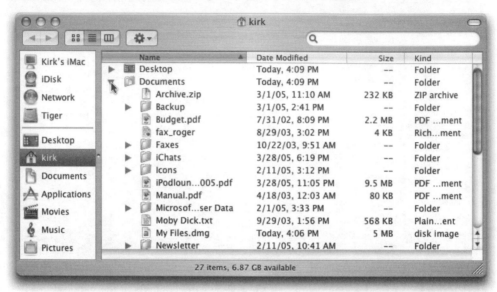

To open a file or application in a List View window, just double-click its icon.

Column View

Column View, which you select by clicking the right-hand section of the View button or by pressing ⌘-3, arranges your files and folders in columns, showing their hierarchical relationship. (See Figure 6-5.) In Column View, you never see the contents of just one folder, and the items shown in Column View are always sorted by name.

 If you're upgrading from Mac OS 9 or earlier, or if you've switched from Microsoft Windows, you'll find that the Column View is a bit unusual. Pre–OS X versions of Mac OS offered Icon and List View, but not Column View. However, you may also find that it is one of the most practical views to use, especially when you move around a lot—Column View always shows a hierarchy and always gives you an idea where you are in relation to other folders.

When you use Column View, you can move horizontally through the hierarchy of files and folders on your Mac, always aware of where you are in relation to other folders. In addition, when you select a file, Column View offers a preview

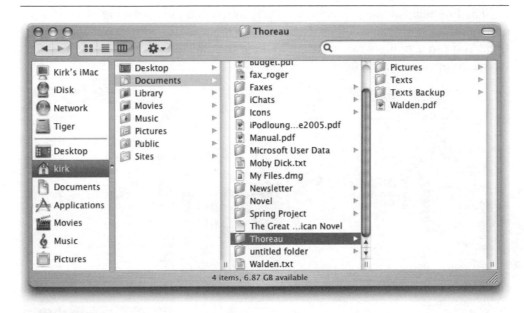

A Finder window in Column View shows the contents of the folder in columns, sorted by name.

column that can show you what the file contains. (This works for some types of files, such as text files, some graphics files, movie files, and more.)

The Preview column is practical since it shows you the beginning of text files and thumbnails of graphics files. But it is even more useful with movies and MP3 files. You can actually watch or listen to these files in the Preview column without having to open an application.

While you wouldn't actually want to watch a movie this small, the Preview column lets you preview it before you open it in another application. You can, however, listen to MP3 files this way—they sound just as good as they do with any other program, though iTunes (see Chapter 16) offers so many great features, you'll want to use that most of the time.

Customize View Options

In addition to offering three different ways to view Finder windows, Mac OS X provides a full range of options so you can customize the way these windows display, and in some cases *what* they display. View options can apply to individual windows, or you can create a set of options that apply to all windows in a given view.

To access view options, click in the window you want to customize, and then select View | Show View Options or press ⌘-J. The View Options window comes in three versions, one for each of the different window views. When you display the View Options window, it floats above other Finder windows. You can leave it visible and click in different windows to change their options—the View Options window changes according to the active Finder window.

Icon View Options

Windows in Icon View offer the most options. You can change the size of the icons displayed, the size of the text labels, the way the icons are arranged, and the window's background. Figure 6-6 shows this window.

The top of the window lets you choose to apply your view options to This Window Only or to All Windows. When you choose All Windows, the settings you choose are saved, and you can apply them to other windows by selecting the All Windows radio button for them. This is practical if you want to have all or most of your Finder windows displayed in one way; but you can still change settings for individual windows by selecting This Window Only for specific windows.

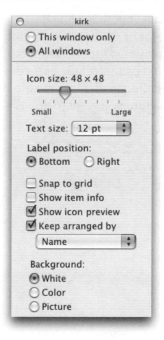

FIGURE 6-6   The View Options window for a window in Icon View

You can customize the following in Icon View:

- **Icon Size**   Move this slider to increase or decrease the size of icons in the window.

- **Text Size**   Choose the size you want for text labels.

- **Label Position**   Icon names can be either at the bottom of icons or to the right. (See Figure 6-7.)

- **Snap to Grid**   This keeps icons aligned on an invisible grid.

- **Show Item Info**   This displays information about the icon. (See Figure 6-8.)

- **Show Icon Preview**   This shows a thumbnail of graphics or movies when selected.

- **Keep Arranged By**   This arranges icons by Name, Date Modified, Date Created, Size, Kind, or Label. Select your choice from the pop-up menu.

- **Background**   You can choose a white background, which is the default, or you can select a color or picture. (See Figure 6-9.) If you select Color, a small rectangle displays next to the Color button. Click this and a color picker opens where you can select the exact color you want to use. If you select Picture, a Select button displays next to the Picture button. Click this button and find the picture you want to use as a background.

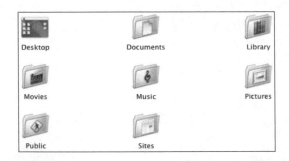 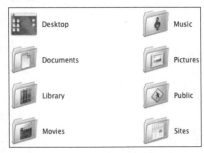

FIGURE 6-7   Icons with label position at the bottom and at the right. Labels at the bottom take up more space vertically, and labels at the right spread icons out more horizontally.

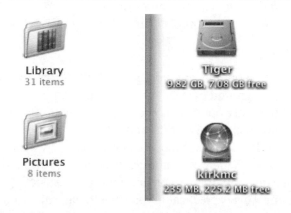

| FIGURE 6-8 | Icons with item info displayed beneath them. For folders, this shows the number of items they contain. For volumes and disks, this shows the amount of space they contain and/or the free space. Some other files show additional information, such as the size of graphics files, the length of MP3 and movie files, and so on. |

| FIGURE 6-9 | This window uses a picture as the background. This is Apple's "Abstract 4" desktop picture. |

 *Pictures align to the top-left corner of windows, so if you use a large background picture, you may not see more than its corner.*

List View Options

List View customization options are more limited than Icon View options—you cannot change the background of your windows, and you only have two choices for icon sizes. But the other options, as shown in Figure 6-10, let you decide which information is displayed about your files and folders.

The top of the window lets you choose to apply your view options to This Window Only or to All Windows. When you choose All Windows, the settings you choose are saved, and you can apply them to other windows by selecting the All Windows radio button for them. This is practical if you want to have all or most of your Finder windows displayed in one way; but you can still change settings for individual windows by selecting This Window Only for specific windows.

You can customize the following in List View:

- **Icon Size**   Choose either small or large icons.
- **Text Size**   Choose the size you want for text labels.

FIGURE 6-10   The View Options window for a window in List View

■ **Show Columns**   Check which columns you want to display. Since you can sort files and folders in List View windows by any of the columns, this gives you a great deal of latitude in your window display.

■ **Use Relative Dates**   If you check this, dates displayed are relative—instead of only displaying the date in day/month/year format, the Finder shows Today and Yesterday for files created or modified on those days.

■ **Calculate All Sizes**   If you check this, the Finder shows sizes for files and folders; if you leave this unchecked, it only calculates sizes for files. If your folders contain a lot of files, it can take a while for their sizes to be calculated.

Column View Options

Column View windows offer the fewest view options. First, you do not have the choice of applying view options to all windows or just one window. In Column View, your view options apply to all windows. As you can see in Figure 6-11, you can only change three options.

FIGURE 6-11   The View Options window for a window in Column View

How to ...   Get the Right Finder Window Settings

The many Finder view options available may seem complicated at first, but as you become familiar with Mac OS X and decide how you want to view your windows, you'll see that they can save you a lot of time and help you better view your files and folders. In most cases, you'll probably want to create global settings for all windows in each view—this makes sure that each time you display a window you know how it's going to be presented.

But in some cases, you'll want certain windows to display differently: these could be specific folders in your home folder, such as Music or Movies, or folders containing projects or archives that are best viewed in certain ways. Take the time to experiment. Getting the right views helps make you more productive and makes it easier to spot your files and folders at a glance when you open a new window.

You can customize the following in Column View:

- **Text Size**   Choose the size you want for text labels.

- **Show Icons**   If this is checked, the Finder displays icons in Column View windows. If you uncheck this, the Finder only displays the names of files, folders, and applications.

- **Show Preview Column**   If this is checked, the Finder shows the Preview column when you select a file. If you uncheck this, the Finder doesn't show the Preview column.

The Finder Window Toolbar

Every Finder window has a toolbar at the top, which gives you access to commonly used functions and lets you quickly search your computer. Let's look at the buttons and icons it contains by default. (We'll see how to change the toolbar in the next section, "Customize the Finder Window Toolbar.")

The first two buttons on the Finder toolbar are the Back and Forward buttons. These work like the same buttons in a web browser, allowing you to navigate through folders and return to where you came from. These buttons are only available if you keep the default Finder behavior, which is to not open folders in a new window. If you have folders open in new windows, these buttons will be dimmed. (If you want to change this, see Chapter 3.)

The View button is a three-part button that lets you change window views in a click: you can choose from Icon View, List View, or Column View. I discussed Finder views earlier in this chapter.

The next button is the Action button, which is really a pop-up menu that displays certain actions you can take on selected items or, if no items are selected, on the folder displayed in the current Finder window. The actions available from the Action button are the same as those you can access using a contextual menu. See Chapter 3 for more on using contextual menus and an explanation of the menu items available from the Finder's contextual menu and Action button.

The Search field lets you enter text to search in the currently visible folder. I look at finding files and folders in Chapter 5.

Customize the Finder Window Toolbar

You can customize the Finder toolbar by changing the icons and buttons it displays, as well as by adding icons for any files or folders you use often. The only limit to customizing the Finder toolbar is space, but there's even a way around that.

NOTE   *If you're upgrading from Mac OS X 10.2 (Jaguar), you'll notice that the Finder toolbar has changed considerably. The toolbar does not present folder icons by default since Apple created the sidebar for this purpose. In addition, the Customize Toolbar window (discussed later in this section) offers fewer icons that you can add to the toolbar. You can still add file, folder, and application icons to the toolbar, but you need to think whether these icons work best in the toolbar or whether—especially for folders— they would be more effective in the sidebar.*

If you want to add a file, folder, or application icon to the Finder toolbar, just drag it to the toolbar. You'll have to hold it over the empty space in the toolbar for a second, and when you have done so, the cursor will change, showing that you can release it to leave the icon on the toolbar.

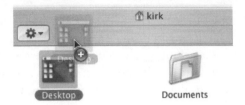

After you have done this, the icon you just dragged shows up in the toolbar. In some cases, as with the folders in your home folder, the Finder gives them special icons that are different from the actual folder icons. For other items, the icons you see in the Finder are the same ones that show on the toolbar.

I said earlier that you are limited by space, but that there is a way around this limit. If you resize your Finder window so it's not wide enough to display all the toolbar icons, it shows a double-arrow indicating that there are more icons. To select one of these icons—this is the same as clicking it—click the double-arrow, and then select the icon you want from the pop-up menu that displays.

NOTE   *When you change the size of a Finder window, its toolbar changes with it. Narrowing the window puts more of the toolbar icons out of view, but they are always accessible from the double-arrow pop-up menu.*

You can change the order of icons in the toolbar by holding down the COMMAND (⌘) key and dragging any of them. You could, for example, move the Search field to the left, and when you add folder, file, or application icons to the toolbar, you'll always have access to the Search field, since it won't be pushed off the visible part of the toolbar.

You can do much more than just add a couple of icons to the Finder toolbar. With any Finder window open, select View | Customize Toolbar. A sheet then

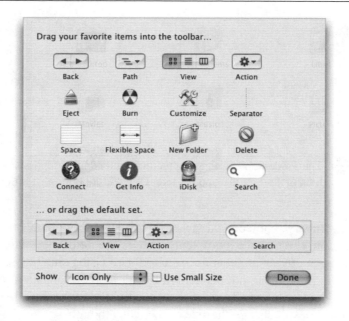

6

FIGURE 6-12   The Customize Toolbar window gives you a wide range of icons to place in the Finder toolbar.

displays, as in Figure 6-12, showing all the functions you can add to the toolbar. Feel free to customize the toolbar to your heart's content. You'll note that there are no folder icons on this sheet; again, Apple considers the best place for folder icons to be the sidebar.

To add any of these items to the toolbar, just click their icons and drag them to the toolbar—you don't need to drag them and hold them, waiting for the cursor to change, when you're on the Customize Toolbar sheet. Drag them wherever you want on the toolbar; the other icons move out of the way to let you place the one you're dragging. To remove items, just drag them off the toolbar. You can choose from the default icon set by dragging the default set strip to the toolbar, or you can mix and match the icons available. No matter which icons you choose in this window, you can still add your own files or folders as explained earlier.

The Customize Toolbar window gives you another useful option: you can choose whether the toolbar shows Icon & Text, Icon Only, or Text Only. By default, the Finder window toolbar displays as icons only, with large icons. The difference between these three options, other than what they display, is the amount of space the Finder toolbar takes up. As you can see in Figure 6-13, choosing Text Only takes

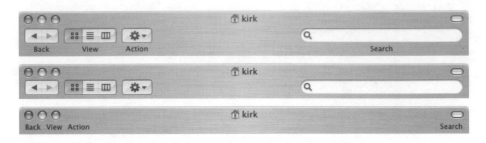

FIGURE 6-13   The Finder toolbar showing the three icon display options: at the top, Icon & Text; in the middle, Icon Only; at the bottom, Text Only

up less space vertically, but Icon Only takes up less space horizontally (not apparent in the illustration, but true for many icons, where the names are wider than the icons), allowing you to put more icons in the toolbar. (Using small icons only affects icons you add to the toolbar, not the default Finder icons.) You can also check Use Small Size on the Customize Toolbar sheet to slightly shrink the size of the text displayed—this doesn't change the size of the icons though.

Since most of the icons are images that remind you what they are for, you don't need their names. However, if you place plain folder icons containing personal files in the toolbar, it might be better to have text displayed.

When you have finished customizing the Finder toolbar, click Done to return to your Finder window.

SHORTCUT   *While you can change the toolbar display from the Customize Toolbar sheet, there's another way you can do so: hold down the COMMAND (⌘) key and click the Hide Toolbar button (the pill-shaped button at the top-right corner of any Finder window). Each time you click this button, the toolbar display changes, cycling through the six available options: Icon & Text, Icon Only, and Text Only, as well as each of the same options with smaller text.*

The Finder Window Status Bar

At the bottom of every Finder window is a status bar, which shows a bit of information about the current window. This bar tells you how many items are in the window, how many are selected (if any), and the amount of free disk space on the disk containing the folder that the window displays.

2 of 8 selected, 6.84 GB available

In addition, the status bar shows whether a window is displayed in Icon View: if it is, a small icon displays, such as that on the left in the preceding illustration.

Hide the Finder Toolbar and Status Bar

The Finder toolbar and status bar are helpful, and can save you a lot of time. They help as you navigate through windows and give you instant access to certain functions. But there are times when they get in the way and take up too much space. When this occurs, you can hide them temporarily—or permanently, if you prefer—with just a click.

To hide the toolbar in a Finder window, click the Hide Toolbar button at the top-right corner of any Finder window (or select View | Hide Toolbar or press ⌘-OPTION-T). Here's what a window looks like without the toolbar:

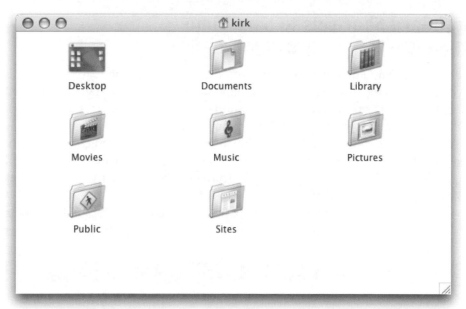

To display the toolbar again, click the Hide Toolbar button (or select View | Show Toolbar or press ⌘-OPTION-T).

You can see that there is now a status bar at the top of the Finder window, beneath the title bar; this provides the same information as the status bar in the brushed metal windows. You can hide this by selecting View | Hide Status Bar, and display it again by selecting View | Show Status Bar. There is no keyboard shortcut for this.

NOTE   *When you hide the Finder toolbar in Mac OS X 10.4, you may be surprised—the changes to the window are much greater than merely hiding the toolbar. The entire window interface changes. The sidebar disappears, as does the toolbar, and windows display a different interface. If you don't like brushed metal Finder windows and sidebars, this is one way to return to a simpler interface.*

Hiding the toolbar and status bar affects only the window you change, so you can use a combination of aqua and brushed-metal windows. You can, however, use the three different Finder window views in these windows. Select one of them from the View menu, or press ⌘-1 for Icon View, ⌘-2 for List View, or ⌘-3 for Column View.

Keyboard Shortcuts to Save Time When Working with Windows

I can't repeat enough how much time you can save when you learn some basic keyboard shortcuts. Pressing a key combination is much faster than clicking and selecting menu items, and when you memorize the main keyboard shortcuts, you'll find you have much greater control over your computer.

The shortcuts shown in Table 6-1 apply to Finder windows, though some of them also work in other application windows. (The shortcuts for Close and Minimize windows are global, for example.) If you learn no other keyboard shortcuts, these will save you a great deal of time.

See the inside back cover of this book for a more complete table of shortcuts you can use in the Finder, as well as standard shortcuts that most applications use.

The Shortcut	What It Does
⌘-N	Open new Finder window
⌘-W	Close window
⌘-M	Minimize current window
⌘-T	Add selected item(s) to sidebar
⌘-J	Show view options
⌘-1	View as icons
⌘-2	View as list
⌘-3	View in columns
⌘-OPTION-T	Hide/show toolbar

TABLE 6-1   Keyboard Shortcuts for Working with Finder Windows

Chapter 7

All about Your Mac's Folders

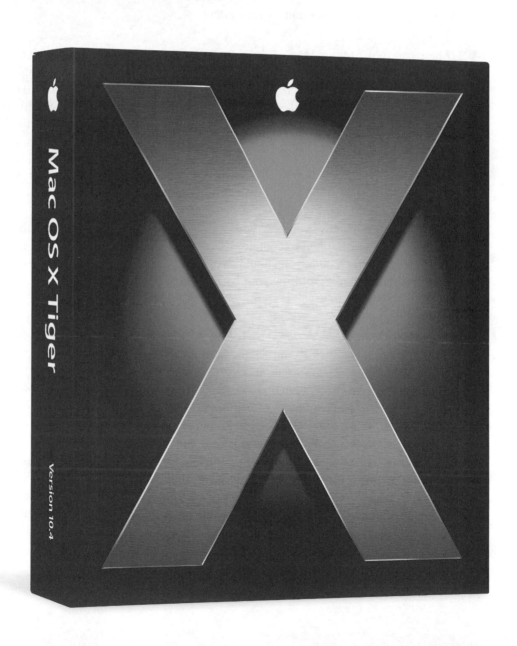

How to...

- Learn what's in your Mac's folders
- Organize your files efficiently
- Use your home folder and its subfolders

When you look at your Mac's folders, you'll see that they are organized in a somewhat rigid structure. Some of these folders are very important and are used by Mac OS X in special ways. Other folders are designed to provide order and help you store your files logically. While this organization may seem to be a constraint, it actually helps you by giving you specific locations for storing different types of files.

If you've moved to Mac OS X from earlier versions of Mac OS, or from Microsoft Windows, you'll find this structure a bit disconcerting. But you'll quickly get used to these folders, and you'll find that they help you become more organized and more productive.

In this chapter, I'll show you how your Mac's folders are organized, and the types of files they're designed to contain. I'll also explain which folders you can put files into, and which ones you should avoid. After reading this chapter, you'll have a better understanding of how your Mac is organized, and why.

Looking Inside Your Mac's Folders

If you look at the top level of your Mac's hard disk, you'll see four folders (see Figure 7-1): Applications, Library, System, and Users. (If you installed the Xcode Developer Tools, you'll also have a Developer folder here. If you installed the Classic Environment, you'll have another folder there called System Folder.) To see these folders, click your hard disk icon in the sidebar.

Within these four folders, Apple has placed all the files, folders, and applications that you use when working on your Mac. Each of these folders is meant to hold certain types of files, and, while you could put other files into some of them, it's a good idea to follow Apple's organization. In fact, unless you have an administrator account, you can't put files in some of these folders; and you shouldn't anyway.

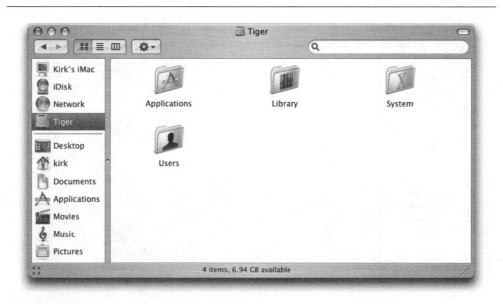

FIGURE 7-1   These four folders contain the guts of Mac OS X.

The Applications Folder

The *Applications* folder contains, as its name suggests, applications—programs
that you use to carry out specific tasks. All the applications included with Mac OS X
are installed here, and most applications you install later are also placed in this
folder. (Figure 7-2 shows some of the applications in this folder.) Mac OS X is
a multiuser operating system (OS), which means you can set up user accounts
for yourself, your spouse, and your kids; or each of your coworkers can have
accounts; or each student using a school computer can have their own account.
(For more on user accounts, see Chapter 8.) While your personal files are stored
in your home folder (discussed in the section "The Desktop Folder," later in the
chapter), Apple puts an Applications folder at the top level of your hard disk, so
every user can access all the computer's applications.

You can open any of these applications by double-clicking their icons. Since
you'll probably be going to this folder pretty often, Apple places a shortcut to it
in the sidebar: clicking the Applications icon in the sidebar of any Finder window
opens this folder.

FIGURE 7-2   Some of the applications included with Mac OS X: you can see Address Book, Dictionary, iCal, iChat, and others.

 *You can also open this folder by selecting Go | Applications or by pressing ⌘-SHIFT-A in the Finder.*

The Library and System Folders

While you can put files in many of your Mac's folders, such as your home folder or its subfolders, there are some folders on your Mac that you shouldn't touch. The *Library* folder is one of these. It contains essential system files, including fonts, preferences, plug-ins, and caches. You may never have to open this folder, since anything that needs to go there is usually taken care of by applications or their installers.

The *System* folder contains other files that you don't want to touch. If you have an administrator account on your Mac—which you have if you are its only user or if you are responsible for setting the Mac up for others—you are allowed to access these folders, and you have permission to move, copy, and delete their files. Messing with the System folder, or with the Library folder, could prevent your Mac from functioning correctly, or at all.

CAUTION   *The previous comments are serious. Unless you know what you're doing, don't even think of fiddling with the files in these two folders. You could severely damage your Mac's system, and you might have to reinstall Mac OS X.*

The Users Folder

The *Users* folder is the center of the world for the people who use your Mac. It contains individual folders for each user on your Mac. If you are the only user, you'll just see two folders: one with your name on it and another called Shared. Each user folder is labeled with the user's short name, in lowercase letters—mine is called "kirk"; yours will be labeled with whatever short name you entered when you set up your Mac.

Where Applications Belong

While most applications are installed in the Applications folder, some tools get installed in the Utilities folder that's inside the Applications folder. There you'll find a number of tools and utilities included with Mac OS X, and other utilities you may install later. (See Chapter 19 for more on utilities.)

In addition, you can actually install a lot of software wherever you want. Some software, which comes in disk images or on CD-ROMs, doesn't use Apple's Installer application and just tells you to drag the application or its folder to your hard disk. While you can put these programs anywhere, it's a good idea to keep them all in your Applications folder.

If you don't have an administrator account, you won't be able to install software into the Applications folder, nor will you be able to drag programs there. However, you can create an Applications folder inside your home folder and add your own programs there. In fact, if you do this, the folder will display the same icon as the main Applications folder.

Don't move *any* of Apple's programs from their initial folders. When you update these programs, Apple's Installer usually expects to find these programs in either the Applications folder or the Utilities folder, and, in some cases, does not update them correctly if they are not in these default locations.

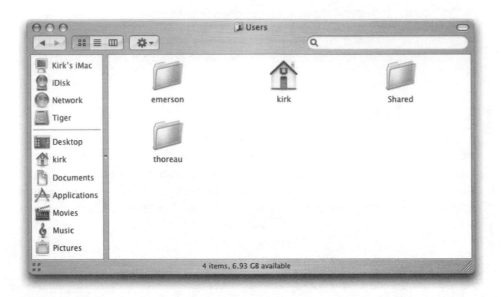

NOTE   *If you have more than one user on your Mac, each user's folder displays here, but only the currently logged in user's folder has the home icon.*

I'll show you the contents of the home folder in the next section, but first let's look at the Shared folder. Since Mac OS X is a multiuser system, each user only has *permissions,* or access rights, to certain files and folders. If you look inside another user's folder, you'll see that most of their subfolders have little red Do Not Enter icons on them (see Figure 7-3)—you can't access their files, with the exception of those in the Public and Sites folders (see the next section, "Your Home Folder").

The *Shared* folder is the one location where every user can place files. If you want to leave files for someone else to copy or look at when they use your Mac, put them here. When other users log in on your Mac, they can access any of the files in this folder and copy them to their personal folders.

Your Home Folder

To paraphrase Ralph Kramden, a person's home is their castle. Your home folder is that castle, and you are the queen or king of that castle. Your home folder is your personal domain, and it's where you put all your files and folders. As you can see in Figure 7-4, each home folder contains eight subfolders.

SHORTCUT   *You can go to your home folder by clicking the home icon in the sidebar of any Finder window, or by pressing ⌘-SHIFT-H.*

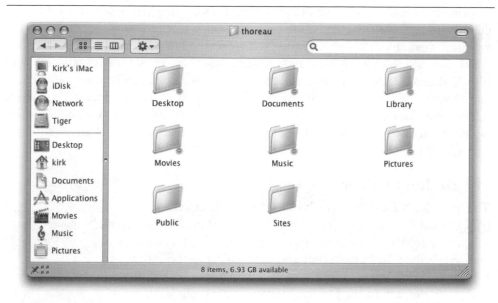

FIGURE 7-3   Most of the subfolders inside another user's home folder are off-limits.

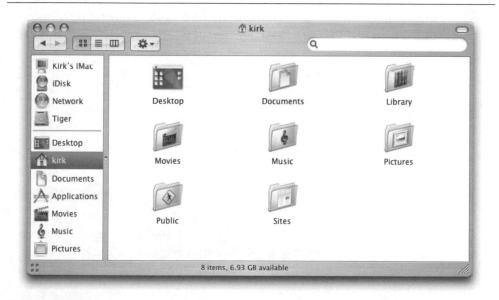

FIGURE 7-4   These eight subfolders, with distinctive custom icons so you can recognize them more easily, are inside each user's home folder to help organize files.

These subfolders help you organize your files by suggesting where you should put certain types of files. These are only suggestions, but there are several reasons to follow them. First, this organization is logical. The main folders you'll put files in are Documents, Movies, Music, and Pictures, and this is a good way to organize your files. The second reason is that certain programs will automatically place their data in these folders. When you start up iTunes, for instance, it creates a folder in your Music folder; when you launch iPhoto, it puts its library folder in Pictures. If you follow this organization, it will be easier to back up your files. (For more on backing up files, see Chapter 19.)

The Desktop Folder

The Mac OS X Desktop, which I discussed in Chapter 4, is the background for your Mac's windows and a part of the Finder, but it is also a folder. You can put files and folders on the *Desktop* and access them from there, but you can also get to these files and folders from the Desktop folder itself. There's an icon for this folder, by default, in the Finder window sidebar; click this icon and you'll see what's on your Desktop.

Desktop

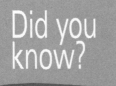

You'll notice one small difference between the contents of your Desktop folder and your actual Desktop: only files and folders appear in the Desktop folder, while the Desktop itself also displays hard disks, network volumes, audio CDs, CD-ROMs, DVDs, or other removable media. (You can change what the Desktop displays in the Finder preferences. See Chapter 4 for more on this.)

Did you know?

Your Desktop Belongs to You Alone

Unlike the Desktop in Mac OS 9 and earlier, the Mac OS X Desktop is user specific. In Mac OS 9, for example, whatever files or folders are on the Desktop appear there for all users. But in Mac OS X, the contents of the Desktop belong only to the user who placed them there. As I mentioned earlier, each user has a Desktop folder. So when you log out and another user logs in, the other user won't see the files you have left on the Desktop.

You'll probably use the Desktop from time to time for your personal files and folders: you might use it to save files before placing them in other folders, to temporarily store files you've downloaded from the Internet, or to copy files you're working on. Yet files on the Desktop are never really there (on the Desktop, that is); they are in the Desktop folder. Each user has a separate Desktop folder, and only the files in a user's Desktop folder show on that user's Desktop.

The Documents Folder

The *Documents* folder is designed to hold all your personal files (with the exception of certain types of files like music files, movies, or pictures): it's the catchall for your word-processing files, spreadsheets, presentations, lists, and that great American novel you've been working on. As you can see next, this folder can contain files and other folders, and some applications install folders here to store their data.

Documents

7

There are a couple of ways to get to the Documents folder. The easiest is to click the Documents icon in the Finder window sidebar. You can also get there by clicking your home folder icon in the sidebar and then double-clicking the Documents folder. Either way, this will likely be the folder you use the most, so become familiar with one way of getting to it quickly.

You don't have to put your personal files in your Documents folder. You can create your own folders within your home folder if you want, or even in any of its other folders, though don't put any personal folders in the Library folder; I explain why this is dangerous in the following section. Also, don't put personal files in the Public folder, unless you want other users to be able to access them. If you have a second hard disk or if your hard disk has more than one partition, you can put your files on a different disk or partition. But the Documents folder remains the most logical place for your files, and keeping all your personal documents in one location makes it easier to back up your files.

The Library Folder

You saw earlier that there is a Library folder at the top level of your hard disk. There is also another one inside the System folder, as well as one inside each user's home folder. All these Library folders store similar types of files, but each one has a different purpose. The *Library* folder in your home folder stores personal files, such as application preferences, favorites, web-browser

Library

bookmarks, and other user-specific files, as opposed to system-wide files, which are stored in the other Library folders. If you use Apple's Mail program for e-mail (see Chapter 10), for example, your mailboxes are stored here as well. You don't need to go into this folder any more than you need to fiddle around in the other Library folders, and if you delete any of the files or folders it contains, you could harm your Mac OS X system. However, you should back up your e-mail if you use Mail; I'll look at backing up files and your mailboxes in Chapter 19.

The Movies Folder

Apple includes a *Movies* folder inside each user's home folder to store movies in. If you use iMovie to edit your videos, the application will suggest that you save new movies in this folder. If you don't use iMovie or another video-editing program, you'll probably never use this folder, but nothing can stop you from placing other files here.

Movies

Digital video takes up a lot of disk space. If you work with video a lot, you should consider buying an additional hard disk, either one you can install internally on tower Macs or an external FireWire hard disk.

The Music Folder

The *Music* folder is meant to hold digital music files, in formats such as AAC, MP3, AIFF, WAV, and so on, that you create from your own CDs with iTunes, or that you buy from the iTunes Music Store or other online music sites. This folder also holds other files and folders used by other music applications. When you start up iTunes for the first time, it creates an "iTunes" folder inside your Music folder and puts any music files you create with iTunes (as well as your playlists) in this folder.

Music

NOTE *If you have a lot of digital music files, your Music folder will contain a lot of data, more than you could ever back up on a CD or other removable medium (though you might be able to fit the files on a DVD). The only way to back up these files is to a second hard disk.*

The Pictures Folder

Just as the Movies and Music folders are meant to hold movies and music, the *Pictures* folder is designed to hold your digital photos. If you use Apple's iPhoto, the application creates an *iPhoto Library* folder inside the Pictures folder, and when you download photos from a digital camera, this is where they are stored. You can store other pictures in this folder if you want as well.

Pictures

NOTE *When Apple released Mac OS X 10.3, or Panther, it included some of its iApps, such as iTunes, iPhoto, and iMovie. Shortly thereafter, Apple decided to bundle these applications (together with iDVD and GarageBand) in a package called iLife. Since these programs are no longer free (with the exception of iTunes), they are not a part of Tiger. Nevertheless, the folders for working with these programs—the Pictures and Movies folders—are still part of your home folder. If you don't have these programs, these folders may remain empty. Don't worry, they don't take up much space.*

The Public Folder

Earlier in this chapter, I explained how the Shared folder lets you put files in a location where other users can access them. The *Public* folder inside in your home folder works in a similar way. When users log in on your Mac, they can access any folders here, or they can copy files to the Drop Box, which is inside the Public folder. (They can also use the Shared folder, which I mentioned earlier in this chapter, to leave you files. Any user can access files in the Shared folder, but only you have permission to use the files in your Drop Box.)

If other users connect to your Mac over a network, they can access your home folder—they see a list of user names in the connection dialog, and select one to connect to. When the connection is made, they end up inside your Public folder, and view or copy any files you have placed there. However, if they want to send you files, they can only place them in the Drop Box (but cannot access any of the other folders in your home folder). For more on sharing files on a network, see Chapter 12.

The Sites Folder

Mac OS X includes one of the most respected web servers available: Apache. This web server can be used to share files on a local network over a web-based interface (see Chapter 12) or can turn your Mac into a full-fledged web server open to the Internet. In either of these cases, you can put your web server files in the *Sites* folder—though if you use your Mac as a web server open to the outside world, you'll want to put them in the /Library/WebServer/ Documents folder. Note that using a web server to provide access to your files over the Internet is beyond the scope of this book.

Sites

Chapter 8

Create and Manage User Accounts

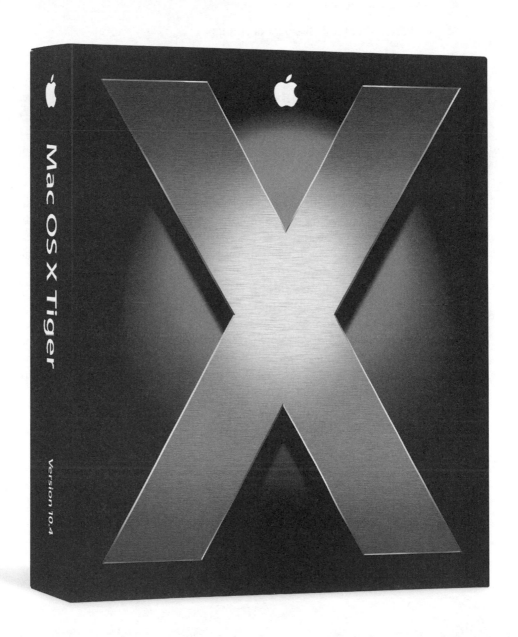

How to...

- Log in and out of your Mac
- Use fast user switching
- Manage user accounts
- Set parental controls for user accounts
- Set login options

Mac OS X is a multiuser operating system. This means it is designed to work with several user accounts on the same computer. While you may be the only user on your Mac, you can set up dozens of accounts for different people if you need to: family members, coworkers, students, or even friends. Each user has the right to access *only* his or her files and folders, yet all users can run applications installed on the Mac. Each user's files are organized in individual user folders (home folders) and are inaccessible to other users.

The advantage to working with a multiuser environment is the ability to seal off each user's files from other users. This protection is pretty strong; other users really can't access your files, though administrative users can in some circumstances. (In some situations, the administrator may want to know all the users' passwords. This is normal since an administrator is responsible for managing a computer and needs access to certain files to perform tasks such as backing up files, troubleshooting, and maintenance. An administrator can also access users' files in other ways.)

In this chapter, I'll show you how to log in and log out of your Mac, how to use fast user switching to change users without logging out, how to set up and work with user accounts, how to set up parental controls to limit what some of your users can do, and how to delete accounts. If you need to set up two or 20 accounts on your Mac, you'll learn how to do that in a jiffy.

Log In and Out

Only one user can be active at a given time on your Mac. You can have user accounts for each member of your family, each student in a class or school, or each employee in a company. Since each of these accounts is protected by a password, only the user with this password (or an administrator who knows all the users' passwords) can access the account.

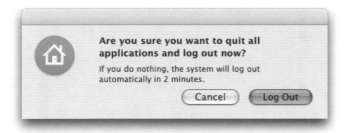

Are you sure you want to quit all applications and log out now?

If you do nothing, the system will log out automatically in 2 minutes.

Cancel   Log Out

FIGURE 8-1   If you don't reply to this alert within two minutes, the system logs out automatically.

NOTE *While only one user can be active at a time, Mac OS X's fast user switching lets you change active users without actually logging out. See the following section for more on fast user switching.*

When you're working on your Mac and want to log out, select Apple Menu | Log Out or press ⌘-SHIFT-Q. An alert displays, asking you to confirm that you really want to log out. (See Figure 8-1.)

Click Log Out to log out, or click Cancel to keep your session open.

After you log out, another window displays all the users on your Mac (Figure 8-2).

Click your user name, and then enter your password in the Password field and click Log In (or press the ENTER or RETURN key). If you enter an incorrect password, the Login window shakes back and forth, as if nodding its head no. You have three tries to enter your password. If after these three tries you still haven't entered the right password, a hint displays if you have entered one in the Accounts preference pane (see the section "Create User Accounts," later in this chapter). This hint should help you remember your password.

NOTE *Your password is very important. If you lose your password, check with your Mac's administrator. If you're the administrator, or the only user, you will have to reset your password by starting your Mac from the Mac OS X installation DVD and using the Utilities | Reset Password function available from the Installer. Suffice it to say that you should keep a copy of your password in a safe place in case you forget it.*

8

FIGURE 8-2   The Login window shows all the users who have accounts on your Mac.

Switch Users with Fast User Switching

While only one user can work on a Mac at a time, it is possible to have several accounts open at any given time using *fast user switching*. Unlike logging out from one user account and logging in to another, which means you must quit all active applications, fast user switching lets you switch from one account to another without logging out of the first account. You can switch this way among several accounts, needing only to select their names from the User menu and enter the appropriate password.

If you have created more than one user account on your Mac (see the section "Create User Accounts," later in this chapter, for more on creating user accounts) and have turned on Fast User Switching (see the section "Set Login Options," later in the chapter), you'll see a User menu at the right end of your menu bar. This menu displays either the full name of the current user, the short name of the current user, or a User icon; if you click this menu, it shows a list of all the other user accounts on your Mac (open accounts are indicated by an orange check icon).

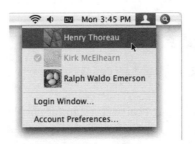

To switch users, just select a user from this menu; a Login window displays showing that user's name. Enter the user's password and then click Log In or press ENTER or RETURN. The new user's account will activate, but the current user's account will remain open in the background, with all the user's applications running and documents open.

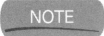
As you'll see if you have different user accounts, each user's environment is individual. When you customize your Finder's appearance (see Chapter 3), you may change the items in Finder window sidebars, put your own picture on the Desktop, and accumulate files on the Desktop as well. But when other users activates their accounts, they won't see any of this; their accounts only use their customizations and preferences, and only display their files.

Another way to switch users is to select Login Window from the User menu. This displays a login window (similar to that shown in Figure 8-2) where you can choose a user account with which to log in.

When you want to shut down your Mac, you need to either have all its users log out or enter an administrator's password. (I'll tell you about the administrator's account in the next section, "Manage User Accounts.") If you can't do either of these, you won't be able to shut down your Mac; for this reason, it's important that users log out when they've finished working so they don't prevent you from doing so.

Manage User Accounts

You can create as many user accounts on your Mac as you want, providing each user with their own home folder where they can put their files and allowing them to customize their environment individually. You can also manage these accounts, giving users specific rights, such as which applications they can use and which functions they can access. For example, you can set some accounts to provide full access to all applications, and you can configure other accounts so specific users can only use selected applications.

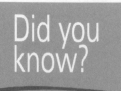

The Flip Side of Fast User Switching

Fast user switching is a very useful feature, but it comes with its share of caveats. As I mentioned earlier, you need to be able to log out all users to shut down your Mac. If you are an administrator, that's easy; you can just enter your user name and administrator's password in a dialog that displays when you try to shut it down. But if you don't have an administrator's account, you can only shut down your Mac if all other users have logged out. (You can, however, put your Mac to sleep; if you can't shut it down, this is almost as good.)

But there are other issues to consider. First, your Mac has only a limited amount of memory, and each user account that is open (whether it's active or not) uses some of that memory. If you have several user accounts open, you'll find that your Mac may function slowly. Second, while most applications will open in every account that is running, some won't. Finally, if someone does decide to shut down the Mac, and your account is in the background, you'll lose any unsaved changes to your documents; make sure you save your files before switching to another user.

To create and manage user accounts, you must be an *administrator*. An administrator is a user who has the right to create, edit, and delete user accounts, as well as install software and perform certain system maintenance tasks. If you are the first user on your Mac, you are automatically an administrator. While each Mac must have at least one administrator, you can allow several users to be administrators, or even all users if you wish. You can choose this when creating or editing user accounts (see the following section).

You manage user accounts in System Preferences. You can open the System Preferences application by clicking its icon in the Dock or by selecting Apple Menu | System Preferences. Click the Accounts icon in the System section of the System Preferences; this opens the Accounts preference pane (see Figure 8-3). Then, to make changes to existing accounts or create new accounts, click the padlock icon and enter your administrator's user name and password.

The left column of the Accounts pane displays all the users on your Mac. You can see in Figure 8-3 that the top of this column is labeled My Account, and beneath

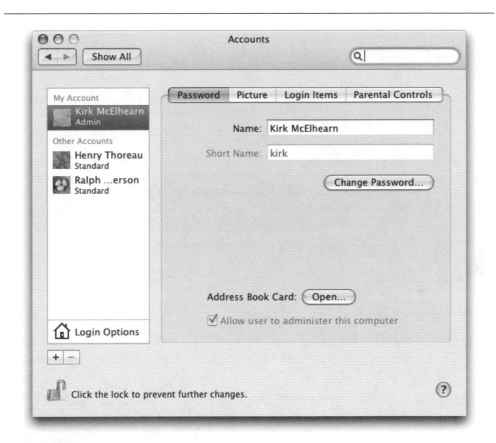

FIGURE 8-3   You create, edit, manage, and delete user accounts from the Accounts preference pane.

this is a section labeled Other Accounts that shows all the other user accounts on your Mac. This preference pane is where you can add new users, edit or delete existing users, and set login options.

Create User Accounts

To create a new user account, click the plus (+) button below the user account list. This displays a new user sheet where you enter information about the user.

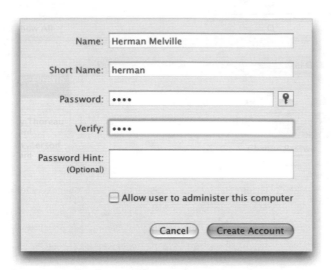

There are five fields where you enter information about a user:

- **Name**   Enter the user's real name.

- **Short Name**   This is the name that appears on your user's home folder and is also a name your user can enter when logging in to your Mac remotely; users don't need to use their full names. Your Mac will suggest a short name here; in most cases, this is just the user's name in lowercase letters. You can change this if you don't like the suggestion. You might want to do this if the short name is too long.

- **Password**   This is your user's password. It must be at least four characters long and is case sensitive. (This means that capitals count; "PassWord" is not the same as "password".) If you are in a company or school, use a password that's hard to figure out; computer security professionals tell you to use something with random letters and numbers. (If you click the key icon next to the Password field, you'll see the Password Assistant, which helps you determine the quality of your password; this assistant can also suggest passwords for you.) But if you're using your Mac at home, use something that you'll never forget. Don't worry too much about security in such a case.

- **Verify**   Enter the password again to confirm it.

- **Password Hint**   This is optional, but is useful if you think your users may forget their passwords. Enter a hint that will help the user remember the password. This hint is displayed if the user enters a wrong password three times. Try to choose a hint that's not too obvious a giveaway for your password. If you do use your spouse's name, your child's name, or your pet's name as a password—which is not a good idea—don't use a hint such as "my wife's name." Someone might be able to figure it out. If you only use your Mac at home, though, don't worry too much about this.

When you've filled in all the preceding information, click Create Account to create the account and move on to set other options for the account. (See Figure 8-4.)

FIGURE 8-4 After creating a new user's account, it displays in the Accounts list.

You can also choose to allow the user to administer this computer. If you check this option, the user will have rights to create and manage users, to install software, to change all the system preferences, and to perform certain other tasks that regular users cannot perform.

If you want to change the user's picture—which is displayed in the Login window—click the Picture tab. Choose from one of Apple's pictures, or choose your own by clicking Edit, then Choose, and navigating to a picture file. You can also just drag a picture file from the Finder to the Images box, which displays when you click Edit. You can change the scale of the picture by moving the slider below it; when you've finished, click Set to use the picture.

Use Administrator Accounts

As you've seen, there are two types of user accounts: administrators, who can do just about anything on your Mac, and standard users, who have limited access to files, folders, and settings. It's important to understand what an administrator account allows you to do and what limits it has.

As the administrator of your Mac, you have access to all the System Preferences, and you can change settings that affect the overall operation of your computer. Standard users can only change settings that affect their environments and the way they work. Administrators can also install software, using Apple's Installer program, which standard users cannot do. Finally, administrators can access files and folders in the netherworld of their Mac, including those in the System and Library folders (see Chapter 7 for a discussion of these folders). The Finder displays an authentication dialog when you attempt to access these files and folders, and if you enter your administrator user name and password, you'll be allowed to continue.

One thing administrators cannot access, however, is other users' files contained in their home folders. These files, as long as they are not in the Public or Sites subfolders, are only accessible to their creators. (Administrators, however, *can* turn on special *root* access to be able to go anywhere they want, including users' home folders—but that's beyond the scope of this book.)

While you need to be an administrator to do certain tasks, this power can be dangerous. In fact, many users find it safer to create two accounts for themselves: an administrator account for installing software or changing system-wide settings and a standard account for everyday use. Even if you're careful, it's always possible that, as an administrator, you might accidentally delete important files or make changes that cause problems to your Mac.

In fact, if you work with two accounts, you'll rarely need to log in with your administrator account. To access any of the System Preferences that standard users can't change, just click the Lock button and then authenticate by entering your administrator account user name and password. If you need to access any files in the Library or System folders, or make any other system-level changes, authenticate this way as well. While you'll type your user name and password a bit more often, it will ensure that you can't make any blunders as an administrator.

Set Parental Controls

After you set up a user account, you can establish parental controls, restricting what the user can do and which applications he or she can access. These controls are not just for parents, however; you can use them if you are setting up a Mac that several people will use in a school or work environment as well. To set parental controls, click a user's name in the Accounts list to select it, and then click the Parental Controls tab.

You can set parental controls for five applications:

- **Mail**   You can add e-mail addresses to a list of names with which the user can exchange e-mail. Add addresses to the list, and the user will *only* be able to send e-mail to or receive e-mail from those addresses. You can also check Send Permission Emails To, and enter your e-mail address, to allow the user to ask permission to send mail to other users. (This only works if both requester and authorizer use Mac OS X 10.4 and Apple's Mail.)

- **Finder and System**   This offers two choices: Some Limits and Simple Finder, each of which is described next.

  - **Some Limits**   This lets you choose from a number of actions that you might want to disallow the user to perform, such as Open All System Preferences, Modify the Dock, and Burn CDs and DVDs. It also lets you limit their usage to selected applications. To do this, check This User Can Only Use These Applications. Check or uncheck the boxes next to the four categories: Applications, Utilities, Applications (Mac OS 9), and Others. To allow or disallow access to specific applications, click the disclosure triangle to show all the applications and uncheck the ones you don't want your user to use. You can uncheck any applications to prevent users from launching them, and check applications to allow them, effectively creating user accounts that can only use one or two applications if you want.

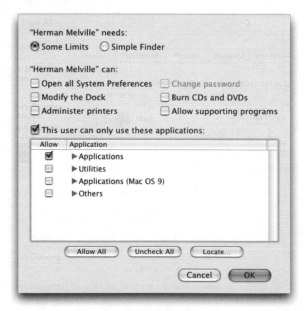

■ **Simple Finder**   This presents a simplified Finder to the user. It offers
fewer menu choices and gives the user fewer chances to mess things up.
As with the Some Limits setting, you can choose which applications you
want them to use, and these applications appear in the My Applications
folder in the Dock. This can be a good way to configure access to your
Mac for a young child, only allowing them to launch games they play and
preventing them from fiddling with any other programs.

The Simple Finder is a truly simplified interface and one that is entirely
kid-safe. As you can see in Figure 8-5, a minimal Dock is displayed
(with just three folders), and Finder windows are as Spartan as possible.

| FIGURE 8-5 | The Simple Finder: in the Dock, the three folders are My Applications, Documents, and Shared. |

The three folders are, from left to right, My Applications, which contains aliases to the applications the user is allowed to use, Documents, which contains any documents the user creates, and Shared, which allows you to exchange documents with the user via the Shared folder. (See Chapter 7 for more on using the Shared folder.) These items display as icons in the Simple Finder window, and only one window displays at a time.

Even though the Simple Finder is simplified, you, as the administrator, can access full Finder menus if you need to. Select Finder | Run Full Finder, and then enter your administrator's user name and password. You'll be able to move and copy files around and change Finder preferences as needed. (You won't be able to access the System Preferences, though.) To return to Simple Finder, select Finder | Return to Simple Finder.

■ **iChat**   As with Mail, you can create a list of approved contacts for iChat. Check this option; then enter any iChat user names you want to allow the user to chat with.

■ **Safari**   Check Safari, and then click Configure; a dialog tells you to log in as the user you are restricting and then add sites that you want them to be able to access. Type the URL of a web site; if it is not allowed, Safari displays a dialog telling you this. Click the Add Website button, enter your administrator's user name and password, and then add the site as a bookmark in the Bookmarks Bar. (See Chapter 10 for more on Safari and bookmarks.) When you set parental controls for Safari, the user can only access sites in the Bookmarks Bar; for this reason, you may want to remove some or all of the default sites that Apple has placed in this bar.

■ **Dictionary**   Finally, you can choose to prevent the user from "viewing certain words, such as some profanity" by checking the Dictionary box.

Set Login Options

The Accounts preference pane offers several login options, which you can set by clicking the Login Options button at the bottom of the Accounts list. This lets you activate such options as fast user switching, choose a user for automatic login, and decide how to display the Login window.

The first choice on this screen is automatic login. If you have more than one user on your Mac, you can choose to have a specific user log in automatically whenever you start up. This saves you from having to select your user and enter your password each time. To do this, check Automatically Log In As and select a user from the pop-up menu. A sheet displays, showing the user name and asking you to enter that user's password.

Next is a choice for the way to display the Login window. If you choose List of Users, all the users who have accounts are listed in the Login window. For users to log in, they click their user name and then enter their password. If you choose Name And Password, the Login window only displays two empty text fields. Users must type their user names (either their full name or their short user name) and passwords in these fields. In most cases, List of Users is the best choice, since users will see their names and not have to remember exactly what they are. However, if you have a lot of users (such as in a school environment or in a company), Name And Password is better; it saves users from scrolling through a long list.

After entering the user's password, click OK. The next time you start up your Mac, that user's account will automatically log in.

Choosing Name And Password adds a bit more security to your Mac since anyone who wants to log in needs to know both a user name and a password. It's not much in the way of protection, but an intruder who knows the user names on the computer has one less hurdle to overcome; so this option could make it more difficult for unauthorized users to access your Mac.

Use automatic login with care. When a user is logged in automatically, your Mac starts up and then provides access to that user's files. If you're not sure you'll be in front of your computer when it starts up, you probably should not turn this on (unless you only use your computer at home).

Another option lets you show the Sleep, Restart, and Shut Down buttons. This only affects the Login window, but if you uncheck this, these buttons are not displayed and no users can perform these operations from the Login window. (They will be able to do so from the Finder, however, unless you have configured their accounts to use a Simple Finder.)

You can choose to display the Input menu in the Login window; if you do this, users will be able to change keyboard layouts before typing their passwords. This is only useful if your users will be working with different keyboard layouts and languages. You can also choose to use VoiceOver, Apple's assistive technology, in the Login window. This provides speech for users who are visually disabled. And you can turn on password hints in the Login window as well; if you check this option, a hint is displayed (if you have entered one for the user) after three unsuccessful attempts at entering a password.

Finally, if you want to use fast user switching, which I described earlier in this chapter, check the Enable Fast User Switching check box. You may *not* want to use this in certain situations, especially in schools or labs where many users access your Mac. As I explained earlier, having multiple user accounts open can use a lot of memory, and if your users get into the habit of using fast user switching instead of logging out, it may slow down your Mac.

Edit User Accounts

To make changes to any of your user accounts, you must be an administrator. Open the Accounts preference pane in the System Preferences and click the user name in the account list. (You can only make changes to a user account if that user is not logged in. If that user is logged in, you must switch to the user's account and log out to be able to make changes.) You'll be able to change just about everything concerning that user's account. The only thing you cannot change is the user's short name because this is the name of the user's home folder.

Delete User Accounts

Administrators can delete user accounts at any time, except when that user is logged in. To delete a user account, click the user's name in the Accounts list and then click the minus (–) button at the bottom of the Accounts list. An alert asks you to confirm this deletion. If you're sure you want to delete the account, click OK.

When you delete a user's account, your Mac saves the contents of the user's home folder as a disk image in a folder called Deleted Users, found inside the Users folder. This way you can be sure that none of the user's files are lost. If you click Delete Immediately in the alert, then this disk image will not be saved, and all your user's files will be deleted right away.

If you save a deleted user's home folder, you'll be able to access it in the Deleted Users folder. To access these files, double-click the disk image file, which then mounts a disk image on the desktop. Open that disk image to access all the deleted user's files.

Modify a Non-Administrator Account

Even if you're not an administrator, you are allowed to change some of your user account information and settings. You can change your full name, your password, and the picture used in the Login window. You can also set login items (see the following section). Open the System Preferences and click the Accounts icon.

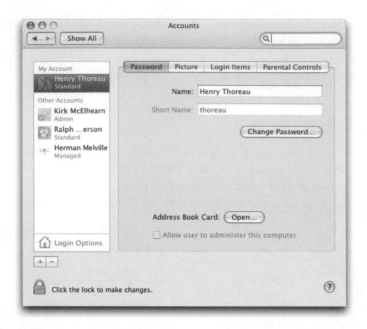

You can change everything but your short name on the Password tab; you can see in the preceding illustration that it's dimmed. You can also access your Address Book Card and change its information. (See Chapter 15 for more on the Address Book.)

You can change your picture on the Picture tab (see the earlier section "Create User Accounts" for more on choosing pictures).

Start Up Applications When You Log In

If you use certain applications all the time, you may find that you spend the first few minutes opening these applications every time you turn on, or log in to, your Mac. You can set any items you want—applications, files, or folders—to automatically open when you log in, saving you time and getting your Mac ready for you to work more easily.

As with everything in this chapter, you set *login items* from the Accounts preference pane of the System Preferences. Click your account in the Accounts list (whether you are an administrator or regular user), and click the Login Items tab.

If you've upgraded from Mac OS X 10.3, Panther, Login Items is what Apple used to call Startup Items.

To add an application to the Login Items list, click the plus (+) button and find the application you want to open automatically. The application is added to the list. (See Figure 8-6.)

   *If the item you want to add as a Login Item is visible in a Finder window or on the Desktop, you can just drag it to the Login Items list to add it.*

If you want the application to hide so its window(s) don't appear on screen, check the box in the Hide column. If you do this, you can make the application visible, after it launches and hides, by clicking its icon in the Dock.

To remove an application from this list, click its name and click the minus (−) button.

You're not limited to automatically opening just applications—you can also open files or folders in this way. Just add them to the list the same way you add applications to have them open automatically. Figure 8-7 shows an application, a folder, and a file in this list.

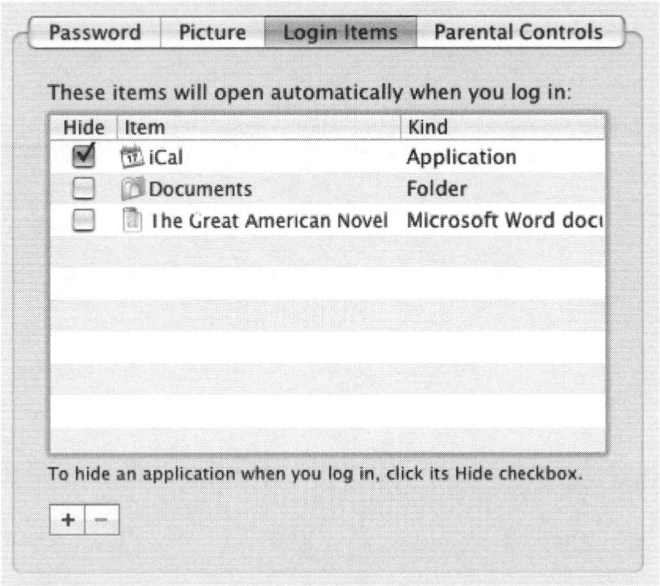

8

| Password | Picture | Login Items | Parental Controls |

These items will open automatically when you log in:

Hide	Item	Kind
☑	📅 iCal	Application
☐	📁 Documents	Folder
☐	📄 The Great American Novel	Microsoft Word docu

To hide an application when you log in, click its Hide checkbox.

+ −

FIGURE 8-6   iCal will open automatically and then hide at each login.

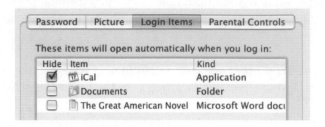

FIGURE 8-7   You can add applications, folders, and files to the Login Items list.

As with applications, you can check the Hide check box to have folders and files hidden after they open. Their icons display in the Dock, and you can make them visible by clicking them.

Chapter 9

Customize Your Mac

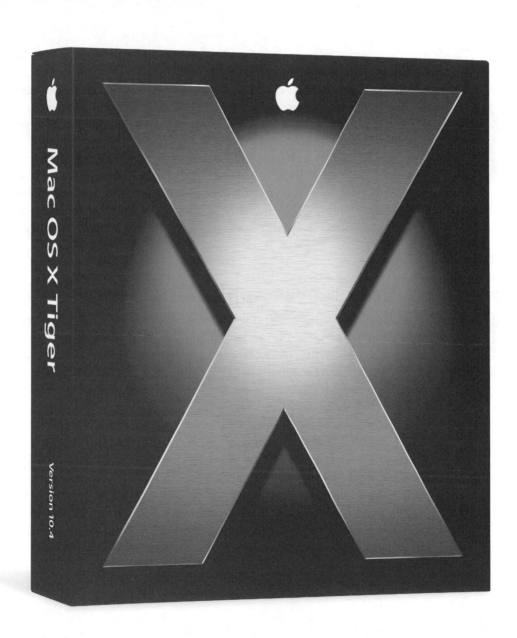

How to...

- Set personal preferences
- Customize your environment
- Set hardware preferences

There are many ways you can change, adjust, set up and configure your Mac, customize your environment, and make your computer perform the way you want. Mac OS X uses the System Preferences application to centralize settings that affect both your computer and your personal environment. With some two dozen preference panes, this application gives you many ways to change how you work with your Mac and control how your Mac works for you.

In this chapter, I'll show you the preference panes you can use to customize your Mac and explain what each of them is used for. You'll learn how to adjust the way your Mac works, personalize your environment, set up such things as networking, printing, and screen display, learn how to automatically set your Mac's date and time, and find out how to use special features for people who have difficulties using their computer.

The System Preferences Application

You can adjust all the preferences and settings for your Mac from the System Preferences application, which is a central repository for *preference panes,* individual modules that control specific types of preferences. Each preference pane controls a precise part of your Mac's operations, and the names of the panes tell you exactly what settings they cover: Network, Print & Fax, Dock, Displays, Accounts, and so on.

NOTE *System Preferences cover aspects of your Mac that can be configured globally—that is, it doesn't configure specific applications. Most applications, including the Finder, have their own preferences. It's easy to confuse the Finder and the operating system, but if you look at the Finder preferences (see Chapter 3), you'll quickly notice the difference between Finder settings and the global settings that you can change in the System Preferences. Many of the changes you make to the System Preferences affect only your user account, but some affect the entire system.*

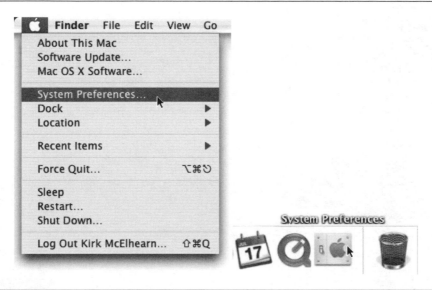

FIGURE 9-1   Two ways to open the System Preferences: from the Apple menu (left) or the Dock (right)

You can open the System Preferences by clicking its icon in the Dock, or by selecting the Apple menu | System Preferences, as shown in Figure 9 1.

The System Preferences application contains some two dozen icons (see Figure 9-2), each of which opens a preference pane where you can change settings for a specific part of the operating system.

When you open the System Preferences, its icons are displayed in four categories:

■ **Personal**   These preference panes control personal settings, such as the way the Dock displays, your Desktop background and screen saver, Dashboard and Exposé settings, Spotlight preferences, and the type of keyboard layout you use.

■ **Hardware**   These preference panes control your Mac's hardware: the way your Mac reacts when you insert a CD or DVD, the way your mouse works, your screen resolution, and more.

FIGURE 9-2   The System Preferences application is an interface for almost two dozen preference panes.

■ **Internet & Network**   This is where you enter Internet and network settings such as account information, your .Mac settings, and whether you want to share items on your Mac across a network.

■ **System**   This category deals with system functions such as setting the date and time, updating your Mac's software, and managing user accounts.

To access any preference pane, just click its icon once; the System Preferences window changes to display that preference pane, changing size if necessary.

At the top of the System Preferences window is a search field where you can enter keywords to find which preference pane controls the settings you want to change. As you type, Spotlight highlights the preference panes that apply to your search string, and a small pop-up menu displays below the search field showing you functions available in the different preference panes.

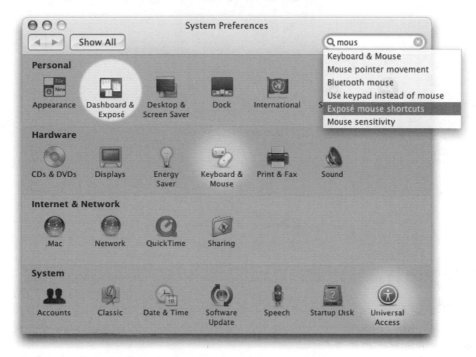

If you find a function in this list that corresponds to your search, click it with your pointer, or use the DOWN ARROW key to move down the list, and then press RETURN to open the corresponding preference pane.

The System Preferences application has a toolbar, where you can click a Back or Forward button to move through the preference panes you have visited, and a Show All button that returns you to the global view, as seen in Figure 9-2.

You can also access any of the preference panes from the View menu, which is shown in Figure 9-3. Just select the preference pane you want to view from this menu.

This menu also lets you choose how you want to display the preference pane icons. The default display is Organize By Categories, which is shown in

FIGURE 9-3   To display any of the preference panes, select it from the View menu.

Figure 9-3, but you can also choose Organize Alphabetically to display them in alphabetical order.

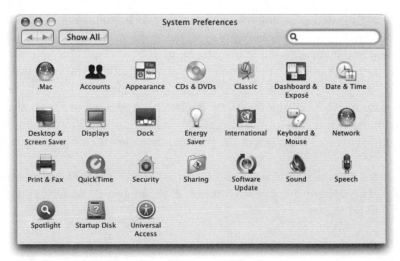

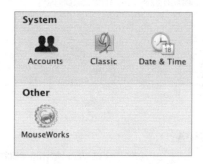

FIGURE 9-4   Third-party preference pane icons are added to the bottom of the window, in the Other category.

Some software, especially software used to control hardware devices, installs preference panes on your Mac so you can configure these devices. These preference pane icons are placed in an additional category called "Other" at the bottom of the System Preferences window. (See Figure 9-4.) This Other category only displays if you have non-Apple preference panes installed on your Mac.

NOTE   *If you don't have an administrator account (see Chapter 8 for more on administrator accounts), you won't be able to change all the System Preferences. Some of these preferences, such as most of those in the Personal category, are accessible to all users, since they only affect your individual environment. But other preferences, such as Startup Disk, Network, and Sharing, which affect all users on your Mac, are only accessible to administrators. Unfortunately, the category groupings don't correspond to this distinction: for instance, the Security preference pane, in the Personal category, contains both user-accessible and administrator-only settings; the .Mac preference pane, in the Internet & Network category, is a user-accessible preference pane, but other panes in the same category, such as Network and Sharing, are not.*

Set Personal Preferences

The Personal preferences section contains seven icons for preference panes that let you set user-specific preferences. With the exception of some settings in the

Security preference pane, changes you make to these preferences only apply to your user account.

Appearance Preferences

The Appearance preferences (Figure 9-5) let you adjust certain appearance settings, change the number of recent items shown in the Apple menu, and set font smoothing options. Click the Appearance icon to display this preference pane.

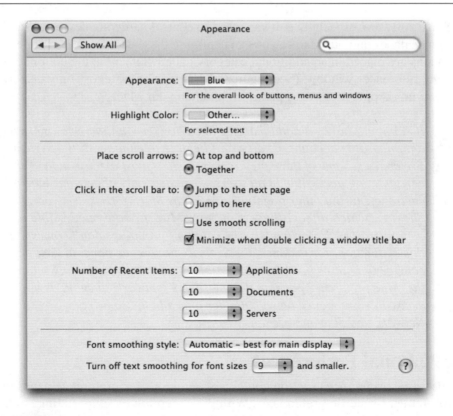

FIGURE 9-5   The Appearance preference pane allows you to change some display options.

You can set the following options in the Appearance preference pane:

- **Appearance**   Choose either Blue or Graphite for buttons, scroll bar controls, highlights, the Apple menu, the Spotlight icon, menu selections, and window items.

- **Highlight Color**   Choose from eight preset colors for text selections and list highlighting, or choose your own color by selecting Other and picking a color from the Color window.

- **Place Scroll Arrows**   Choose whether you want scroll arrows at the top and bottom of windows or together at the bottom of the scroll bar.

- **Click in the Scroll Bar To**   Choose from Jump To The Next Page or Scroll To Here. If you choose Jump To The Next Page, this makes documents or windows scroll one window up or down when you click in the scroll bar. If you choose Scroll To Here, your scroll bar is considered to be proportional to the size of the entire window or document, and clicking in the scroll bar moves to a position relative to the location where you click.

- **Use Smooth Scrolling**   This scrolls pages at a uniform speed, making scrolling smoother.

- **Minimize When Double Clicking a Window Title Bar**   If you check this, double-clicking a title bar minimizes a window, sending it to the Dock; this is the same as clicking the yellow Minimize button.

- **Number of Recent Items**   Choose the number of recent Applications, Documents, and Servers that display in the Apple menu. (See Chapter 3 for more on the Apple menu.)

- **Font Smoothing Style**   Mac OS X offers font smoothing, which smoothes the display of fonts on your screen. Choose from four types of font smoothing, depending on the type of screen you have.

- **Turn Off Text Smoothing**   Choose the smallest size fonts you want smoothed. If very small text is smoothed, it can be hard to read.

9

TIP

To get more information on this or any preference pane, click the ? icon at the bottom of the pane's window. This opens the Apple Help Viewer at the section that corresponds to the current preference pane. (For more on using the Apple Help Viewer, see Chapter 20.)

Dashboard & Exposé Preferences

Dashboard & Exposé preferences let you choose active screen corners and keyboard and mouse shortcuts for use with Dashboard and Exposé. For more on Dashboard and Exposé, and these settings, see Chapter 3.

Desktop & Screen Saver Preferences

The Desktop & Screen Saver preferences let you change your Desktop picture and choose a screen saver. See Chapter 3's "Customize Your Desktop" section for instructions on setting a Desktop picture.

To choose and configure a screen saver, click the Desktop & Screen Saver icon and then click the Screen Saver tab.

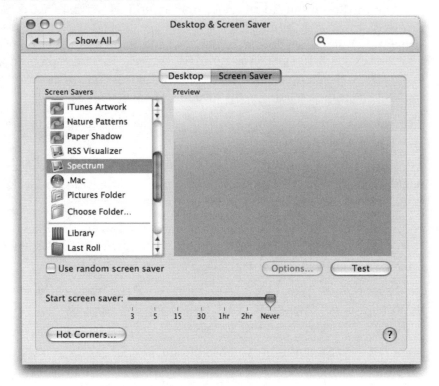

This tab shows you a list of available screen savers at the left, a preview at the right, and several settings at the bottom of the window.

Choose a screen saver in the Screen Savers list; the preview window shows you a small version of your choice. Some screen savers offer options—if the Options

Did you know?

About Screen Savers

In the old days of computers, it was possible for your screen to get a *burn-in* effect when its display remained the same for too long. This problem affected screens displaying text interfaces more than graphical interfaces. But CRT manufacturers have changed the way screens work, so this problem is rarely, if ever, seen now.

Screen savers were designed to protect screens from this burn-in, but in most cases they did little more than amuse computer users, displaying flying toasters or other strange items. This is the case today—screen savers don't *save* your screen but can show you that your computer is still on and provide attractive graphics when you're not busy.

However, LCD screens may actually be damaged by screen savers—if, instead of dimming the screen, your LCD displays a screen saver, it could shorten the lifespan of the screen's backlight. In the Energy Saver preference pane, you can set your screen to dim after a certain time, which offers much more protection than any screen saver.

9

button is available, click this to configure the selected screen saver. You can also click Test to get a full-screen preview of it. Move your mouse to return to the preference pane.

If you want to use a random screen saver, check the Use Random Screen Saver check box. To choose when the screen saver starts, set a value in the Start Screen Saver slider.

NOTE   *Some screen savers, such as Flurry, are dynamic and change automatically; others, such as Cosmos and Forest, are sets of pictures that fade from one to the other. You can also choose a .Mac slide show, if you have uploaded your own pictures to your .Mac account, or you can subscribe to another user's .Mac slide show. Choosing the Pictures Folder or another folder (click Choose Folder and select a folder) creates a screen saver from your own pictures. You can choose the iTunes Artwork screen saver to display album art from the music files in your iTunes Music Library, or you can choose the RSS Visualizer to display headlines from an RSS feed (see Chapter 10 for more on RSS feeds), or the Spectrum screen saver to display a range of flowing colors.*

You can choose to set hot corners for your screen saver. You can set whether moving your pointer to that corner turns the screen saver effect on immediately or prevents it from activating. To set hot corners, click the Hot Corners button. A sheet displays showing pop-up menus for the four hot corners. It's possible that some of these are already assigned to Dashboard or Exposé functions (see Chapter 3 for more on Dashboard and Exposé); if so, you can choose to change these hot corners to screen saver functions. If you want to use a hot corner to turn on your screen saver, select Start Screen Saver from the pop-up menu in that hot corner. To use a hot corner to *never* turn on a screen saver (for example, if you use your Mac to watch DVDs), select Disable Screen Saver for that hot corner.

TIP   *Want more screen savers? Mac OS X doesn't come with a big choice. You can download plenty of free screen savers from the Web. Some web sites for movies or bands, and some fan sites, offer screen savers you can download and use with Mac OS X. (For example, if you're a Lord of the Rings fan, go to www.lordoftherings.net to download some neat screen savers.) You can also search for "screen saver" at Version Tracker (www.versiontracker .com) or MacUpdate (www.macupdate.com), two web sites that list Mac software and provide links for downloads.*

Dock Preferences

The Dock preferences let you change the position and size of the Dock, its visibility, and other options. See Chapter 3's "Customize the Dock" section for instructions on using this preference pane.

International Preferences

The International preferences (Figure 9-6) let you adjust certain settings relative to the country you are in: language, date and time format, number format, and the input menu. Click the International icon to display this preference pane.

This preference pane has three tabs:

- **Language**   Drag languages to your preferred order in the left section. Your Mac OS X interface is in the topmost language shown in this list. If you want to use Mac OS X in a different language, change the language order and log out, and then log in again. (But if an application does not have language resources for the preferred language, it displays in the next available language in the list.) Click the Edit List button to add or remove languages from the list. The Order For Sorted Lists pop-up menu lets you choose how lists (such as when you view a Finder window in List View) are sorted. And the Word Break pop-up menu lets you select how words are separated.

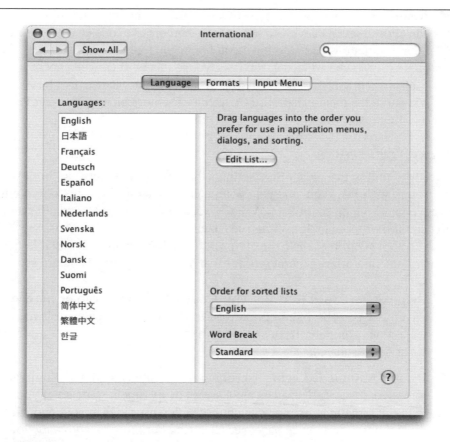

FIGURE 9-6 The International preference pane is where you choose settings relative to your country.

- **Formats** Choose your desired date, time, and number formats here. For dates, you can choose by country or customize the way dates are displayed. For times, choose your desired time format here, and select whether you want time displayed in a 12-hour or 24-hour format. Click Customize to change the way dates display. The Calendar pop-up menu lets you select from several calendars, such as Gregorian, Buddhist, Hebrew, Islamic, and Japanese. For numbers, the format is applied according to the country or region you select at the top of the window and the currency you select at the bottom. You can also choose your preferred currency and whether U.S. (feet and inches) or metric measurement units are used.

■ **Input Menu**   Choose the type of keyboard layout you want to use. You can choose several keyboard layouts, and if more than one layout is chosen, an input menu is added to the menu bar of all applications. If you use an alternative keyboard layout, such as Dvorak, this is where you choose it. This is also where you can choose to display the Character Palette and Keyboard Viewer in the input menu. (See Chapter 14 for more on the Character Palette and Keyboard Viewer.)

Security Preferences

The Security preference pane offers settings that affect the security of both your user account, with FileVault, and your computer in general. The top section of this preference pane, which controls FileVault, is accessible to all users and affects only your account. For more on FileVault, see Chapter 17.

The bottom section of the Security preference pane is only accessible to administrators, and offers general settings that help make your Mac more secure.

■ **Require Password to Wake This Computer from Sleep or Screen Saver**   If you check this option, you'll need to enter a password when you wake your computer from sleep or when you reactivate it after a screen saver has displayed.

■ **Disable Automatic Login**   Checking this disables automatic login and forces your Mac to display its login screen every time it starts up. If you want to use automatic login, you can choose which user logs in automatically on the Accounts preference pane; see Chapter 8 for more on automatic login.

■ **Require Password to Unlock Each Secure System Preference**   If you check this option, users will have to enter a password each time they want to access a secure system preference, even if they have an administrator account. If you don't check this, administrators will never have to enter their password to access secure system preferences.

■ **Log Out After ... Minutes of Inactivity**   This setting logs out your Mac, no matter which account is active, after a set period of inactivity. Enter a number of minutes in the field, or change the time by clicking the arrow buttons.

■ **Use Secure Virtual Memory**   This encrypts virtual memory files that are written to your hard disk so no one can recover data from these files after you have shut down your computer.

Hardware Preferences

The Hardware preferences category contains six icons for preference panes that let you set preferences for your hardware. (See Figure 9-7.)

Any changes you make to these preferences only apply to your user account, with the exception of Energy Saver and Print & Fax preferences, which apply to all users of your Mac.

CDs & DVDs Preferences

The CDs & DVDs preferences (Figure 9-8) let you choose how your Mac acts when you insert a CD or DVD. Click the CDs & DVDs icon to display this preference pane.

Use this pane to choose what your Mac should do when you insert a blank CD or DVD. You can select from the following:

- **Ask What to Do**   The Finder asks you what you want to do.

- **Open Finder**   This prepares the disk for copying in the Finder.

- **Open iTunes/Open iDVD**   If you insert a blank CD, this opens iTunes and prepares the disk for copying in iTunes. If you insert a blank DVD, this opens iDVD.

- **Open Disk Utility**   This opens Disk Utility, which you can use to burn CDs or DVDs.

- **Open Other Application**   If you use a different application to burn CDs or DVDs, choose it here by selecting this menu item and then browsing to that application and selecting it.

FIGURE 9-7   The Hardware preferences category

The CDs & DVDs preference pane and its five options

■ **Run Script**   If you want to run an AppleScript when inserting a blank CD or DVD, choose this menu item, and then browse to the location of the AppleScript and select it.

■ **Ignore**   If you want nothing to happen when you insert a blank CD or DVD, choose this.

When you insert a music CD, a picture CD, or a video DVD, the bottom three choices let you decide what to do. You can have the default applications open automatically (iTunes, iPhoto, if you have iLife installed, and DVD Player), or you can choose to have your Mac open another application, run a script, or ignore the disk.

Displays Preferences

The Displays preferences (Figure 9-9) let you choose your Mac's screen resolution, color depth, and refresh rate. You can also adjust its contrast and brightness, and, if you have multiple monitors, choose how they are displayed. Click the Displays icon to display this preference pane.

This preference pane may be different depending on the type of Mac you have; in addition, the name it displays in its title bar corresponds to the type of monitor you have. In Figure 9-9, there are three tabs, but you'll have a fourth tab if more than one monitor is connected to your Mac.

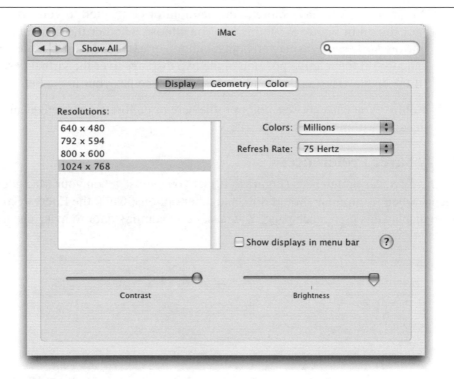

The Displays preferences pane, where you can adjust your monitor's settings

■ **Display**   Choose your resolution, colors, and refresh rate. You can adjust the contrast and brightness using the sliders at the bottom. And if you check Show Displays In Menu Bar, a menu extra lets you change resolution and color depth on-the-fly by clicking the menu extra and selecting one of its choices. If you have more than one display connected to your Mac and the second display does not show up, click Detect Displays to tell the system to find it.

■ **Geometry**   If you have a CRT screen connected to your Mac, or if you have an all-in-one Mac with a CRT screen (a nonflat panel iMac, or an eMac), this tab lets you adjust your screen's geometry: height, width, rotation, and so on.

- **Arrange**   If you have more than one monitor connected to your Mac (not shown in Figure 9-9), this lets you choose whether the display is mirrored (the same display on both monitors) or extended (side by side). You can also set the relative position of the two displays over the virtual desktop (if the display is extended) and choose which one has your menu bar.

- **Color**   You can choose a color profile here or calibrate your screen and make a custom ColorSync profile.

Energy Saver Preferences

The Energy Saver preferences (Figure 9-10) let you choose when your Mac goes to sleep, when its monitor should dim, and other options. Click the Energy Saver icon to display this preference pane. You must be an administrator to make changes

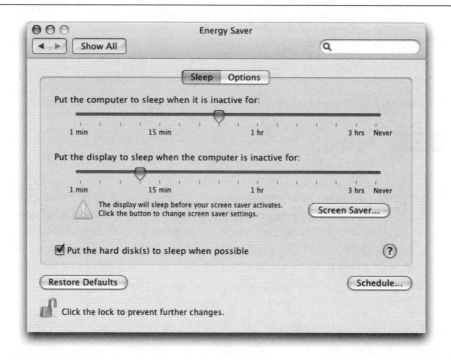

FIGURE 9-10   The Energy Saver preference pane lets you choose when to put your Mac to sleep.

to this preference pane. If the lock icon at the bottom left of the pane shows a closed lock, click the icon and then enter your administrator's password to make changes.

Choose whether you want your Mac to go to sleep and after how long, and choose whether you want to put the display to sleep to save energy. If you click the Schedule button, you can choose whether you want to start up your computer at a specific time every day, on weekdays or on weekends, and whether you want it to go to sleep or shut down at a specific time. The Options tab gives you some additional options, such as waking when the modem detects a ring or restarting automatically after a power failure.

Figure 9-10 shows the Energy Saver preference pane on a desktop Mac. If you have an iBook or PowerBook, it is slightly different. You have two views: a simple view that lets you choose from a group of preset energy settings, and a detailed view, which lets you select more options. (Click the Show Details button to see this view.) You can also choose different settings for when your laptop is running on battery power or when it's plugged into a power adapter.

TIP   *Want to use your Mac as an alarm clock? It might be overkill, but you can set it to start up at a specific time each day, and choose to open, say, an MP3 file at startup (see the "Start Up Applications When You Log In" section in Chapter 8 for more on launching files at startup).*

9

Keyboard & Mouse Preferences

The Keyboard & Mouse preferences (Figure 9-11) let you choose a key repeat rate and the delay until repeat when you hold down keys on your keyboard, as well as let you control a Bluetooth keyboard and mouse. They also allow you to turn on Full Keyboard Access, for users who cannot use a mouse or other pointing device. Click the Keyboard & Mouse icon to display this preference pane.

The Keyboard tab lets you adjust settings for typing. The Key Repeat Rate slider allows you to set the speed at which keys repeat when you hold them down. And you can use the Delay Until Repeat slider to choose the time before keys start repeating when you hold them down. If you have a 17-inch G4 PowerBook (or one of certain later PowerBook models), you'll also have options to illuminate the keyboard and control how long the keys remain illuminated when you're not using your computer.

The Mouse tab of this preference pane lets you adjust your mouse's tracking speed, scrolling speed (if you have a scroll wheel), and double-click speed.

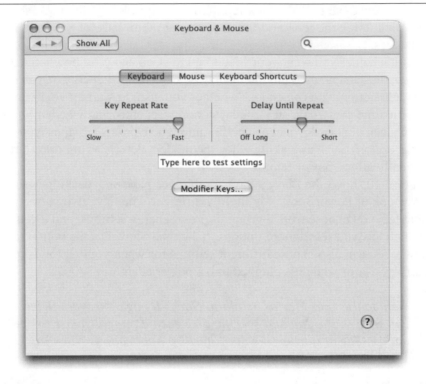

FIGURE 9-11   The Keyboard tab of the Keyboard & Mouse preference pane

You can also choose the primary mouse button; if you are a left-hander, you might prefer using the right button as the primary mouse button.

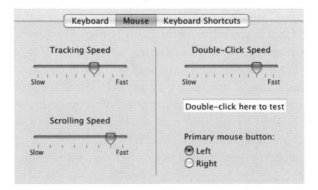

Choose a tracking speed, scrolling speed, and double-click speed for your mouse. If you use a third-party mouse with its own driver, use that device's preference pane or settings application; those settings override the Mouse preference pane.

If you have an iBook or PowerBook, this preference pane is different; it contains a second tab for trackpad settings and options.

As with the Mouse tab, you can set tracking and double-click speed, and you can also choose from several specific trackpad options. You can use the trackpad for clicking (which means that when you tap the trackpad it is the same as a mouse click), or for clicking and dragging. You can also use Drag Lock, so you can tap, drag, and then tap again to release the item you dragged.

You can also have the trackpad ignored while you are typing. This is practical since you may rub your thumbs against it, moving the cursor to another line when you are typing. If you check Ignore Trackpad When Mouse Is Present, the trackpad is turned off when you have an external mouse plugged into your Mac.

If you have a Bluetooth adapter in your Mac, there will be an additional tab (bctween Mouse and Keyboard Shortcuts) called Bluetooth. That's where you set the options for wireless Apple mice and keyboards, and where you check your battery levels.

The Keyboard Shortcuts tab lets you change or assign keyboard shortcuts to specific system functions, such as screen captures (pictures of your screen) or universal access. You can also set the keyboard shortcut for hiding and showing the Dock, and you can change or set the keyboard shortcut for any menu item in whichever application you use.

9

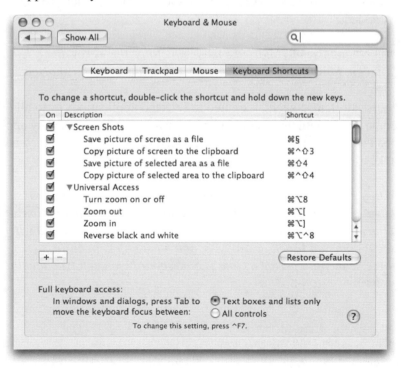

To change a preset shortcut, click the Shortcut column for the action whose shortcut you want to change. When the text becomes highlighted, type a new keyboard shortcut. This shortcut is applied immediately.

To set a keyboard shortcut for an application, click the + button. A sheet displays.

Select an application from the Application pop-up menu by choosing one of the applications shown in the menu, selecting Other to browse and find another application, or choosing All Applications to apply your keyboard shortcut to all applications on your Mac.

Enter the *exact* name of the menu command in the Menu Title field, and then enter a keyboard shortcut in the Keyboard Shortcut field. Click Add and this shortcut is added.

NOTE *You cannot use any shortcuts made up of just the ⌘ key and a letter key. You can, however, use any ⌘-number combination as a shortcut.*

Keyboard shortcuts, whether applied to selected applications or to all of them, don't become active until the next time you launch the applications. Any applications that are open while shortcuts are applied must first be closed and restarted before the changes take effect.

NOTE *When entering a menu command to use with a keyboard shortcut, this menu command must be exactly as it appears in the application's menu. This means that you must respect case (capital letters), and when you see a command such as Save As, you must enter an ellipsis (…), not three sequential periods. On a U.S. keyboard, you can type an ellipsis by pressing OPTION-; .*

CAUTION

When setting keyboard shortcuts, you may choose a shortcut that is already used by a specific application for another menu command. If you do so, you'll find that one of the two shortcuts (usually the one already used by the application) won't work. Check carefully in your application before applying any shortcuts.

If you decide you want to delete all your keyboard shortcuts and reset them to their defaults, click the Restore Defaults button.

TIP

When you change any keyboard shortcuts, your applications show these new shortcuts in their menus. If you have forgotten which shortcuts you have set, just look in your menus for a reminder.

The final option on this screen, Full Keyboard Access, lets you choose how Full Keyboard Access works. This feature enables users who cannot work with a mouse or other pointing device to use their Mac more efficiently; it also allows any user to quickly navigate through the Mac's interface by pressing the TAB key. You can choose to have this apply to Text Boxes and Lists Only, or to All Controls. If you choose All Controls, you'll be able to press the TAB key to change the focus among different items. Try it in this preference pane; if you select All Controls and then press the TAB key, you'll see blue highlighting around different items as they are selected (buttons, text fields, tabs, radio buttons, and so on). When one item of a group (say a tab or radio button) is highlighted, you can use the arrow keys to move to other items in that group. Press RETURN to activate the selected item.

Print & Fax Preferences

The Print & Fax preferences (see Figure 9-12) let you choose certain settings for printing and for sending and receiving faxes. You can choose your default paper size and your default printer, and you can set up your Mac to receive faxes and to share its printer if it is connected to a network. Some of the settings on this preference pane are accessible to all users, but to set up printer sharing and faxing you must have an administrator account.

To add a printer to the Printer list, click the + icon below the list. You can also view print jobs, by clicking the Print Queue button, and information about the selected printer by clicking Printer Setup. See Chapter 14 for more on adding and setting up printers.

9

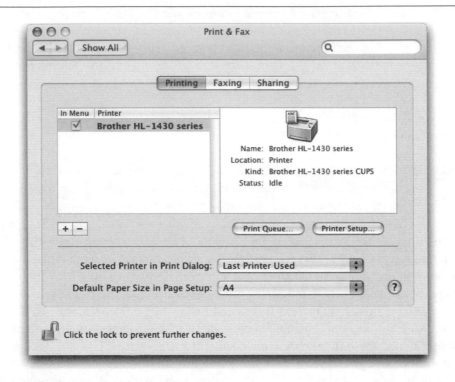

FIGURE 9-12   The Printing tab of the Print & Fax preference pane lets you choose certain printing settings.

At the bottom of this window, you can choose which printer to display in print dialogs: select a printer from the pop-up menu, or select Last Printer Used, so each time you print, the last printer is automatically selected. (If you only have one printer, you won't need to worry about this.)

Select a Default Paper Size in Page Setup, so all your applications know what size paper you use. The pop-up menu gives you a dozen choices, including US Letter, US Legal, A4, and many others.

The Faxing tab lets you set up your Mac to receive faxes.

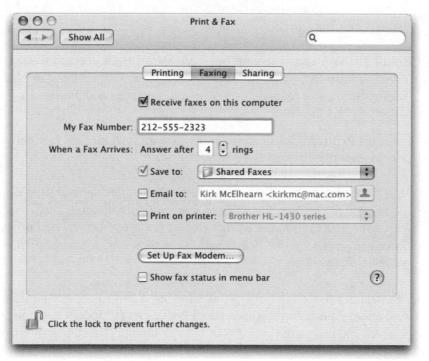

To turn on fax reception, check Receive Faxes On This Computer. Enter your telephone number in the My Fax Number field; this number is displayed on faxes you send from your Mac.

Choose how you want your Mac to react when receiving a fax:

- **Answer after … Rings**   Enter a number here; you probably want to choose a number around 4 or 5 if you use the same line for a telephone; if you have a dedicated line, choose 1.

- **Save To**   Select a folder to save faxes you receive. Incoming faxes are saved as PDF files, which you can view with the Preview application or with Acrobat Reader. Choose from Faxes (which is located in your home folder), Shared Faxes (located in the /Users/Shared folder), or select another folder.

If you have multiple users on your Mac and you want all users to have access to incoming faxes, choose Shared Faxes. All your users will be able to view and copy files in this folder.

- **Email To**　You can have your Mac send the PDF files of all incoming faxes to the e-mail address of your choice. Enter an e-mail address, or click the Address Book icon to display a list of your contacts, and then select a person to send the fax to.

- **Print on Printer**　Select a printer if you want incoming faxes automatically printed after they arrive.

You must select at least one of the three choices telling your Mac what to do when a fax arrives, but you can select more than one if you want: you can have faxes saved and e-mailed, for example, or saved and printed. In any case, it's a good idea to save them so you always have archives of your incoming faxes.

To view the fax list, click Set Up Fax Modem. You can check and edit information about your fax, and you can double-click a fax modem in the list to view its current and completed jobs. (Your fax modem may not appear in this list until after you try to send a fax. To do this, open any document you can print; then select File | Print. Click the PDF button and select Fax PDF. From the sheet that displays, select your modem in the Modem menu. Click Cancel; then you can return to the fax list and make changes to your modem's name and other information.)

To view a status icon in the menu bar, check Show Fax Status In Menu Bar. You'll be able to check the status of your fax modem from this menu.

The Sharing tab lets you turn on printer and fax sharing. Check Share These Printers With Other Computers, and then select the printer(s) you want to share. If you do this, other computers on your network will be able to use your printer(s). Check Let Others Send Faxes Through This Computer if you also want to share your fax modem.

Sound Preferences

The Sound preferences (Figure 9-13) let you choose alert sounds and adjust your computer's volume. They also let you choose your input and output devices if you have other sound hardware. Click the Sound icon to display this preference pane.

FIGURE 9-13   The Sound preference pane lets you set sound volume, alerts, and more.

The Sound preference pane has three tabs:

■ **Sound Effects**   Choose an alert sound, alert volume, and output volume. Decide whether you want interface sound effects (when you move files to the Trash or empty the Trash, for example) and whether you want audible feedback when you raise or lower the volume with the volume keys. Check Show Volume In Menu Bar if you want a menu extra displayed at all times. Click this menu extra and move the slider to change your Mac's volume.

■ **Output**   This lets you choose a sound output device (if you have one other than your internal speakers), its balance, and its volume.

■ **Input**   This lets you choose a sound input device (such as an internal or external microphone, or any other sound input device) and its volume.

Internet & Network Preferences

The Internet & Network preferences category (see Figure 9-14) contains four icons for preference panes that let you set preferences for Internet use, networking, and your .Mac account (if you have one).

Changes you make to the .Mac and QuickTime preferences only apply to your user account; changes to Network and Sharing preferences apply to all users on your Mac, and you must be an administrator to make them.

.Mac Preferences

The .Mac preference pane lets you configure your .Mac account (if you have one) and manage your iDisk. See Chapter 11 for more on using .Mac.

Network Preferences

The Network preferences are where you enter important information so your Mac can access either an internal network or the Internet. This is where you enter the name of your Internet service provider and where you set up your modem or other network interface. See Chapter 12 for instructions on using this preference pane.

QuickTime Preferences

QuickTime is Apple's multimedia software architecture that handles audio and video playback on your Mac. The QuickTime preferences (Figure 9-15) let you adjust the way QuickTime works.

In most cases, QuickTime's default settings are appropriate. One setting you might want to check is the Streaming Speed setting on the Streaming tab (see Figure 9-15). You should choose the speed at which you connect to the Internet to make sure that media is downloaded properly. If you connect to the Internet over an internal modem, the connection speed is probably 56 Kbps.

FIGURE 9-14   The Internet & Network preferences category

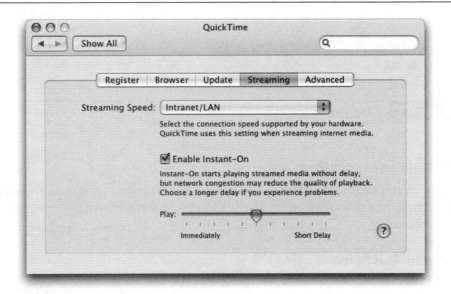

FIGURE 9-15   The Streaming tab of the QuickTime preference pane

If you have an ISDN, cable, or DSL connection, check with your Internet service provider for the correct speed. If you are on a company network, check with your network administrator.

Sharing Preferences

The Sharing preferences are where you turn on file sharing, printer sharing, Internet connection sharing, and more. See Chapter 12 for instructions on using this preference pane.

System Preferences

The System preferences category (see Figure 9-16) contains seven icons for preference panes that let you choose settings for system features.

Changes you make to the Classic, Software Update, Speech, and Universal Access preferences only apply to your user account; changes to Accounts, Date & Time, and Startup Disk preferences apply to all users on your Mac, and you must be an administrator to make them.

FIGURE 9-16   The System preferences category

Accounts Preferences

Mac OS X is a multiuser operating system, and this preference pane lets you create, edit, manage and delete user accounts. See Chapter 8 for instructions on using this preference pane.

Classic Preferences

The Classic preference pane (Figure 9-17) lets you choose where your Mac OS 9 System Folder is, if you have one, and lets you start or stop the Classic environment.

Select where your Mac OS 9 System Folder is located in the Start/Stop pane. You may need to click the disclosure triangle next to the name of your volume to see its System Folder.

> **TIP**
> *In some cases, your System Folder may be dimmed in the Classic folder list. If this is the case, close the Classic preference pane and open the Startup Disk preference pane. Select your Classic folder as a startup disk, and then close this preference pane and save your changes. Go back to the Classic preference pane; you should now be able to select your System Folder to use for Classic. (Don't forget to go back to the Startup Disk preference pane and change your startup disk back to your Mac OS X volume!)*

You can start the Classic environment by clicking Start; this button changes to Stop when Classic has started running. You can stop it by clicking the Stop button. If Classic ever freezes, click the Force Quit button to shut down the Classic environment.

You can check Start Classic When You Login and Hide Classic While Starting if you wish. It's only useful to start Classic on login, though, if you plan to use it every day. Check Warn Before Starting Classic to have your Mac display an alert before launching the Classic environment, and check Show Classic Status In Menu Bar to display a menu extra showing Classic status and giving you quick access to Classic functions.

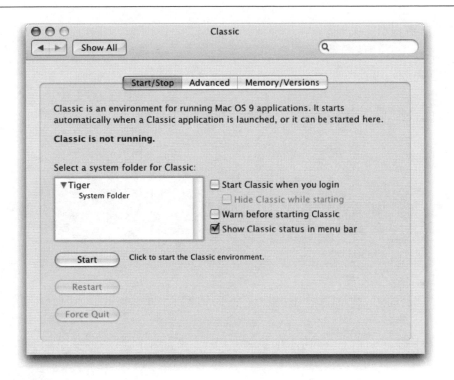

FIGURE 9-17   The Classic preference pane lets you manage the Classic environment.

NOTE   *In Chapter 13, I tell you more about using Classic and working with Classic applications.*

The Advanced and Memory/Versions tabs let you manage advanced features of the Classic environment and view the memory usage of Classic applications. For more on using the Classic environment, see your Mac's online help.

Date & Time Preferences

The Date & Time preferences (Figure 9-18) let you set your Mac's date, time, and time zone, as well as synchronize its clock with a network clock, and choose settings for the display of your menu bar clock. Click the Date & Time icon to display this preference pane.

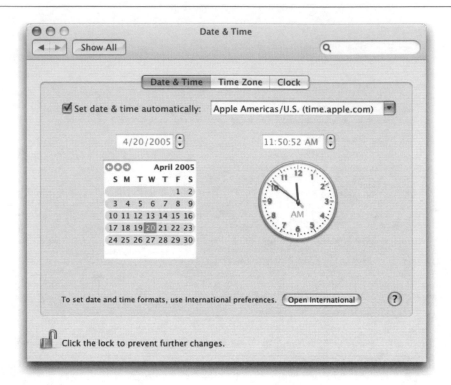

FIGURE 9-18 The Date & Time preference pane lets you adjust your Mac's date and time, and manage other date and time settings.

This preference pane has three tabs:

■ **Date & Time** Set your Mac's date and time here and make sure your Mac is always on time by synchronizing its clock with a network clock.

■ **Time Zone** Select your time zone here.

■ **Clock** Choose settings for your Mac's clock: whether it is displayed in the menu bar or as a window, whether it shows as digital or analog, and whether it shows seconds, the day of the week, and more. You can even have your Mac announce the time using Apple's text-to-speech technology.

Software Update Preferences

Mac OS X provides a built-in software update program that checks your Mac's software and offers to download new versions when they are available. See Chapter 19 for instructions on using this preference pane.

Speech Preferences

Your Mac can both talk to you and understand speech (within limits). The Speech preferences (Figure 9-19) let you choose settings for these functions, if you choose to use them. Click the Speech icon to display this preference pane.

Apple's Speech Recognition is not a technology that lets you dictate and have your words converted to text but a feature that lets you give orders to your Mac, using preset phrases, so your Mac can do things at your command. You can tell it to open and close windows, switch applications, check your e-mail, copy or paste data, and more. The Speech Recognition tab lets you control this function.

The other speech technology on your Mac is text-to-speech. This lets certain applications speak their text, reading out loud to you in a synthetic voice. While these voices are not perfect, they can be very helpful for people with visual impairments. You can control this function by selecting various options on the Text To Speech tab.

To learn more about these two speech features, see your Mac's online help.

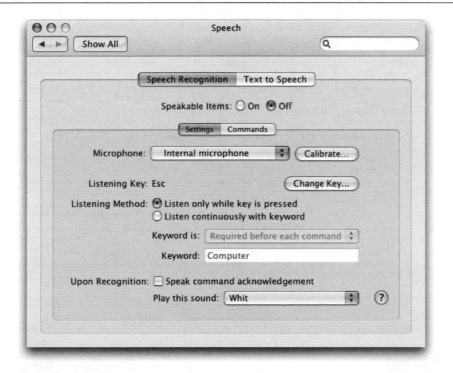

FIGURE 9-19   The Speech preference pane lets you control how your Mac talks to you or listens to you.

Startup Disk Preferences

The Startup Disk preferences (see Figure 9-20) control which disk or volume your Mac starts up from. Click the Startup Disk icon to display this preference pane. You must be an administrator to make changes to the Startup Disk preferences.

If you have more than one disk or volume in your Mac or if you have external hard disks, use this pane to choose which disk to use. You can also choose Network Startup if your Mac can start up from a network. If you are on a network, check with your network administrator for more about this.

To change the startup disk, click one of the system folders in the list and then close the preference pane to save your settings. If you wish to restart right away, click the Restart button. Your Mac will display an alert asking you to confirm that you want to restart, and then it will restart from the disk you selected.

NOTE
Macs made before 2003 can start up in Mac OS 9 or Mac OS X (if they are supported by Mac OS X). Some Macs made in 2003 can start up in Mac OS 9 as well, but most models released in 2003 or later can only start up in Mac OS X.

FIGURE 9-20   The Startup Disk preference pane is where you choose which disk or folder your Mac uses to start up.

You can also click Target Disk Mode to restart your Mac in this manner. If you connect your Mac to another Mac with a FireWire cable and start up in this way, your Mac mounts as an external hard disk on the other Mac. You can use this to transfer files from one Mac to another, or if you are installing Mac OS X on a new Mac and want to copy over files from an old Mac, starting up the older Mac in target mode allows the Migration Assistant to copy the previous Mac's files. (See Chapter 18 for more on using target mode to transfer files when installing Mac OS X.)

Universal Access Preferences

The Universal Access preferences (Figure 9-21) let you turn on special features for people who have difficulties with seeing, hearing, or using the keyboard or mouse. Click the Universal Access icon to display this preference pane.

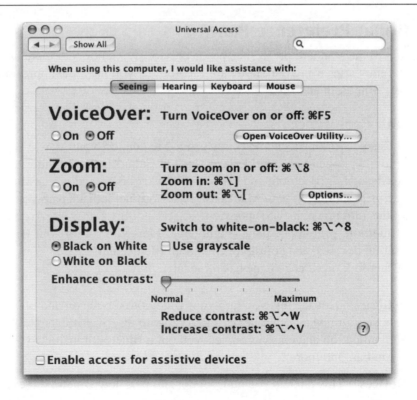

| FIGURE 9-21 | The Universal Access preference pane lets you turn on special functions to help disabled people use a Mac. |

This preference pane has four tabs:

- **Seeing**   This tab lets you turn on special functions for people who have difficulties with seeing: you can zoom your screen, change the display to white on black, change the display to grayscale, enhance the contrast, and more.

- **Hearing**   This tab lets you turn on functions useful for people who have difficulties with hearing, offering visual feedback instead of alert sounds.

- **Keyboard**   This tab offers functions for people who have difficulty pressing more than one key at a time or repeating keystrokes.

- **Mouse**   This tab offers functions for people who have difficulty using a mouse or other pointing device.

Additional Preference Panes

In addition to the standard preference panes previously mentioned, there are two others that may appear in your Hardware category (if you have the appropriate hardware): Bluetooth and Ink.

Bluetooth Preferences

Bluetooth is a networking technology you can use to connect your Mac to Bluetooth-enabled mobile phones and other devices, such as Palm PDAs and more. You can exchange files using Bluetooth and use a wireless keyboard and mouse, including Apple's wireless models. If your Mac doesn't have a Bluetooth adapter, you can buy one that plugs into one of its USB ports.

The Bluetooth preference pane (Figure 9-22) lets you set up your Bluetooth adapter, set up devices, and configure Bluetooth file exchange.

The Bluetooth preference pane has three tabs:

- **Settings**   This tab lets you turn your Bluetooth device on and off, lets you choose if you want other devices to be able to discover it, lets you turn on authentication and encryption, lets you put a Bluetooth menu extra in your menu bar, and more.

- **Devices**   This tab lets you add, set up, and pair new Bluetooth devices.

- **Sharing**   This tab lets you control how your system behaves when you exchange files using Bluetooth and allows you to turn on browsing for other Bluetooth devices, as well as choose a folder for them to browse.

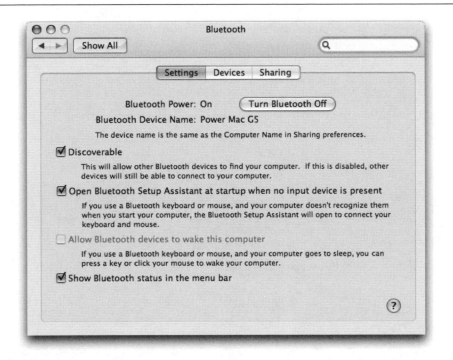

FIGURE 9-22   The Bluetooth preference pane lets you set options for using Bluetooth devices.

Ink Preferences

Ink is a handwriting recognition technology that you can use with a graphics tablet. You can write on the tablet, and the Ink technology converts your writing into text. The Ink preference pane (Figure 9-23) lets you configure Ink handwriting recognition and allows you to turn on and off gestures and create your own word lists for uncommon words.

The Ink preference pane has four tabs:

- ■ **Settings**   This tab lets you fine-tune your handwriting style and choose the recognition language and display font, as well as other options.

- ■ **Language**   This tab is where you choose your language.

FIGURE 9-23   The Ink preference pane lets you configure handwriting recognition using a graphics tablet.

■ **Gestures** This tab lets you turn on and off gestures for punctuation, spaces, and other nonalphanumeric characters.

■ **Word List** This tab lets you add your own uncommon words to Ink's recognition dictionary.

Part III

Connect to the World

Chapter 10

Surf the Internet

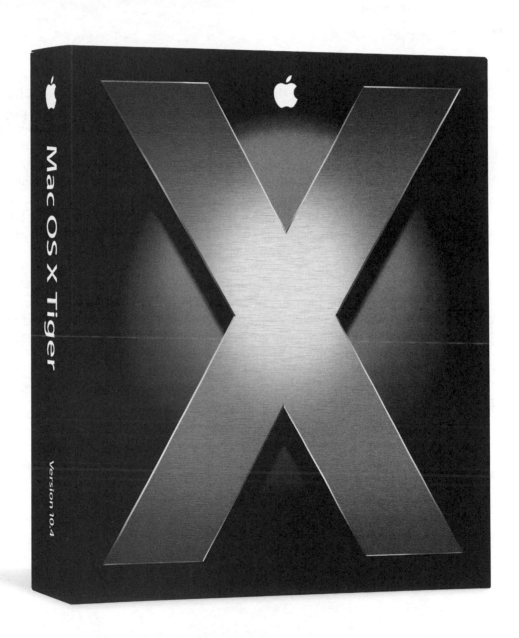

How to…

- ■ Set up your Mac for the Internet
- ■ Use e-mail
- ■ Surf the Web
- ■ Chat with your friends

For many people today, the main reason to own a computer is to use the Internet. Whether it is to use the Web for school or hobbies, to use e-mail for professional reasons, to keep in touch with family, to buy things online, or to play games online or share photos and home videos, the Internet is the essential tool for today's computer users.

In just a few years, the Internet has gone from a little-known network used by researchers and computer buffs to an essential tool for work and play. You can buy just about everything over the Internet, you can play games on it with users all around the world, and you can keep in touch with friends and family by e-mail, sending text, pictures, and even videos. You can also chat with people using Apple's iChat AV, an instant messaging tool that lets you carry out text, audio, and even video chats.

Macs have long been the easiest computers to connect and configure for the Internet, and today's Macs are no exception. In this chapter, I'll show you how to set up your Mac to use the Internet and how to connect to your Internet service provider. I'll tell you about using e-mail and Apple's Mail program, about surfing the Web, and about using text, audio, and video chats with Apple's iChat. If you're not surfing the Web yet, you will be by the end of this chapter.

Set Up Network Preferences

In most cases, when you first set up your new Mac, you enter the information necessary to connect to the Internet in an assistant that walks you through the setup procedure and records your basic data: your name, address, and e-mail address, along with your Internet service provider (ISP) information, such as your user name, password, and dial-up phone number. When you do this, your Mac stores the information you enter in the Network preference pane. If you didn't enter this information when setting up your Mac, or if you didn't have an Internet connection at the time, I'll explain how to do so in this section.

 *If you've upgraded from an older version of Mac OS X, such as Jaguar, you'll find that the Network preferences have been reorganized and include many of the settings that were previously in the Internet preference pane.*

Configure Network Preferences

The Network preference pane (Figure 10-1) is where you enter information that your Mac needs when using the Internet and other networks. You can access this preference pane by opening the System Preferences (either click its icon in the Dock or select the Apple Menu | System Preferences) and clicking the Network icon.

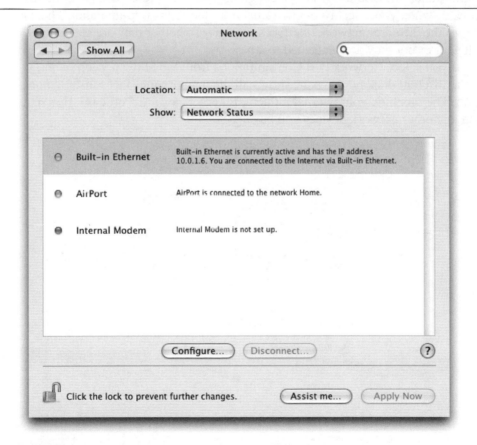

FIGURE 10-1   The Network preference pane is where you enter information needed by your Mac to connect to the Internet or other networks.

NOTE   *You may see different entries on the Network preference pane, depending on the type of hardware and network interfaces your Mac has. All new Macs include at least Built-in Ethernet and an Internal Modem, as shown in Figure 10-1; some new Macs also include a wireless AirPort card, and if you don't have an AirPort card, you can purchase one and install it in most recent Mac models.*

The Network preferences affect your connection both to a local network (if you use one) and the Internet. This preference pane contains a number of different displays, as well as several tabs, depending on the type of hardware your Mac has and the type of connection you want to make. Figure 10-1 shows the Network Status pane; this displays when you open the Network preference pane the first time, or when you select Network Status from the Show pop-up menu. This pane shows the different network interfaces you have, whether they are set up, and whether or not they are connected to a network.

If you select Network Port Configurations from the Show pop-up menu, you'll see a different display: this pane shows all the network interfaces installed on your Mac. They include your internal modem, Ethernet card, AirPort card, FireWire, and any other network devices you have.

You can activate or deactivate your network interfaces on this pane by checking or unchecking the boxes next to their names. You can also change the order with which your Mac uses these interfaces to make a connection by dragging them in the list; your Mac tries the topmost network interface first, then the next one, and so on, until it can create a connection.

The easiest way to configure your Mac to use a network is to use the Network Setup Assistant. You can open this assistant by clicking the Assist Me button at the bottom of the Network preference pane and then clicking Assistant. This assistant asks you a series of questions about how you connect to a network or to the Internet and records the settings you need.

NOTE   *If you use America Online (AOL) for your Internet access, see the instructions included with AOL's software to find out how to configure your Mac.*

The first screen of the Network Setup Assistant asks you to enter a name for the location it's going to create. A *location* is a group of network settings, which includes the network interface you use to connect to a network and the way this interface goes about connecting. Enter a name for the location in the Location Name field; this could be anything, such as My Connection, or the name of your ISP; you could name it home, office, or something similar. Enter a location name, and then click Continue.

10

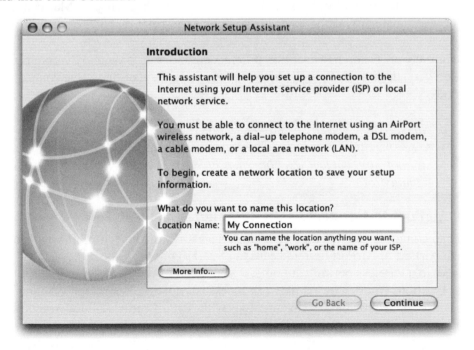

TIP

You can set up as many locations as you want, and you can switch locations by selecting the Apple Menu | Location, and then the name of the location from the submenu that displays. Locations are practical if you switch network configurations for any reason, such as if you have a PowerBook or iBook and use it both at home and at the office, or if you use your modem sometimes and another network interface at other times.

The next screen asks you how you connect to the Internet. You have five choices:

- **I use AirPort to connect to the Internet wirelessly.** Check this if you have an AirPort card in your Mac and either an AirPort base station or another Mac sharing a connection via AirPort.

- **I use a telephone modem to dial my ISP.** Check this if you use your Mac's internal modem, or an external modem, to connect to your Internet service provider.

- **I use a DSL modem to connect to the Internet.** If you have a broadband DSL connection, check this.

- **I use a cable modem to connect to the Internet.** Check this if you have cable Internet access.

- **I connect to my local area network (LAN).** Check this if your Mac connects to a local network that provides Internet access.

The Network Setup Assistant asks different questions according to the connection method you check here. The following sections cover each of these five connection methods.

NOTE

Not sure how you connect to the Internet? Click the More Info button to see the different types of connections and hardware used. If you're still not sure, contact your Internet service provider or your computer's administrator.

Use AirPort to Connect to the Internet Wirelessly

You can connect to the Internet using a wireless AirPort connection. If your Mac has an AirPort or AirPort Extreme card (an 802.11b or 802.11g card), you can connect to a wireless network at home, if you have an AirPort base station, or in other locations where wireless network access is available. You can also share a wireless connection among several Macs with AirPort cards. (I'll tell you how to set up an AirPort network in Chapter 12.)

The assistant asks you here to choose the wireless network you want to join. It displays a list of all available networks. Click the one you want to join, and then click Continue. The next screen asks if you're ready to connect. Click Continue.

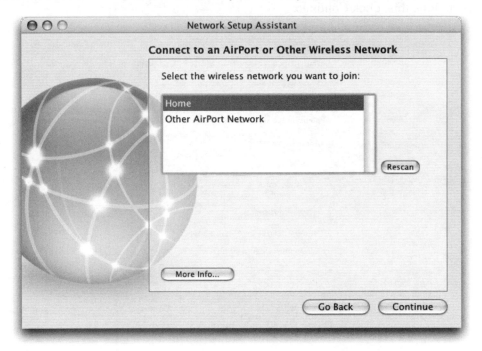

The assistant opens the connection—this may take a few seconds—and your location is now saved with the settings you've chosen.

NOTE   *If the wireless network you choose requires authentication, a password field will appear when you select it. Also, some networks don't broadcast their names. If you know there's a wireless network available, click Other AirPort Network and you'll be able to enter the network's name and password.*

Use a Modem to Connect to the Internet

Most new Macs include internal modems, though modems are becoming less popular as high-speed Internet connections abound. These modems operate at a speed of 56 Kbps, which is fine for casual web surfing and e-mail use but is pretty slow for downloading music, pictures, or movies from the Internet. In many cases, modems are only really used by people on the road with PowerBooks or iBooks who cannot connect to a wireless network.

If you choose to connect to the Internet with a modem, the assistant asks you to enter some information such as your account name, your password, your ISP's phone number, and whether you need to dial a prefix to get an outside line. When you've done this, click Continue.

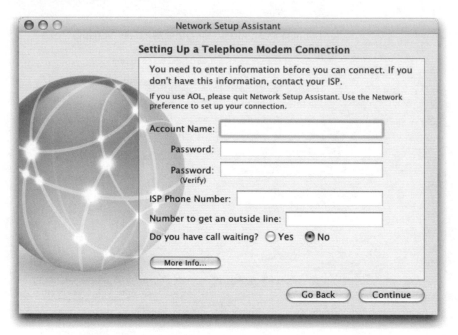

The Modem pop-up menu on the next screen lets you choose from a number of modem scripts, which tell different modems how to connect. If you are not using the standard Apple internal 56K modem, choose your modem from this list. If you are using the Apple modem, you have four choices for modem protocols: V.32, V.34, V.90, and V.92. These are different ways for your modem to talk to your ISP's modems. Try V.90 first, and if you have connection problems, try the other three or call your ISP and ask them which is the best protocol to use. Select the appropriate modem and click Continue.

The assistant opens the connection—this may take a few seconds—and your location is now saved with the settings you've chosen.

Use a DSL or Cable Modem to Connect to the Internet

For people who use the Internet a lot, or who want to be able to send and receive large files, broadband is the way to go. Broadband offers two advantages over modem connections. First, it gives you higher bandwidth. Think of bandwidth as a pipe. If a modem connection is like a water pipe in your home, broadband is like a water main. You get more water through the pipe in a given amount of time.

Broadband is the same: you get much more data in or out of your computer in the same amount of time, making downloads and uploads faster. The second advantage is that broadband is generally always on, meaning you don't need to wait to connect (and listen to the screechy noises of your modem), and that you can use services that require a permanent connection.

There are two main types of broadband connections: cable and DSL (though if you are connected to a local network, that is technically broadband as well). Many cable and DSL connections use the PPPoE protocol (Point-to-Point Protocol over Ethernet) to connect through a special type of modem, called a cable or DSL modem, to your ISP.

If you plan to connect via broadband, some ISPs offer two types of modems. One connects via Ethernet, and the other via USB. Choose the Ethernet model, if you can, since USB models require you to install additional drivers; the Ethernet models connect directly and are easier to set up and troubleshoot.

The Network Setup Assistant can automatically connect to the Internet in many cases; this depends on the type of DSL or cable modem you have, and the way you connect. Try clicking the Continue button to see if you can connect immediately.

If you can't connect to your ISP automatically, you'll need to enter some connection information: you may have a DHCP Client ID; if so, enter that in the first field. If not, you'll be connecting by PPPoE. Select that option, then enter your account name and password, and then click Continue.

10

If the Network Setup Assistant can't connect you to your ISP, contact them to make sure your connection information is correct.

Connect to the Internet via a Local Network

Another way of connecting to the Internet is over a local network. If this is how you access the Internet, the next screen in the assistant attempts to connect to your network. Make sure you are physically connected to the network via an Ethernet cable, and then click Continue.

If the assistant can't connect automatically, the next screen asks you to enter some information such as an IP address, a subnet mask, a router address, and one or more DNS hosts. If you don't know this information, contact your network administrator.

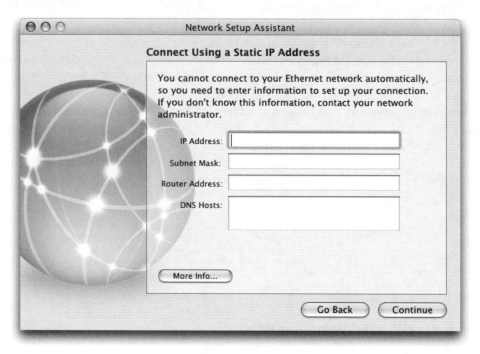

After you've entered this information, click Continue, and the Network Setup Assistant connects your Mac to your local network.

If you have several Macs, either at home or in an office or school, you can configure one of them to connect to the Internet and share its connection to other computers on the network. I'll tell you how to do this in Chapter 12.

Internet Connect

| FIGURE 10-2 | The Internet Connect application icon |

Open an Internet Connection

If you are using a broadband Internet connection, or if you connect via a local network and the Network Setup Assistant was able to connect immediately, then you won't need to open an Internet connection when you want to surf the Internet. However, if you are using a modem or certain DSL or cable modem connections (connected via PPPoE), you'll need to use the Internet Connect application to open and close your Internet connections. (See Figure 10-2.)

Internet Connect, located in your Applications folder, is a program that manages your Internet connection by dialing your modem (or activating your DSL or cable modem) and establishing a connection with the ISP you have specified using the Network Setup Assistant or in the Network preferences. Once you are connected, as you can see in Figure 10-3, it shows your connection speed and the amount of time you are connected, and it lets you disconnect.

The Summary pane of Internet Connect, shown in Figure 10-3, shows the different types of connections available. The Internet Connect toolbar gives you access to information and settings for the connections you have available.

| FIGURE 10-3 | This shows a computer connected to the Internet via AirPort. |

10

To connect to the Internet, click one of the icons in the toolbar, either Internal Modem or AirPort. The Network Setup Assistant will have entered all the necessary information so Internet Connect can function. Click Connect to open a connection. If you connect with a modem, this should take a few seconds, and you'll probably hear a series of strange noises as your modem negotiates with your ISP's modem and then finally connects.

After you've connected, the Internet Connect screen shows your connection speed and the IP address you're connected to, how long you've been connected, how much time remains (if you have a time limit), your IP address, and a set of Send and Receive gauges that show when data is being sent from, and received by, your Mac.

When you want to disconnect, just click the Disconnect button.

You can check Show Modem Status In Menu Bar, from the Internal Modem pane of Internet Connect. If you do this, a menu extra displays in the menu bar to help you connect using your modem.

You can use the menu extra to open Internet Connect quickly; just click the Modem menu extra and select Open Internet Connect. You can also connect and disconnect directly from the Modem menu extra by selecting Connect or Disconnect from its menu.

Work with E-mail

E-mail is one of the essential tools of today's business and is a great way to keep in touch with your family and friends. Everyone needs an efficient e-mail program, and Apple includes its Mail application with Mac OS X. This program is a full-featured e-mail client, with many advanced features such as a powerful junk mail filter, the possibility to use multiple accounts, customizable rules, and much more.

How to ...   Change Your Default E-mail Program

You don't have to use Apple's Mail for e-mail; you can also use other e-mail programs, such as Entourage (included with Microsoft Office), Eudora, PowerMail, or others.

Some applications will open your e-mail program automatically or will even open new messages to specific addresses when you click links or buttons. However, Apple's Mail is the default e-mail application and will open when other programs request your e-mail program, unless you change this default setting. Apple has unfortunately hidden this setting very well; the only way you can change your default e-mail program is from within the preferences of Apple Mail.

To do this, open Mail, and then select Mail | Preferences and click the General tab. The Default Email Reader setting shows the current default program. To change this, click the pop-up menu and select another program; if your e-mail program is not listed, click Select and browse until you find it, and then click Select again.

You can now quit Mail and be sure that your e-mail program is configured as the default. But even if you don't use Mail, you shouldn't delete it; if you ever need to change this default e-mail program again, there's no other way.

10

Set Up Mail

Most e-mail programs are easy to use, and Mail is no exception. You set up an e-mail account with your user name, password, and mail servers, and you connect to the Internet to check your mail. To open Mail, click its icon in the Dock or double-click its icon in the Applications folder.

Mail

If you didn't enter your e-mail account information in the Internet preference pane, or in the assistant that helped you set up your Mac when you first turned it on, you can configure accounts manually with Mail. When you first open the program, an assistant displays and helps you set up your account. Click Continue on the Welcome screen to move ahead to the General Information screen for your account.

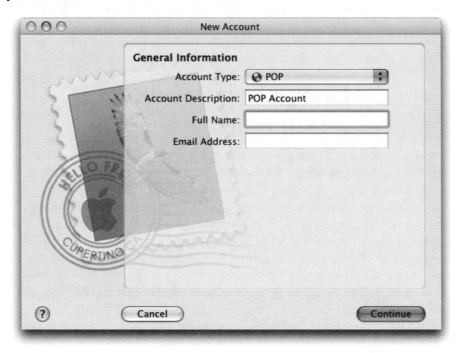

NOTE   *If you've upgraded from a previous version of Mac OS X, Mail will import your existing account information and mailboxes automatically, so you can start working with the program right away.*

Select your account type (most e-mail accounts are POP, though if you have a .Mac account you can select this), and then enter an account description, your name, and your e-mail address. Click Continue, and then enter your incoming mail server, user name, and password in the appropriate fields. If you're not sure about what to enter here, check with your ISP or network administrator. Click Continue to move to the next screen.

In this screen, enter your outgoing mail server, and if necessary, check Use Authentication and enter your user name and password. (Again, check with your ISP if you're not sure what to enter.) Click Continue. You'll see an account summary on the next screen; click Continue to create this account. After this, the Conclusion screen displays.

 **Import E-mail from Another E-mail Program**

When you first launch Mail and after you set up your e-mail account, the program displays a dialog asking if you want to import mailboxes. If you previously used another program, such as Microsoft Entourage, Outlook Express, Claris Emailer, Eudora, or the like, this feature lets you import all your e-mail into Mail.

To do this, click the Import Mailboxes button. (If you don't do it right away, you can do so later by selecting File | Import Mailboxes.) Click the radio button next to the name of your program, and then click the Continue button.

Select the items to import on the next screen, and then click Continue. Follow the remainder of the instructions to import all your mailboxes. You'll now be able to use your saved e-mail in Mail.

If you have an IMAP account, you won't need to worry about importing mail—the principle behind this type of account is that your e-mail resides on a central server, so you don't have to import anything.

You now can choose to import existing mailboxes, create another account, or click Done to open Mail and start using the account you just set up.

If you need to edit your e-mail account information at a later time, or if you want to add another account, you can use the Accounts pane in Mail's preferences (see Figure 10-4). Select Mail | Preferences, and then click Accounts. Click the + button to configure a new account.

The procedure for creating a new account from this location is similar to the one just described; the assistant walks through the procedure, displaying several screens where you enter your account information.

> **NOTE** *If you need to set up an IMAP or Exchange account to use with a corporate network, check with your network administrator to find out what settings to use. For other types of accounts, check with your ISP or other e-mail provider.*

FIGURE 10-4   The Accounts pane in Mail's preferences

Work with Mail

The main things you'll want to do with Mail are to compose mail, send mail, and receive mail. Mail's interface is simple and easy to understand (see Figure 10-5): the default display uses two panes, with mailboxes and folders in a list to the left, and with a toolbar containing icons for the most common actions you use.

In Figure 10-5, you can see the main elements of Mail's interface:

■ **Toolbar**   At the top of the window, a toolbar holds buttons for the most common actions you use with Mail.

■ **Message List**   This is a list of messages in your mailbox. Click one to display its body in the bottom pane.

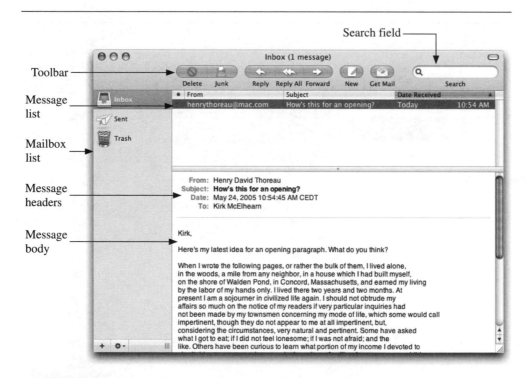

FIGURE 10-5   Mail's interface is clear and easy to understand.

- ■ **Headers**   This shows you who a message is from, the sender's address, the date and time it was sent, and the message's subject.

- ■ **Message Body**   This is the text of the message.

- ■ **Search Field**   You can enter text in this field to search among the messages in the selected mailbox.

- ■ **Mailbox List**   This displays all your mailboxes and folders, including a Trash folder.

The main tasks you perform with Mail are checking your e-mail, reading messages, replying to messages, and sending new messages. Many of the toolbar buttons let you do these tasks with just one click:

- ■ **Delete**   This deletes the selected message.

- ■ **Junk**   This sets the selected message as junk mail and helps Mail's junk mail filter learn from the message. If Mail thinks the selected message is junk, this icon says Not Junk. Click it to tell Mail that it is not a junk message.

- ■ **Reply**   This creates a new message in reply to the selected message.

- ■ **Reply All**   This replies to the selected message, sending the reply to the sender and all of its recipients.

- ■ **Forward**   This forwards the selected message; you select the address for the new recipient from the new mail message created after clicking this icon.

- ■ **New**   This opens a new, blank mail message.

- ■ **Get Mail**   This checks all your accounts for new messages.

Check Your Mail

Click the Get Mail button to check your e-mail. Mail checks your account(s) and downloads any messages waiting for you. These messages go into your Inbox. Click the Inbox icon in the mailbox list to see what messages await you.

You can also press ⌘-SHIFT-N to check for new mail.

10

NOTE   *Mail is set to check your mail automatically every five minutes. You can change this time or turn off automatic checking in Mail's preferences. Select Mail | Preferences and click the General icon. Select a time in the Check For New Mail pop-up menu. If you're not connected to the Internet all the time, set this menu to Manually, so that your Mac doesn't try to open an Internet connection every five minutes.*

All your messages then display in the top pane of Mail's main window. Click a message to display it; the message body shows in the bottom pane. You can read your message there, and if you want to delete it, just click the Delete button.

Reply to a Message

To reply to a message, select it in the top pane, and then click Reply. A new window displays with the To address set to that of the sender of the message you are replying to. The message body contains the entire message you're replying to, set off as quoted text in a different color. You can type your reply at the top of this message, or you can put your reply in different places throughout the message.

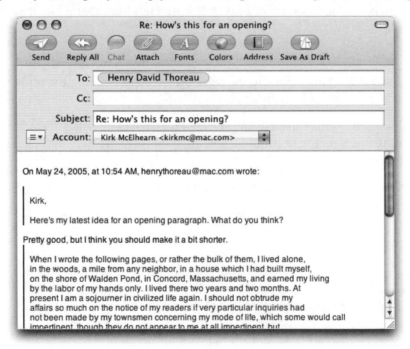

SHORTCUT *You can press ⌘-R to reply to a selected or open message.*

When you've finished composing your reply, click the Send button. This sends your message immediately. If you want to wait until later, just close the message and save it as a draft, or click Save As Draft, and then reopen the message from the Drafts folder when you're ready to send. (You won't have a Drafts folder until you save a message as a draft.)

When replying to messages, you have several choices: if the message was sent only to you, you can click Reply to send a reply to the sender. If you were one of several recipients, however, and you want all the recipients to read your reply, click Reply All; this sends your reply to both the sender and all the other recipients of the original message. Finally, if you want to forward a message to another recipient, click Forward. This sends the original message to a recipient of your choice, indicating that you forwarded it. You can add your own comments to this message.

Compose a Message

When you want to compose a new e-mail message, click the New button in Mail's toolbar. This opens a new message window.

10

Composing E-mail Offline

If you're not connected to the Internet all the time, you'll find that you need to work a bit differently when composing new messages or replying to messages. When you click Send, Mail tells your Mac to open an Internet connection and send your message. But if you have a dial-up connection, you won't want to connect for each e-mail message you compose, nor will you want Mail to try to connect every five minutes.

Select Mailbox | Go Offline to save your messages in the Outbox instead of sending them immediately. When you work offline, sending a message puts it in the Outbox, and to connect to the Internet and send the waiting messages, you must select Mailbox | Go Online. When you do this, Mail sends all messages in your Outbox as soon as you connect to the Internet.

You need to enter an address for the person you're sending the e-mail message to. Click the To field, and then type the recipient's address. If you already have that person's address in your Address Book, or if you've recently sent him or her a message, you'll see that Mail automatically completes the address after you type a couple of letters. If the address that Mail proposes is not the one you want, type another letter or two. If you know seven people named Henry, for example, you may need to type this first name plus one or two letters of the recipient's last name to find the right one.

You can also select addresses by clicking the Address icon in the New Message window. Just double-click an address, or drag it to the To field. You can send messages to multiple recipients by entering several addresses, or by dragging them from the Address window. If you type them, you must separate multiple addresses with commas; if you drag them, just drag one address after another, or select multiple addresses (by pressing the ⌘ key and clicking on several addresses) and drag them together.

NOTE   *You can send messages to recipients by entering their address in the To field, and also send copies of the message to other recipients by entering their addresses in the Cc field.*

After you have entered your recipient's address, enter a subject for the message in the Subject field.

Work with Attachments

Attachments are files sent with e-mail messages. You can send text files, photos, or even music and video files if you have a fast enough Internet connection, and if both your and your recipient's mailboxes allow you to send large files. (In many cases, e-mail accounts limit the size of attachments. This can be 5MB or 10MB, or another size. If you need to transfer files larger than this and you have a .Mac account, you can use your iDisk. See Chapter 11.)

If you want to send files with your message, just drag them from a Finder window or the Desktop into a message window. You can also add attachments by clicking the Attach button in the new message toolbar and browsing to find the file(s) you want to attach. (If you're sending files to a Windows user, or if you're not sure whether your recipient uses a Mac or a PC, click the Attach button, find the file you want to send, and check Send Windows Friendly Attachments in the dialog.)

The attachments you add to your message appear in the message body section of the window. In the next illustration, you see a file sent as an attachment; but if you send one or several pictures, they will display in the message.

10

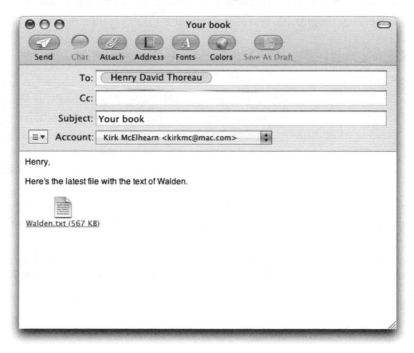

You can delete any of these attachments by clicking them to select them and pressing the DELETE key.

When you receive messages with attachments, they display at two locations in your incoming message. First, you'll see the files' icons in the body of the message. You can save the files by just dragging these icons to the Desktop or to a Finder window, or you can open them to view their contents by clicking their links.

Attachments are also listed in the headers of your incoming message.

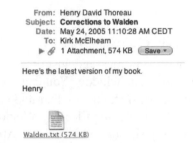

You'll see the number of attachments and their sizes, followed by a Save All button. Click this button to open a standard Save dialog where you can choose a folder to save these attachments. You can also click the disclosure triangle at the left of this line; click this triangle to display your attachments. From there, you can drag them from the display to the Desktop or any Finder window.

Sort Spam with Mail's Junk Mail Filter

Spam is the scourge of the Internet. If you don't get any, you're lucky; in fact, you're probably one of the only three people in the world who don't. If you do, you are familiar with the litany of messages offering to help you get rich quick, to increase the size of certain body parts, or to sell you all kinds of medication and more. Some of this is annoying, and some of it is downright offensive.

One of the most powerful features of Apple's Mail application is its built-in junk mail filter. If you use Mail, you can filter spam, or junk mail, into a special Junk folder and then check it occasionally to make sure there are no messages that really were intended for you, or set it to delete its contents automatically every day, every week, or at whatever frequency you want.

When you first start up Mail, its junk mail filter is set to Training (see Figure 10-6). This means the filter is in a learning mode; it tries to figure out which messages are junk, and you confirm its choices.

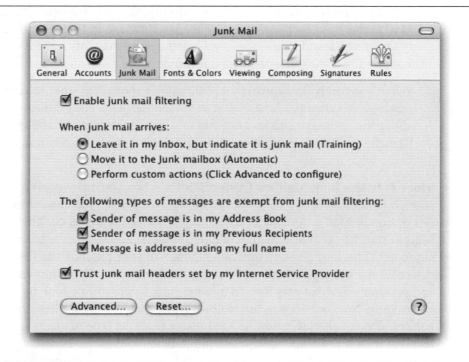

FIGURE 10-6   The Junk Mail preference pane when you first start up Mail

You can view the Junk Mail preference pane by selecting Mail | Preferences and clicking the Junk Mail icon in the preferences window toolbar.

Junk mail filtering is enabled by default when you first use Mail. This allows you to choose from several settings that tell Mail how to classify messages as junk.

You have two choices as to how Mail reacts when junk mail arrives:

■ **Leave It in My Inbox, but Indicate It Is Junk Mail (Training)**   This tells Mail to stay in training mode. When in this mode, Mail indicates any messages it considers junk by changing their color to brown and showing a Junk header at the top of each message.

■ When you receive messages that are indeed junk mail, just delete them. Mail learns from each message and keeps a database to filter out junk. If Mail has flagged a message as junk and it's not junk, click the Not Junk button at the top of the message window.

■ When you receive junk mail that Mail has not spotted as junk, select the message and click the Junk button in the toolbar. This adds information about this message and its contents to Mail's junk mail database. Remember, Mail is in training mode and needs your help sometimes to know what is junk.

■ **Move It to the Junk Mailbox (Automatic)**   When you have received enough junk mail for Mail to be accurate in its judgment, you can select this option in Mail's Junk Mail preference pane (see Figure 10-6). This tells Mail to start filing your junk mail into its Junk mailbox without asking you anymore. (This also displays the Junk mailbox in your mailbox list.) You can still set a message to junk by clicking the Junk button in the toolbar, and set a message that gets filtered into the Junk folder to Not Junk by clicking the Not Junk icon in the toolbar. While this junk mail filter is not perfect, it gets better over time as Mail learns from the type of spam you receive. It won't stop you from receiving junk mail, but it will prevent you from having to read it. It is best to check your Junk folder before deleting its messages, though, in case any real messages get flagged as junk.

The Junk Mail preferences let you choose to exempt three types of messages from junk filtering:

■ **Sender of Message Is in My Address Book**   If this is checked, no messages from people in your address book are flagged as junk.

■ **Sender of Message Is in My Previous Recipients**   Check this to exempt messages from anyone you have recently sent messages to from being considered junk, even if they are not in your Address Book.

■ **Message Is Addressed Using My Full Name**   Since most junk mail is addressed to e-mail addresses only, and sometimes with your first name, this exempts messages that are addressed to your full name. This may allow some messages to get through the junk mail filter, but if you do business over the Internet and get e-mail from strangers regularly, this helps you spot real messages.

Finally, you can check Trust Junk Mail Headers Set By My Internet Service Provider if your ISP uses special junk mail headers. It's best to leave this checked.

Create Mailboxes and Smart Mailboxes

When you fire up Mail for the first time, you only see an Inbox, a Trash folder, and a Sent folder. If you save a message as a draft, you'll see a Drafts folder, and if you turn on automatic junk mail filtering, you'll also see a Junk folder.

Mail lets you create other mailboxes, both to store your e-mail archives, and to display certain types of messages. You can create two types of mailboxes: normal mailboxes, which work and look like folders, and smart mailboxes, which search your e-mail and display only messages that meet certain criteria.

Normal mailboxes are great for storing e-mail, or for routing e-mail from certain mailing lists or senders. To create a new mailbox, select Mailbox | New Mailbox and then select the account (or On My Mac, if you don't want to store it on your e-mail account server; this is only the case for IMAP accounts) and name the mailbox. Click OK to save the mailbox, and it will be added to your mailbox list.

Smart mailboxes are more interesting, since they let you choose a set of criteria to display only certain messages. For example, you can create a smart mailbox to display only messages from family members, or from specific friends; you can create a smart mailbox to display messages that come from your work account; or only those messages that you haven't yet read. Let's look at this latter example.

To create a smart mailbox, select Mailbox | New Smart Mailbox. In the sheet that displays, enter a name for the smart mailbox (this is the name that displays in the mailbox list) and then select criteria for what types of messages the smart mailbox displays. You'll notice that this concept is similar to that used for smart folders in the Finder (Chapter 5) and smart playlists in iTunes (Chapter 16). In this example, choose Message Is Unread from the first pop-up menu. (If you choose other criteria, such as From, Subject, and so on, then you'll see other conditions, where you can enter an e-mail address, specific text, and more.)

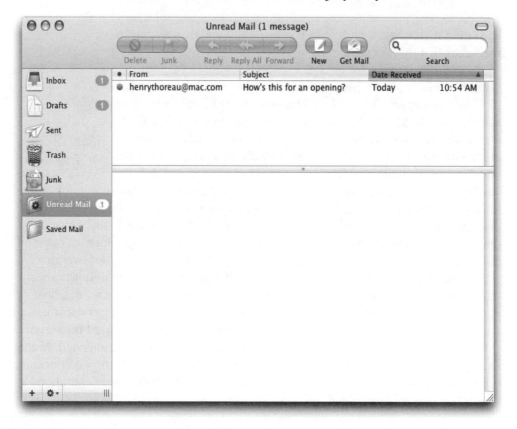

Click OK to save the smart mailbox; this now displays in your mailbox list.

You'll see in the preceding illustration that the Unread Mail smart mailbox displays with a gear icon, as on smart folders in the Finder, and that it shows one message. This is the same message that is in the Inbox in this example; the Inbox shows the number of unread messages to the right of the mailbox icon. But having an Unread Mail mailbox lets you see, at a glance, all your new, unread messages.

You can create as many smart mailboxes as you want, to sort your messages in many ways. Try a few different combinations of criteria, especially if you want to sort mail from specific addresses or accounts. Remember that smart mailboxes don't actually *contain* your e-mail messages; they merely display them. Nevertheless, you can work with messages from these smart mailboxes just as you do in other mailboxes.

Create Rules

When you receive a lot of e-mail, you need to have a way of managing all those messages. For some people, e-mail may come in droves from their jobs; for others, who subscribe to e-mail mailing lists, messages may come on specific subjects and interests. In all cases, creating rules to manage your e-mail and route it into different mailboxes is a great way to improve your productivity and make your e-mail easier to read and file.

Mail includes a function for creating *rules,* or setting conditions for sorting messages. You saw in the preceding section how smart mailboxes use criteria to determine which messages they display. Rules work in the same way, examining messages and applying actions according to the presence or absence of the criteria you choose.

Mail manages rules in its preferences. Select Mail | Preferences and then click the Rules icon. You'll see that, by default, there is one rule already there: called News From Apple, it tells Mail to change the background color of any messages sent by Apple to blue. It lists some two dozen possible Apple e-mail addresses, covering all the bases, with addresses from different countries, from the iTunes Music Store, and from Apple itself.

You can create your own rules to filter and move messages automatically as well. Click Add Rule, and the Rule sheet displays. Enter a name for your rule, such as the name of a sender, for example, or a mailbox such as Work or Family. From the first menu in the first criterion (the menu marked From), select a criterion you want to use—there are about two dozen of them, including the From address, the To address, the Account, the Date Sent, and much more.

10

Select one of these criteria, then select from the second menu an operator, such as Contains, Begins With, or Is Equal To. In the field after this menu, enter a text string, such as an e-mail address, a name, or a keyword you want to find in a message subject.

Next, in the Perform The Following Actions section, click the first menu to see the possible actions.

You can choose, for example, to move the message to a specific mailbox, change its color, reply automatically, or even delete a message. Each choice leads to different possibilities. Play around with these possibilities to see the many things you can do with rules. While most people will find them useful to move specific messages into mailboxes or change message colors to make them stand out, your options are vast.

NOTE   *If you have a .Mac account, you can also manage your e-mail on the .Mac web site. See Chapter 11 for more on using .Mac.*

Surf the Web

Surfing the Web is simple on your Mac. You can use Apple's Safari, the fastest browser available for Mac OS X, or one of the many other browsers available (Internet Explorer, Firefox, Netscape, Camino, OmniWeb, and so on). Mac OS X comes with Safari and Internet Explorer, but Safari is the default web browser, and its icon is in the Dock.

Safari

To open Safari, just click its icon in the Dock or double-click its icon in the Applications folder.

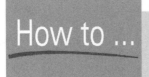 *While Apple's Safari is the fastest web browser available for Mac OS X, you may need to use Internet Explorer for some web sites. Some e-commerce and banking sites, as well as some internal networks (intranets) may not work with Safari, but Apple has been very attentive to users' comments and its progressive upgrades have improved compatibility with most web sites. You can download Internet Explorer from Microsoft's web site: www.microsoft.com/mac/.*

Surfing the Web with Safari is simple: when you start up the program, it opens to its preset home page. At press time, this is Apple's "start" page, which gives you news about Apple products, new releases on the iTunes Music Store, and links to the rest of Apple's web site.

How to ... Change Your Home Page

Safari uses a default home page that Apple has set for you. You may like this page, but you might want to change to a different home page—for instance, you might want to have Safari open to your personal web site, a news site, or even the .Mac web site. To do this, select Safari | Preferences and then click the General icon in the toolbar. You'll see a field labeled Home Page. Enter a URL, or web page address, in this field to set a different home page.

Another way to change the default page is to select the New Windows Open With pop-up menu and choose either Empty Page or Bookmarks. If you choose Empty Page, you'll just see a blank page when you launch Safari; you can type whatever URL, or web address, you want in the Address field at the top of the window. If you choose Bookmarks, your bookmarks will display, and you can double-click any of them to open their pages. If you choose one of these two options, your Mac won't try to connect to the Internet as soon as you open Safari—you may find such connect attempts to be a bit of a headache, especially if you connect with a modem.

Work with Safari Bookmarks

Safari includes some preset bookmarks in its Bookmark Bar. Click one of these buttons to go to that page, or click the Apple or News pop-up button to select one of the bookmarks it contains.

A bookmark is an essential tool when browsing the Web, allowing you to return to a page you use often. When you want to bookmark a page, select Bookmarks | Add Bookmark. A sheet displays asking you to name the bookmark and select a location for it.

Enter a name for the bookmark, and then select a location. You can save bookmarks in the Bookmarks Bar or in the Bookmarks menu. You can also store bookmarks in a number of preset bookmark collections.

Some web pages have titles that are very long and even misleading. By entering your own name for the page, you'll find it easier to work with your bookmarks.

To manage your bookmarks, click the Bookmarks button in the Bookmarks Bar, or select Bookmarks | Show All Bookmarks.

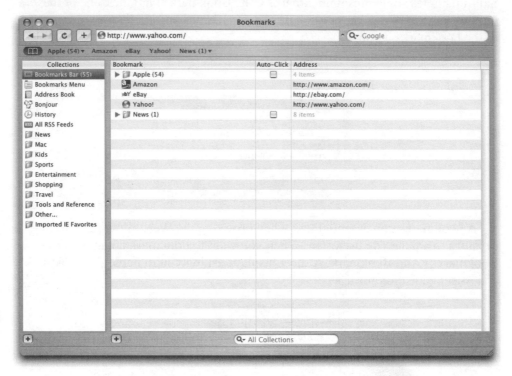

This window displays all your bookmarks: the Bookmarks Bar, the Bookmarks menu, as well as a group of preset bookmark collections. You can go to any page by double-clicking a bookmark in this window. You can also go back to previous pages by clicking History, looking at all the web addresses you have visited in the past few days, and then double-clicking one of them.

If you want to organize your bookmarks in folders within your Bookmarks menu, just click the Bookmarks Menu icon in the Collections column and then click the + button at the bottom of the Bookmark section. Type a new name for the folder that displays. This folder displays in the Bookmarks menu as a menu item with a submenu. Drag any bookmarks you want into the folder, and then you'll be able to select them from this submenu.

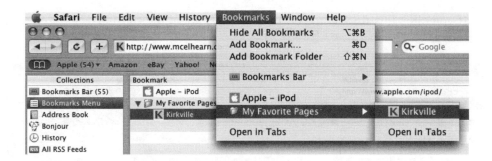

SnapBack

One of Safari's interesting features is SnapBack, which lets you mark a web page and return to it with a click. Say you want to browse Apple's web site. When you go to the main page, select History | Mark Page For SnapBack. Browse around the site a bit, and then when you want to return to the SnapBack page, just click the orange arrow icon at the right of the URL field.

If you don't mark any page, the SnapBack button takes you back to the first page you viewed, in the current window or tab, when you began browsing. You no longer need to click the Back button a dozen times to get back where you started. (But if you manually type an address in the Address field, this is automatically set as your new SnapBack page.)

Safari RSS

New in the Tiger version of Safari is support for RSS, or Really Simple Syndication. RSS is a way that web sites can provide capsule descriptions of their stories, and RSS readers—or Safari—can display these brief descriptions so that you can decide if a story is interesting enough to read.

In most cases, when a web site has an RSS *feed,* or a special RSS file it makes available, Safari displays an RSS icon in its address bar.

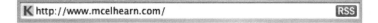

10

If you click this RSS icon, you'll see the display of the capsule descriptions of stories.

You can see in the preceding illustration that the pointer is above the Apple Digital Campus article; it is in the hand form, showing that this is a link to the entire article. You can click any of the titles to read their articles.

At the right of the window, you have several options. You can move a slider to change the length of article summaries that display; this depends, in part, on the length of summaries provided by web sites, but at the shortest position, it merely displays titles and dates. You can sort articles by date, title, source, or whether the articles are new. You can look at recent articles by time period (All, Today, Yesterday, etc.). And you can go to the source page or click a link in the Actions section, such as Mail Link To This Page, which creates an e-mail message with a link to the page.

To return to the normal, non-RSS view, just click the RSS icon in the address bar again.

You can use RSS feeds in Bookmarks Bar folders as well. You'll notice that the default folders—the Apple and News folders—will display numbers in parentheses at times. This is the number of unread stories on the sites contained in those folders.

To save a bookmark for an RSS feed, click the RSS button when you find a site that contains an RSS feed, and then save the RSS page as a bookmark. You'll be able to return to the summary page by selecting that bookmark; if you save the bookmark in the Bookmarks Bar, or in one of its folders, you'll see the number of new articles automatically.

If you get hooked on RSS—and many people do—check Safari's Bookmarks window (click the Book icon at the left of the Bookmarks Bar). Click All RSS Feeds to see a few dozen web sites that Apple has chosen to include by default.

Google Searches

Another great Safari feature is the built-in Google search field (see Figure 10-7). Google is one of the most effective search engines for the Web. When you want to search Google, you don't need to go to the Google site; just enter your search terms in the Google search field and press RETURN or ENTER. This sends your search to Google and returns a page with the search results.

To clear the Google search field, just click the x icon at the right of the field.

You can also click the arrow next to the magnifying glass icon to select previous search terms and return to previous results.

10

> **TIP** *You can combine SnapBack (see the preceding section, "SnapBack") with Google searches. After visiting pages in the Google search results, just click the SnapBack button in the Google search field to come back to the search results page.*

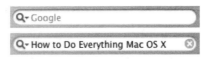

FIGURE 10-7   The Google search bar: empty (top) and with search words entered (bottom)

Access Web Services with Sherlock

Apple's Sherlock is an interface to web services, providing specific types of information much more quickly than web browsers. Using columns and panes, it provides access to practical and useful information, such as stock quotes, movie information, yellow pages, airline flight information, and more (see Figure 10-8). Sherlock comes with a set of channels for a number of basic services and can accept plug-ins for additional channels.

To access one of Sherlock's channels and search for information, click a channel icon. Each channel displays its information and search fields in a different way. Figure 10-9 shows the airline flight channel, which you can use to search for flights by airline, flight number, departure city, and arrival city.

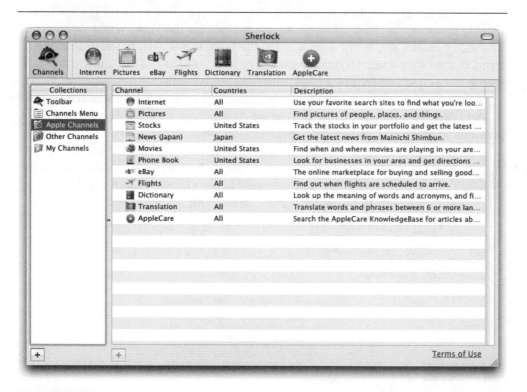

FIGURE 10-8   Sherlock's basic interface, showing its list of available channels

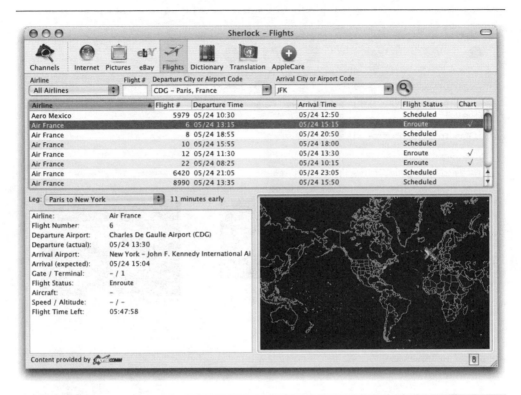

FIGURE 10-9   The Flights channel lets you search for airline flights and returns a list matching your criteria.

Some Sherlock channels just return text, but others return graphics and even video clips. In Figure 10-9, you can see the current location of a selected flight.

Another useful channel is the Movies channel. If you enter your town or city, your ZIP code, or the ZIP code of the area where you want to go to the movies, Sherlock returns a list of movies and theaters (Figure 10-10). Not only does it show you the movies, but when you click a movie title, it shows you a summary of the story, a poster, and, if possible, a trailer. In some areas, you can even use Sherlock to purchase movie tickets online.

The best way to get to know Sherlock is to try out its different channels and see what they offer.

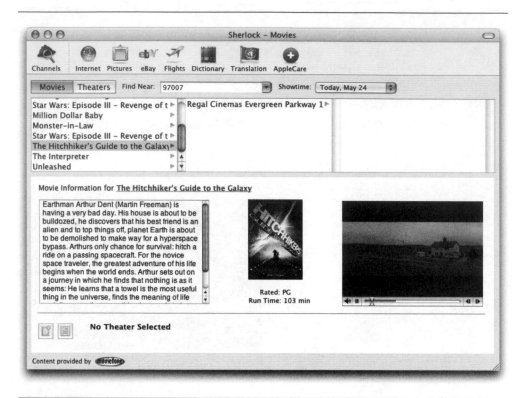

FIGURE 10-10   Want to go to the movies? Let Sherlock tell you what's playing.

Keep in Touch with iChat AV

There are lots of ways to keep in touch with friends, family, customers, and coworkers. E-mail is the easiest, since you can send messages even if your recipients aren't online at the time. But if you want to keep in touch with people with more immediacy, iChat AV, Apple's instant messaging program, is the best way.

iChat AV offers three types of chats: text, audio, and video. You can use text chats with anyone, as long as they have a compatible account (either a .Mac account or an AIM, or AOL Instant Messenger, account). You can use audio chats with anyone using iChat AV who has a microphone and speakers; you can use an internal mike and speakers, or you can plug a mike and speakers, or even a headset, into your Mac. And finally, if you have a fast enough Mac (a 600 MHz G3 or faster, or a G4 or G5 Mac), a broadband connection to the Internet, and a FireWire video camera, you can video chat with others. The new version of iChat AV included in Tiger also lets you set up multiple audio and video chats, with up to ten audio users and four video users. The processor requirements are more stringent for these chats; see the iChat help for more details.

You can also use iChat across a local network, using Apple's Bonjour messaging. You can use iChat for text, audio, and video chats on your local network, as long as you have a fast enough Mac and the required hardware.

NOTE   *iChat is compatible with AIM, but not with another popular instant messaging tool, ICQ (though compatibility with ICQ may be added to a future version of iChat). If you have friends who use ICQ, you can download a Mac OS X version of the program at www.icq.com. The same is the case with other instant messaging services, such as Yahoo Messenger, MSN, and so on.*

Set Up iChat

To use iChat, you need to have either a .Mac or an AIM screen name. This is because iChat stores your Buddy List (your contacts) on its servers, and you need to identify yourself individually; no two people can have the same user name.

If you've already got a .Mac account and have entered this information either when installing Mac OS X or in the .Mac preference pane (see Chapter 11), you won't need to do anything special to use iChat. If not, you'll need to enter your account information when starting up iChat.

When you open iChat AV for the first time, an assistant displays to help you set up your account. The first screen is a welcome screen. Read this and then click Continue.

10

If you have either a .Mac or an AIM account, enter your information in the next screen.

If you don't have an account, click Get An iChat Account. This takes you to a web page where you can sign up for a free 60-day trial .Mac account. (This is not a permanent .Mac account, but if you don't pay for it after the 60-day period, you'll keep your screen name.)

If you have an AIM screen name, select the Account Type pop-up menu and then select AIM Account. You can get a free AIM account by going to http:// my.screenname.aol.com.

After you've entered your account information, click Continue. The next screen asks you if you want to turn on Jabber messaging. Jabber is a type of server that is used in companies. If you use Jabber, check this option and then enter your account name and password. Click Continue.

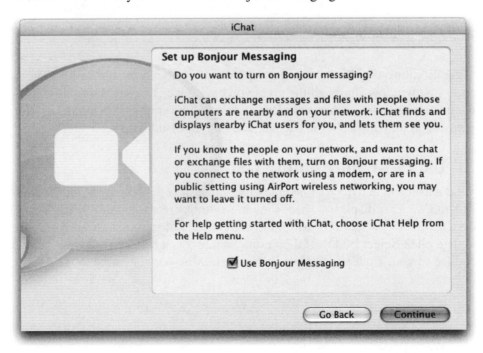

iChat then asks if you want to use Bonjour messaging.

10

Bonjour messaging lets you communicate with other users on a local network. If you use a local network, you should turn this on. Click Continue.

The next screen lets you set up your video camera, if your Mac supports videoconferencing and if you have an appropriate camera. All it does is show if your camera is indeed functioning and show the image your camera displays. Move your camera until the image is correct, and then click Continue.

The final screen tells you that you have successfully set up iChat and are ready to use it. Click Done. When you do this, iChat will display one or two windows: it displays a Buddy List window, and if you've activated Bonjour messaging, it displays a Bonjour window as well.

The Bonjour window shows all available users on your local network. The Buddy List window shows all the users you have added to your Buddy List. If you have just started using iChat, your Buddy List will be empty; if you have used it in the past, you may have several users already in your Buddy List.

Add Users to Your Buddy List

To add a user to your Buddy List, click the + button at the bottom of the Buddy List window. This displays a sheet showing all the contacts in your Address Book. (See Chapter 15 for more on using Address Book.) Select one of these contacts, and then click Select Buddy. If their e-mail address is a mac.com address, they'll be added to your Buddy List. If not, enter their .Mac account name or AIM screen name.

If you want to add a new person to your Buddy List, someone who is not in your Address Book, click New Person. Select the type of account they have (.Mac or AIM) from the Account Type pop-up menu, and then enter their Account Name.

You can also add their first name, last name, and e-mail address, which are recorded in your Address Book. Click Add to add them to your Buddy List. You'll see the user's name in your Buddy List window, followed by one or two icons.

If the user has audio or video capabilities, you'll see a telephone icon (for audio) or a video camera icon (for video); otherwise, you can only carry out text chats with them. You'll also see an icon for the user's picture, if they have set one.

NOTE   *If you see a single telephone or video icon, that means the user is not running Tiger and cannot participate in multiple audio or video chats. If you see icons that look like three overlaid icons, then they have Tiger. However, this does not tell you whether they have the processor power to participate in multiple chats.*

Before the user's name, you'll see one of three icons showing their availability: green means they are available, yellow means they are idle, and red means they are not available. If the user is offline, their name appears dimmed, and there is no colored icon in front of it.

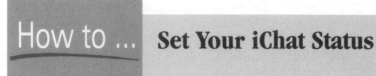

How to ...   Set Your iChat Status

While you may want your buddies to always know when you are online, you may also want to be left alone at times, especially when you're busy. You can change your iChat status to show others whether you're available to chat.

There are two ways to do this: the first is by using the Buddy List window. Beneath your user name is a small pop-up menu that displays your status. Click this menu to choose from Available, Away, Offline, Current iTunes Track (this displays the song you're listening to in iTunes), or Custom status for both Available and Away. If you select one of the Custom menu items, you can type your own custom status in the text field. Select Edit Status Menu to add or delete any custom status messages you create.

You can also change your status by using the iChat status icon in your menu bar. To display this icon, select iChat | Preferences, click General, and check Show Status In Menu Bar.

Click this icon to change your status, to initiate a chat with any of your available buddies, or to display your Buddy List if it is not visible.

FIGURE 10-11   Click the left button to start a text chat, the middle button to start an audio chat, and the right button to start a video chat. If your buddy doesn't have the audio or video capabilities, or if you don't, these buttons will be dimmed.

Chat with Your Buddies

When you want to start chatting with one of your buddies, check to see if they are online and available. There are then two ways to start a chat: if you have the iChat icon displayed in your menu bar, just select the name of one of your buddies. In this case, a window displays (see Figure 10-11) asking how you want to chat.

You can also select your buddy's name in your Buddy List window and click one of the icons at the bottom of the window; these three icons are the same as those shown in Figure 10-11.

When someone wants to start a chat with you, a window will display showing that person's message, along with three buttons at the bottom of the window: Block, Decline, and Accept. To accept the chat, click Accept. You can block the user by clicking Block or turn down their chat by clicking Decline.

If you start a text chat, you can type your first message in the chat window. Your buddy will get a message on their computer and can start chatting with you.

10

> **TIP** *You can change the way chat messages display by selecting iChat | Preferences, and then clicking Messages. You can change text balloon colors, as well as fonts, and you can reformat incoming messages if you want them to always be in a specific color and font. If you don't like the text balloons, select the View menu, and then select Show As Text. You'll see colored backgrounds for each text line, which correspond to the balloon colors set in the Messages preferences. If you don't like the colors, change them, or to turn them off, set them to Clear.*

If you want to start an audio chat, select your buddy and click the audio chat button. When the chat begins, you'll see a window like this:

This window displays your microphone volume at the top and allows you to set your speaker volume by moving the slider at the bottom.

Just speak into your microphone (either built into the screen of your Mac if you have an iMac, eMac, PowerBook, or iBook or an external mike plugged into your Mac), and you can have a conversation with your buddy.

To start a video chat, you need to have an appropriate FireWire video camera, such as Apple's iSight. Just plug this into one of your Mac's FireWire ports, set it up so that it's trained on you (by mounting it on your screen or desk), and start a new chat as described previously. Click the video chat button, and if the other user has a video camera, you'll be able to talk to and see each other.

As you can tell from this illustration, you see yourself in a small image at the bottom right of the iChat window, while your buddy appears in a larger image.

You can do lots more with iChat AV: you can set up group chats, save your chat transcripts automatically, and even transfer files over iChat (see Chapter 12). For more on the many features of iChat AV, see the program's online help.

Chapter 11

Work with .Mac

How to...

■ Set up your .Mac account

■ Use .Mac e-mail on the Web

■ Create your own web site

■ Use other .Mac features

Apple's .Mac is a suite of services that extend the reach of your Mac to the Internet. Offering a wealth of features, .Mac is an ideal way for you to share your files, manage your e-mail, show off your photos, and synchronize data between two or more Macs. Currently sold at $100 per year, or $180 for a five-user family pack, .Mac also gives you access to certain Apple tools, such as Backup, to back up your files, and provides other free software and advantages. While you don't have to use .Mac, its functions are seamlessly integrated into Mac OS X and several of its programs; it provides excellent value to many users.

Apple has overhauled .Mac with the release of Tiger. Not only are new functions built in to Mac OS X (especially the more powerful .Mac Sync function), but the .Mac web site is easier to navigate and your most commonly used features are easily accessible from the main page.

About .Mac

Apple's .Mac offers a wide range of features that help you do more with your Mac.

■ **E-mail**   You get a Mac e-mail account (*your_name*@mac.com), and you can manage your e-mail on the Web using the special .Mac e-mail page. You can also use this web interface to download mail from other mail servers, giving you web access to all your e-mail accounts when you're on the road.

■ **Address Book**   Using the .Mac Sync function built into Tiger, you can synchronize your Address Book contacts between your Mac and your .Mac account on the Web so you can access your Address Book when you use .Mac e-mail over the Web on a computer away from home. This ensures that you're always up-to-date if you use both ways of sending and receiving e-mail. (See Chapter 15 for more on Address Book.)

■ **Bookmarks**   Just as you can synchronize your Address Book contacts, you can synchronize your Safari bookmarks. If you often access the Internet in a cyber café, at the office, or at a school, you can use the same bookmarks as you have on your Mac at home.

How to ...   Log In to Your .Mac Account

Most of what you do with your .Mac account takes place on its web interface. Using Safari, just click the .Mac button in the Bookmarks Bar, or type **www.mac.com**. You'll see a Log In link somewhere on the main page; click this and enter your user name and password. (You may not need to enter your user name if you have already logged in recently from the same computer or if you always use the same computer to access .Mac.)

You'll find a series of links to the different .Mac features on the left side of the main page. Click one of these to access its features. (You may need to enter your password again, for reasons of security.) Some of these features offer easy access to information: for example, the Address Book section has a search field so you can search for your contacts quickly; the iCal section displays the current month, with links to events you have set in a calendar that you sync to .Mac; and the HomePage section has links to your different web pages.

■ **HomePage**   Create your own web site in minutes using .Mac's templates. Use this web site to share files, display photos or movies, or publish your résumé. .Mac is integrated with iPhoto, for example, and you can set up a web-based photo album in a jiffy.

■ **iDisk**   You get 250MB of storage space on Apple's servers (you can purchase more space if you need it) to back up your files or share them with others. (You split this disk space between your .Mac e-mail account and your iDisk.) Your iDisk is seamlessly integrated into Mac OS X, offering the possibility of creating a local copy and automatically synchronizing it with your online iDisk. It also provides an easy way to download some Apple software, from its Software folder.

■ **iCards**   Send all sorts of electronic postcards to your friends and family.

■ **Backup**   Apple's Backup, a tool for backing up your files, lets you back up data to your iDisk, to a CD or DVD, or to another hard disk or folder. (See Chapter 19.)

■ **.Mac Sync**   Synchronize your data, such as your Address Book contacts and bookmarks, so all your Macs can work with the same information.

11

- **iCal**   Use .Mac to share your iCal calendars with others so they can subscribe to your calendars and view your schedule. (See Chapter 15.) You can also view your calendars online, so you have access to your appointments from any computer with Internet access.

- **Learning Center**   The .Mac web site offers a wide range of tutorials for learning more about Mac OS X and other Apple software, such as iLife, iWork, and professional applications for graphics and videos.

In addition to these features, .Mac regularly offers its members free software and services, as well as discounts on software, hardware, and other services.

Set Up Your .Mac Account

If you set up your .Mac account by entering your user name and password when you installed Mac OS X, you have nothing more to do. If you didn't do so then, you can set up your account now. Open the System Preferences application by clicking its Dock icon or by selecting the Apple Menu | System Preferences. Click the .Mac icon.

The .Mac preference pane has four tabs:

■ **Sign In**   If you have a .Mac account, you can enter your member name and password in this tab. If you don't have an account, clicking the Learn More button takes you to Apple's web site, where you can sign up immediately. (At press time, this link lets you sign up for a free 60-day trial subscription to .Mac.) After you enter your user name and password, the name of this tab changes to Account.

■ **Sync**   This tab controls which types of items you want to sync to your .Mac account. You can then sync them to another Mac as well, if you have, for example, a desktop Mac and a PowerBook or an iBook. (I'll look more closely at using the .Mac Sync function in Chapter 15.)

■ **iDisk**   An iDisk is part of Apple's .Mac service. It offers you an online storage space of 250MB for storing e-mail, sharing files, and creating your own web site. (You share this disk space with your .Mac e-mail account and can choose how much to allocate to each usage; you can also purchase more space if you need it.) If you have a .Mac account and enter your member name in the .Mac pane, this tab shows the status of your iDisk. You can choose whether you want a local copy of your iDisk on your Mac and whether it is synchronized with your online iDisk manually or automatically. You can also change your public folder access and set a password to protect your public folder.

■ **Advanced**   This tab tells you which computers you have synchronized with your .Mac account and lets you register new computers or remove any that are registered.

Use .Mac E-mail

Using .Mac e-mail is a lot like using Apple's Mail application—the icons are similar and the overall logic is the same. After logging in to .Mac (see the previous section), click the Mail link to access your e-mail. You'll see any messages that are currently in your Inbox.

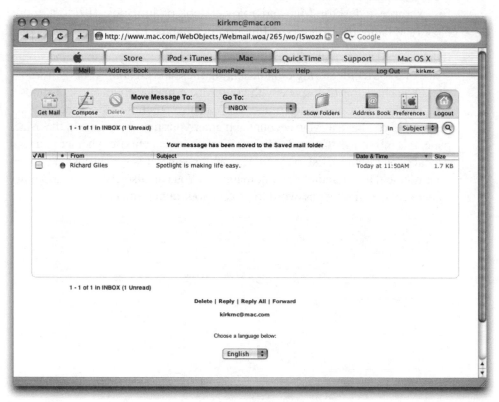

Click one of these messages to read it, and then click Reply if you want to reply to the sender. To delete a message, click the Delete icon. You can also file your messages by selecting a folder from the Move Message To pop-up menu.

To create a new message, click the Compose icon. Enter your recipient's e-mail address and a subject, and then start typing your message. When you've finished, click Send to send it.

 *If you use .Mac Sync to synchronize your Address Book contacts to your .Mac account, you'll be able to use any of these contacts by clicking the Address Book icon.*

The .Mac e-mail interface offers almost as many functions as a stand-alone e-mail client program. For more on using .Mac e-mail, see the online .Mac help: click the Help link in the .Mac toolbar at the top of your screen.

Work with Your iDisk

If you have a .Mac account, you get 250MB of online storage to share between your .Mac e-mail account and your iDisk. (You can choose how much to use for each feature in the Account section of the .Mac web site; click the Storage Settings button to make changes.) You can use your iDisk to back up files, to provide a download location for files you want to share with others, or to create your own home page or photo album. Since Mac OS X 10.3, your iDisk is integrated into the Finder. As you saw in Chapter 3, you can display your iDisk in the Finder window sidebar. In addition, as you saw earlier in this chapter, you can set preferences to use a local copy of your iDisk. When you do this, your Mac creates a mirror of your iDisk on your computer; you can drag files directly into this local copy instead of having to mount your iDisk and copy files manually. You can also choose to have your iDisk synchronized manually or automatically.

If you choose to work with a local copy of your iDisk, then the copy mounts automatically on the Desktop.

11

Your iDisk contains a number of folders where you can store files. You can see that most of these folders have the same names as folders in your home folder. There are three folders that are not in your home folder, though: the Backup folder, which is only used by Apple's Backup application, provided with your .Mac subscription; the Software folder, which contains software that you can download; and the Shared folder, which is available only to users who have purchased a family pack. This folder is available to all users of the family pack, and it functions like a Shared folder in your Users folder.

NOTE   *If you create a local copy of your iDisk, you'll see that four of its folders are a special type of alias: the Backup, Library, Software, and Shared folders. These folders display with a small iDisk icon at the bottom right of their folder icons. As I mentioned earlier in the chapter, the Backup folder is for backing up your data with Apple's Backup program; backups are only made to the .Mac server. The Library folder is for storing bookmarks, Address Book contacts, and iCal data that you have synchronized using iSync. The Software folder contains software that you can download from Apple's servers. Browse this folder to see if there is any software you need: some of this is Apple software, and some is provided either for free or as shareware by other developers. The Shared folder is available only to users of a family pack subscription.*

To copy files to your iDisk, just click the iDisk icon in the Finder window sidebar to display its contents, and drag files into one of its folders. If you've set automatic synchronization in the iDisk preferences, the Sync icon next to your iDisk icon will begin turning as your Mac synchronizes its contents with your online iDisk.

If you've set manual synchronization, the icon looks a bit different, as shown at right. Just click this icon to start synchronizing your iDisk. As your iDisk synchronizes, you'll see its status at the bottom of a Finder window, showing if this window is open to your iDisk or one of its folders.

Syncing iDisk ▭▭▭▭▭ Item 40 of 65: "My Files.dmg"

NOTE   *If your Mac is not always connected to the Internet, you can still use automatic synchronization. If your Mac can't find your iDisk, it will delay synchronization until the next time your Mac is connected.*

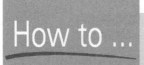

Allow Windows Users to Access Your iDisk

Apple offers an application called iDisk Utility for Windows XP, which allows anyone on a Windows XP computer to access your iDisk and upload or download files to and from your Public folder directly from the Windows XP desktop.

To download this program, click the iDisk link on the main .Mac page, and then look for the Member Central link. Click this link to go to a page where you'll find some software for download (such as Backup and other software), and then click the link iDisk Utility For Windows XP. Download this file, and then install it on a PC running Windows XP.

The iDisk Utility provides a simple dialog offering access to a user's iDisk, with their user name and password, or to any .Mac member's Public folder, with the person's member name.

If you don't choose to create a local copy of your iDisk, you need to mount it to access it. This is simple: just go to the Finder and select Go | iDisk | My iDisk or press ⌘-SHIFT-I. If you use your iDisk regularly, you'll find it practical to have the iDisk display in the Finder window sidebar. (See Chapter 3 for more on the sidebar.)

You can also access other users' iDisks from the Finder's Go menu. Select Go | iDisk, and then select Other User's iDisk or Other User's Public Folder to mount another user's iDisk or Public folder and download or upload files.

   When another user places files in your Public folder, you won't be notified, but if your iDisk automatically synchronizes, these files will be downloaded to your local iDisk. It's best to send an e-mail message to a user to alert them that you've put files in their Public folder so they can know to check there.

For more on using your iDisk, see the .Mac Help page.

Create Your Own Home Page

With .Mac, you can create your own home page, using the many templates available on the .Mac web site. There are page templates for site menus, photo albums, movies, résumés, file sharing, and more. To create a home page, click the HomePage link on the main .Mac page.

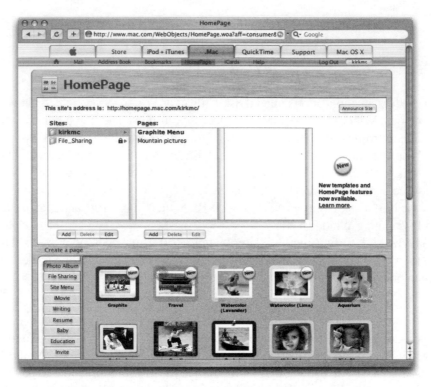

To add a page to your site, click the Add button beneath the list of pages. This takes you to a page where you can select what type of page to add: click the tabs at the left of this page, and then click one of the pages to add it. For example, if you want to add a résumé, click the Resume tab and you'll see a page like the following:

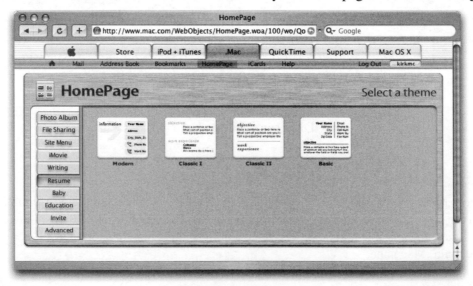

Click one of the résumé templates, and then click Edit. The résumé displays as a series of fields with preset headers. You can enter personal information in the fields to fill in your résumé.

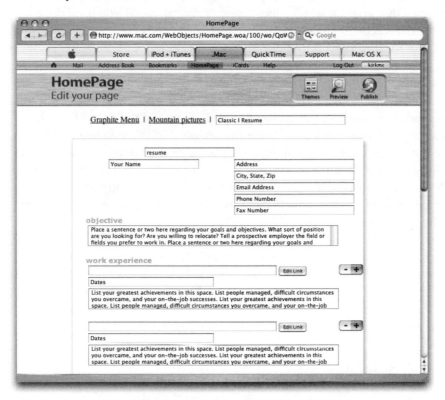

When you've finished, click the Publish button at the top of the page, or click Preview to see what it looks like (and proofread it) before publishing. The next page tells you that your page has been published, shows you its URL (web page address), and offers to send iCards to your family and friends to announce it.

NOTE   *If you want to see an example of a résumé, and an impressive one at that, go to http://homepage.mac.com/steve/Resume.html. This is Steve Jobs' résumé.*

Share Files on the Web

While it's beyond the scope of this book to talk about all the pages available from .Mac's HomePage, there is one type of page that's very useful: File Sharing. This is a special page designed to provide links to files you want to share with others. The links on this page correspond to the files in your iDisk's Public folder; so to share files with other users, whether they have a .Mac account or not—even with Windows users—you can use this page.

First, put some files to share in your iDisk's Public folder. Earlier in this chapter, I explained that you can set up a local copy of your iDisk. If you have done this, just click the iDisk icon in a Finder window sidebar and copy files into the Public folder you see in this window. If you don't have a local copy of your iDisk, select Go | iDisk | My iDisk to mount your iDisk on the Desktop. Double-click its icon, and then double-click the Public folder to open it.

In either case, copying files to your Public folder may take awhile, depending on the speed of your Internet connection and the size of the files. If you have a local copy of your iDisk you'll see the progress of the synchronization at the bottom of the Finder window. (If you have your iDisk set to manual synchronization, click the rotating arrow icon next to the iDisk icon in the Finder window sidebar to start synchronization.) If you copy to an iDisk mounted on the Desktop, you'll see a standard Finder copy dialog showing you the progress of the copy.

To create a File Sharing page, go to HomePage as described previously in the "Create Your Own Home Page" section. Click the Add button, and then click the File Sharing tab to see the File Sharing page templates. As of press time, there are only four—two My Downloads pages, in Archival and Graphite layouts, and two iDisk Public Folder pages, in Graphite and Magenta—but it is possible that there will be more at a later date. Click one of these pages to select it.

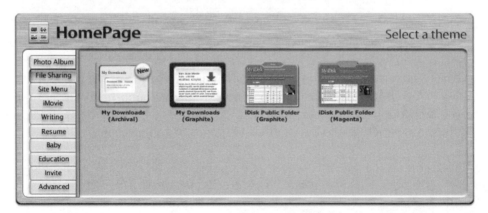

Click Edit to edit some of the text on this page. You can change the header of the page, in the tab at the top of the folder-like graphic, and add text describing its contents. When you've made your changes, click the Publish icon at the top of the page to publish it. When you've done so, you'll see the URL for the page; you can send this to others so they can access your files.

When someone goes to your page, they'll see something like this:

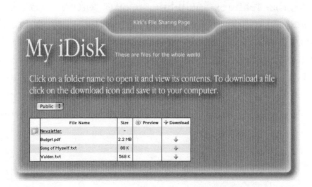

In this example, you can see that there is one folder, Newsletter, and three individual files. To download any of the individual files, just click the arrow icons in the Download column. To view the contents of the folder (which was uploaded as a folder to the Public folder), click the underlined link next to the folder icon. This displays download links for each of the items in the folder.

Create a Site Menu Page

If you have several pages on your site, it's a good idea to create a Site Menu page. You can select one of the available Site Menu pages by clicking the Add button and the Site Menu tab. When you add a Site Menu page, it contains links to all the other pages on your site. When people come to your site, at its http://homepage.mac.com/ *your_user_name* URL, they'll see this Site Menu page and be able to enter any of your other pages by clicking these links.

Create Additional Sites

You are not limited to just one site with .Mac. You can create additional sites, which are actually subfolders within your main site. From the HomePage page, click the Add Another Site button to the right of the Pages list; if you have already created additional sites, click the Add button below the Sites list.

This creates a new subfolder inside your web site. For example, your initial web site's address is http://homepage.mac.com/*your_user_name*. If you create another site in this manner, its URL is http://homepage.mac.com/*your_user_name*/ *site_name*. You can add pages to this site, as explained earlier, or password-protect this site to prevent unauthorized people from accessing it. To apply a password, just turn on password protection when you create the site and enter a password in the Password field.

11

Go Further with .Mac

.Mac offers many other features, including specific software (Backup, and special features of iCal and .Mac Sync) that I examine in other chapters of this book. You can find extensive help on the .Mac web site for all its features, and Apple has been adding new features regularly, as well as new special offers, such as free software or discounts on software and hardware. If you have a .Mac account and you use your iDisk and .Mac e-mail address but not the other features, you should still check the .Mac web page (www.mac.com) regularly to find out about additional features and enhancements.

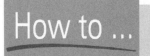

How to ...   Protect Your Public Folder with a Password

If you create a File Sharing page, as described previously, anyone can access the files you put in your Public folder. To prevent strangers from downloading your files, you can apply a password to protect this folder. To do this, open the System Preferences and click the .Mac icon. Click the iDisk tab. At the bottom of this tab, check Use A Password To Protect Your Public Folder. Enter a password in the sheet that displays, and then enter it again to confirm it.

This password protection only applies to users connecting to your Public folder by mounting your iDisk on their Desktop or using the iDisk Utility for Windows XP. If you want to protect access via the .Mac web site, click the HomePage icon, and then look for the text Protect This Site; click the arrow icon next to this.

Follow the instructions and enter a password, and then click Apply Changes. Whenever a user attempts to access your .Mac web site, they'll be greeted by a dialog asking them to enter the password. If they don't have this password, they won't be able to access your site—neither your file sharing section nor the rest of the site.

You can also password-protect only part of your .Mac site. If you create an additional site, as explained previously, you can choose to password-protect only that site. You can create one site for public access, another for family, and another for coworkers, with a different password for each of the additional sites. If you want to password-protect a second site, you'll see a slightly different display. Select the site in the Sites list and click Edit; then enter a password and click Apply Changes. If you ever forget the password, you can always select the site and click Edit; the password will be displayed in clear text, which, while not totally secure, allows you to compensate for a poor memory.

11

Chapter 12

Work with Other Computers on a Network

Mac OS X Tiger

Version 10.4

How to…

- Set up your Mac for networking
- Connect to a network
- Share files with other computers
- Use wireless networking

Macs have long offered simple solutions for networking, or connecting several computers together to share files or network services, such as printer sharing or an Internet connection. In the old days, it was easy to connect two Macs by simple cables and use Apple's AppleTalk networking protocol to transfer files and share data. Today, all Macs come with Ethernet capabilities, so you can plug your Mac into most networks, whether they are Mac-only networks or whether they have Windows or Unix computers as well. And, since you can add an AirPort card to any new or recent Mac, you can even use wireless networking, connecting to networks at home, at work, and in many public places, such as hotels, airports, and coffee shops.

Networking has always been a valuable tool, since computers become more useful when connected to other computers. It has been said that the value of a network increases exponentially as the number of computers on it increases mathematically. Today, the Internet is the ultimate network, connecting computers at all points on the globe. But a local area network allows you to share files with other users, whether at work or at home. Macs can connect to both of these networks easily.

In Chapter 10, I told you all about connecting to the Internet. In this chapter, I'm going to explain how to connect your Mac to a local area network at home, at work, or at school. I'll also tell you how to share files on your network, how to share an Internet connection, and how to use wireless AirPort networking. You'll find that networking with a Mac is simple and efficient, and you'll learn how easy it is to connect your Mac to other computers.

Connect Your Mac to a Network

To connect your Mac to a network, you need to consider two things: hardware and software. You already have the hardware—if your Mac can run Tiger, it has a built-in Ethernet jack. You can connect your Mac to another Mac using an Ethernet cable and create a two-computer network, or, if you want a larger network, use a hub or switch to connect all your computers. As far as the software is concerned, you have all that, too. Mac OS X has powerful networking features built in, and all you need to do is configure your Mac for your network and plug it in.

To understand how network configuration works, think of a telephone system: it uses numbers, and each telephone has a unique number to identify it. A computer network is like that: each computer must have a unique numerical address to identify it so the other computers know how to "call" it. When you set up a network, you give each of your computers an address, or they request one from a router, and this address is used to identify all the data that enters or leaves each computer on the network.

Macs use TCP/IP—the Transmission Control Protocol/Internet Protocol—to connect to networks. This is the main networking protocol used today, and it is the same protocol that makes the Internet work. Computers using this protocol have IP addresses, which are numerical addresses that identify them. They are in the form 111.222.333.444 (four one- to three-digit numbers separated by periods). You don't need to know anything about these terms, but you do need to know their names since you'll see them from time to time, such as in the Network preference pane if you set up your network manually.

Everything you need to configure to connect your Mac to a network is in the Network preference pane in the System Preferences application. You can open the System Preferences by clicking its icon in the Dock or by selecting the Apple Menu | System Preferences.

Click the Network icon to display the Network preference pane (Figure 12-1).

In most cases, your Mac will have set up your network for you when you installed Tiger. If you didn't have network access at the time, or chose not to set up your network, you can do so at any time by using the Network Setup Assistant. To open this assistant, click the Assist Me button at the bottom of the Network preference pane. I explain how to use this assistant in Chapter 10.

12

Manual Network Configuration

In most cases, either installing Tiger or using the Network Setup Assistant, which I mentioned earlier, takes care of your network configuration. But since there may be some cases where you'll want to configure your Mac manually, I'll look at the most common situations next. Unless you need to work in special situations, you probably won't need to worry about the rest of this section. And if you change some of your settings, you might lose your network access. You can always go back to the settings created by the Network Setup Assistant if you have any problems. But even if you don't need to configure your network manually, the following section may help you understand how networking functions.

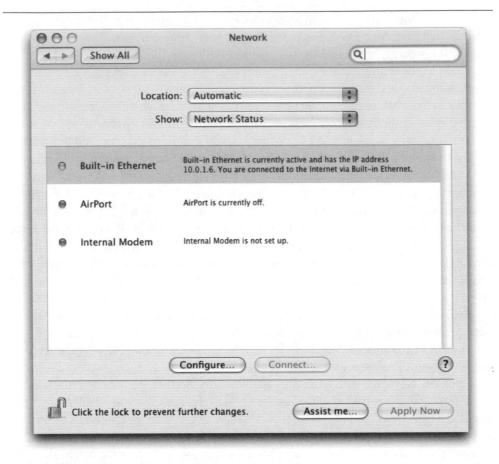

FIGURE 12-1   The Network preference pane is shown here displaying Network Status.
This shows which network interfaces your Mac has and whether they are
configured and/or active.

If you are connecting via Ethernet, make sure the Show menu shows Built-In
Ethernet. The Configure IPv4 menu lets you choose from several ways of setting
up your Mac. I'll look at two of these: Manually and Using DHCP, which are the
main ways you'll be connecting to a network. If you are connecting to a large
network in a company or school, you may set up your Mac differently, but your
network administrator will tell you what to do.

Configure a Simple Network

The simplest type of network is two Macs connected to each other by an Ethernet cable, or a few Macs all connected to a hub or switch. If you just want to connect two or more Macs together to exchange files or access each other's hard disks, select Using DHCP from the Configure pop-up menu in the Network preference pane, and then click Apply Now. This tells your Mac to assign itself an IP address (see Figure 12-2).

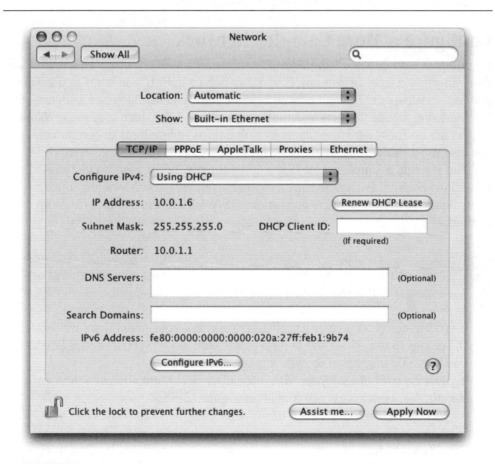

FIGURE 12-2   Using DHCP tells your Mac to request an IP address from its network. You don't need to do anything.

Recent Macs will be able to network by your simply connecting them with an Ethernet cable, but older models will need a special type of Ethernet cable called a crossover cable. The easiest way to connect a couple of Macs is to buy an Ethernet hub, which can cost as little as $20. Connect each Mac to the hub via an Ethernet cable and you've got a network.

Believe it or not, you're ready to connect to another Mac on your network. Just make sure any other Macs on the network are set up like this, and then see later in this chapter to find out how to connect to another Mac.

Configure a More Complex Network

By complex I don't mean complicated, I just mean a network using more hardware than simply a couple of computers and a switch or hub. If you want to use your network to access the Internet as well as share files, you need to have a router—this is a hardware device that acts as a traffic cop, telling data which way to go. While routers are essential for large networks with dozens or hundreds of computers, you can also use a router for a small home network.

You can buy a simple router to use on your network, or you can use an AirPort or AirPort Express base station as a router if some of your Macs are connected using Apple's AirPort wireless networking. (See later in this chapter for more on AirPort.)

 *If one of your Macs shares its Internet connection with other computers on your network, the computer sharing the connection acts as a router and issues IP addresses to the other computers.*

If you are connecting to an existing network, ask your network administrator which settings to use. He or she will probably want to give you a special IP address to make sure you don't conflict with any other computers.

If you want to configure your Mac manually, select Manually from the Configure menu in the Network preference pane. (See Figure 12-3.)

As you can see in Figure 12-3, this Mac is set up with an address of 10.0.1.201. Enter whatever IP address your system administrator has given you, and then enter the Subnet Mask of your network—if in doubt, enter 255.255.255.0. Then enter the Router address; you'll need to check your router's documentation

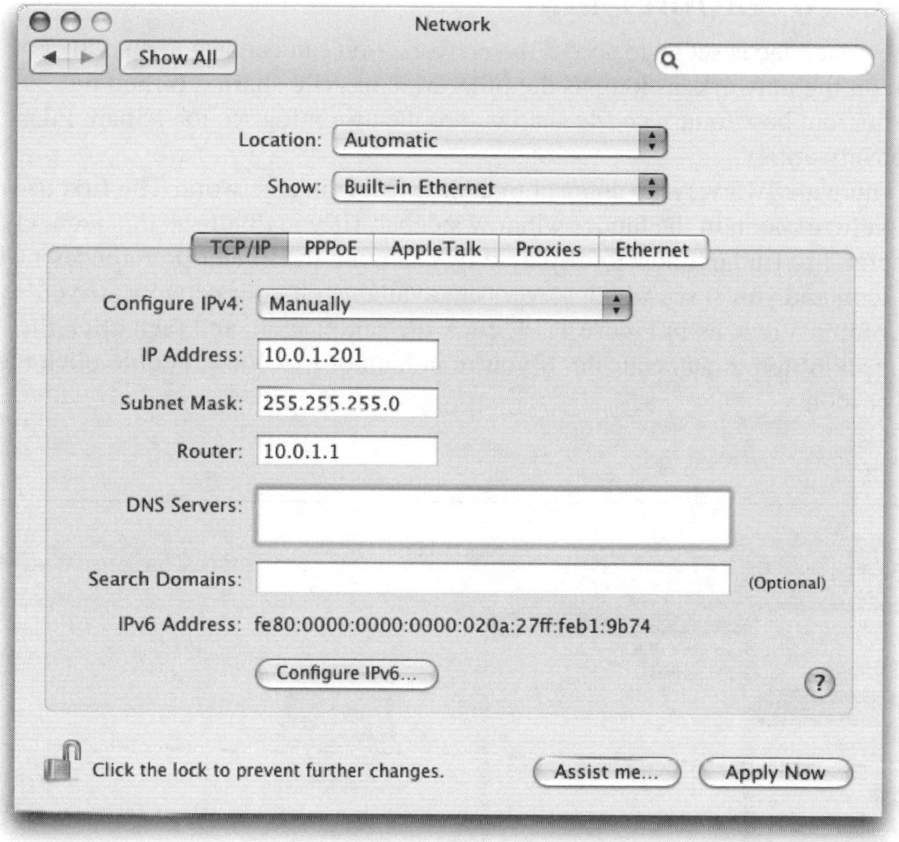

FIGURE 12-3   Configuring a Mac with a manual IP address

for this. In some cases, your Mac will be able to enter the router's address automatically.

NOTE   *If you are using an AirPort base station as a router, its default address is 10.0.1.1.*

Click Apply Now and you're ready to connect to another Mac.

Connect to Another Mac

Once your Mac is set up to access the network, you can connect to any other Mac on the network, as long as the other Mac has file sharing turned on. (To find out how to turn on file sharing, see the upcoming section "Share Files on a Network.")

There are two ways to connect to another Mac on a network. The first uses the Network icon in the Finder window sidebar. (If you don't see this icon, check Chapter 3 to find out how to display it by changing the Finder preferences.) Click this icon and you'll see which servers are available on your network. If you're in Column View, as in Figure 12-4, click the server icon, and then click the Connect button to authenticate. If you're in Icon or List View, double-click the server icon.

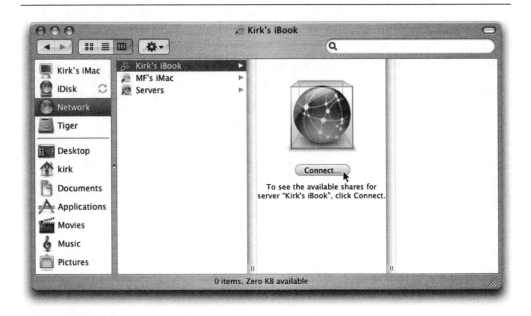

FIGURE 12-4   Click Connect to connect to the selected server.

Enter your user name (if it's not displayed in the Name field) and your password, if you're a registered user (if you have an account on the remote computer) or click Guest if not. Click Connect.

If you connect to a Mac you have an account on, you'll see one or more names, depending on the number of volumes on the server and the permissions you have. If you connect as a guest, you'll see names for each user account on the other Mac. By connecting to one of these accounts, you can access the user's Public folder.

After you *mount* a user's volume, you can click its icon in the Finder window sidebar to access his or her Public folder; you can copy or read any of the files the user has put there, and you can also copy files to the user's Drop Box.

Now that you have access to another user's Public folder, you can share files with that person. When the other user wants you to be able to access files, have the user place the files in his or her Public folder. When you want to send files to the user, put them in the user's Drop Box.

If you let a user connect to your Public folder, it works the same: put files you want to share in the Public folder, and check for files sent by the other user in your Drop Box.

12

If you connect as a registered user, you'll see the same folders under your own account that you would see on the other Mac. For example, connecting from my iMac to my iBook, I see this:

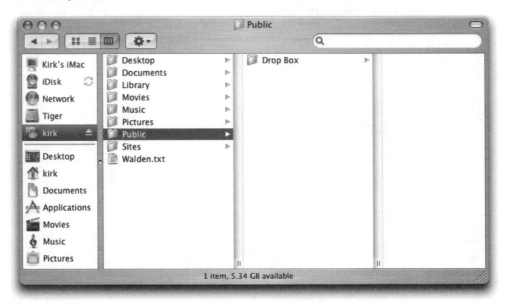

I can access any of the items in my home folder on my iBook, as long as I am connected to the iBook under my user name and password. When you connect to another Mac where you have an administrator's account, you can also mount any disks or volumes available on that Mac. Just select the disk or volume after entering your user name and password and clicking Connect. You'll be able to copy files to and from those volumes as you would on the remote computer.

If you are on a network that contains both Macs and PCs running Windows, you'll see additional icons when clicking the Network icon. (See Figure 12-5.) You'll see icons for all the available servers, both Macs and PCs.

You can connect to the PC on the network by clicking the PC's icon, clicking the Connect button, and authenticating; you can then browse available shares in the next column.

To disconnect from any server, click the Eject icon next to the icon of the server you want to disconnect.

Use the Connect To Server Dialog

Another way to connect to computers on your network is via the Connect To Server dialog in the Finder. This works a bit differently and shows your servers in a different way.

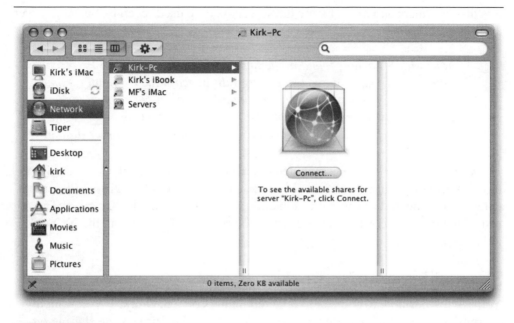

FIGURE 12-5   In this example, Kirk-Pc is an icon for a shared folder on a PC on the network.

From the Finder, select Go | Connect to Server. The Connect To Server window opens.

Recent Servers button

Enter a server address if you know the server's IP address, or a name if you know it. If not, click Browse. This opens a Finder window where you'll connect as you did previously, using the Network icon. If you've previously connected via this dialog, you can also click the Recent Servers button at the right of the window;

this displays a pop-up menu listing the servers you've used recently. Select a server and click Connect.

NOTE *Your Mac's name is found in the Sharing pane of the System Preferences. You can change its name by clicking Edit beneath the Computer Name field. While you can use punctuation and spaces in your computer name, note the way this name is displayed just beneath the Computer Name field. That's the way you'll need to enter it in the Connect To Server dialog.*

After you've entered the computer's name or IP address, click Connect. If you have an account on the computer you are connecting to, click Registered User and enter your name and password. If not, click Guest, and then click Connect. The rest of the procedure is the same as when you connect after clicking the Network icon, as described earlier.

Share Files on a Network

You saw earlier how to connect to other computers on a network. If you want to share files with other users on your network, you need to turn on file sharing on the computer that will be sharing its files. You can do this in the Sharing pane of the System Preferences application. (See Figure 12-6.)

You can share a lot of things on your Mac, and this preference pane lets you turn all of them on or off with a single click:

■ **Personal File Sharing** If you turn on Personal File Sharing, other Mac users can access Public folders and shared volumes on your Mac.

■ **Windows Sharing** If you turn this on, Windows users can access shared folders on your Mac. You'll need to enable one or several accounts to use Windows sharing; click Enable Accounts and select the accounts you want to use; then enter their passwords.

■ **Personal Web Sharing** If you turn this on, other users can access web pages in your Sites folder using a web browser.

■ **Remote Login** This lets users log in remotely using the SSH secure shell protocol.

■ **FTP Access** If you turn this on, users can connect to your Mac and transfer files using the FTP protocol.

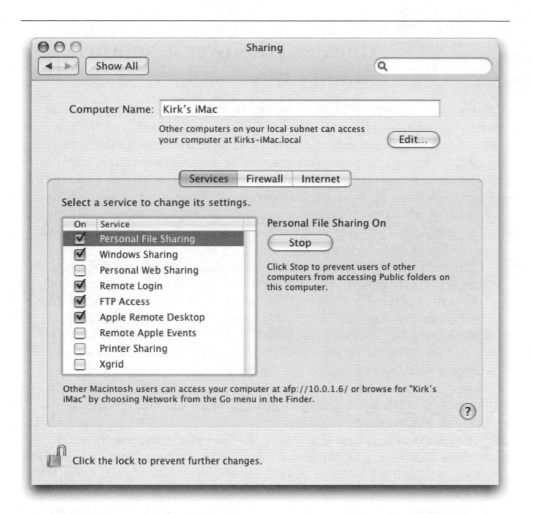

FIGURE 12-6   The Sharing preference pane lets you control what you share on your Mac.

- **Apple Remote Desktop**   If you turn this on, other users can access your Mac using the Apple Remote Desktop program if you have the program installed.

- **Remote Apple Events**   This lets applications on other Mac OS X computers send Apple Events to your Mac.

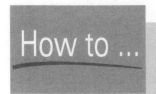

Transfer Files over a Network Another Way

If you have a network of Macs, all using Mac OS X 10.2 or later, you can take advantage of Apple's Bonjour networking. This system automatically finds other Macs on your network and can be used for a number of applications, including printing, file sharing, and more. One such application is iChat, Apple's instant messaging program. When you log in to iChat (see Chapter 10 for more on using iChat) and select Window | Bonjour (or press ⌘-2), you'll see a list of other available users on your network. (Make sure each user has iChat running and is logged in to Bonjour messaging. To do this, users should select iChat | Log In To Bonjour.)

To send files to another user, start a chat session by double-clicking a user's name, and then drag the file or folder you want to send to the text input field at the bottom of the chat window. Press RETURN, and iChat starts sending the file. (Or you can drag a file on the buddy's name in the Buddy List or the Bonjour List.) The other user sees a small window showing the file's name in a clickable link; all the user has to do is click this window and then click Accept to start downloading the file. By default, this file is saved to the user's Desktop. (If you're already in a chat with the person and you send a file, the other person will just see a clickable link in the chat window; the user just clicks this link to start the file transfer.)

You can only send individual files or folders via iChat; if you try to select, say, three files and send them, it won't work. So if you have more than one file to send, put them in a folder or make a compressed archive of them to send them even faster.

The advantage to sending files like this is that they go directly to the user; you don't have to log in to the user's Mac, send files to the user's Public folder, and then tell the user that the files are waiting for them.

■ **Printer Sharing**   This lets you share a printer that is connected to your Mac. (See Chapter 14 for more on printer sharing.)

■ **Xgrid**   This lets you allow Xgrid controllers to access your Mac for use as part of a distributed computing network.

As you can see, your Mac is a ready-made network machine, capable of sharing many things with many computers, whether they are Macs or Windows computers. If you click any of these services, you'll see a brief explanation in the right-hand part of the window. You'll also see a description at the bottom of the pane showing the exact network address that others must use to access your computer using the selected service. (Most of these sharing services are beyond the scope of this book. You'll find some information about using them in your Mac's online help.)

If you do turn on any of these network services, you should be aware that there are related security risks. The Firewall tab in this preference pane helps you protect your Mac against intrusions; I'll tell you about using the Firewall tab and other firewall software in Chapter 17.

Use Wireless AirPort Networking

Wireless networking (Wi-Fi or 802.11 networking) is one of the great advances in computer technology in recent years. No longer do you need to be connected by a cable to another computer or network device to share files, access servers, and use the Internet. If you install an AirPort card in your Mac, or buy an AirPort-ready Mac, you can use wireless networks and access network services so easily that you may forget that they are on other computers.

If your Mac has an AirPort card, you're ready to set it up for wireless networking. If not, you can buy one from Apple and install it yourself on some models. But you'll need something to connect to: either another computer or an AirPort base station. (You can also connect to most third-party 802.11 wireless networking hardware.)

NOTE   *There are two types of AirPort cards: the original model and the current AirPort Extreme models. The AirPort Extreme (820.11g) card gives you higher throughput and is backward compatible with original AirPort (802.11b) cards, but doesn't work in older Macs. The same is true for AirPort base stations: the AirPort Extreme base station works with computers running older cards as well. Unfortunately, Apple no longer sells original AirPort cards, but you may find them from some Mac vendors. If you have an older Mac that doesn't accept AirPort Extreme, you'll have to look around to find the appropriate card.*

If you want to set up a wireless network just to transfer files between two computers, all the computers need are AirPort cards; you can create a computer-to-computer network. If you want to use one computer as a software base station

12

to share an Internet connection, you need that computer to be connected to the Internet by wires and to have an AirPort card. This lets your other Mac access the Internet without any cables. Finally, if you want the greatest flexibility, an AirPort or AirPort Express base station serves as a router for your network, allowing many Macs to connect to it and share its Internet connection, as well as share files. It can even connect to a wired network, acting as a bridge between your wireless computers and your wired machines.

Whichever solution you choose, setting up AirPort is simple. The easiest way is to open the AirPort Setup Assistant, which is located in the Utilities folder inside your Applications folder. This assistant (Figure 12-7) walks you through the steps required to set up a wireless network.

To set up AirPort wireless networking, just answer the questions the Assistant asks you. Once you have set up your AirPort network, you can connect to other Macs as described earlier in this chapter; there's no difference in the way you connect, only the medium changes. In addition, if you turn on Internet Sharing (see the next section), you can share an Internet connection to other Macs over AirPort.

FIGURE 12-7   When you want to set up a wireless network, the AirPort Setup Assistant handles everything for you.

Share an Internet Connection

If one Mac is connected directly to the Internet, either by modem or by any other type of connection, it can share its Internet connection across a network to other Macs. To do this, you need to set up both the server, the Mac sharing the connection, and the clients—that is, the other Macs using that shared connection.

First, on the server, open the System Preferences and click the Sharing icon. Click the Internet tab. This tab, shown in Figure 12-8, is where you turn on Internet Sharing. Like most networking configuration on the Mac, this is done with just a couple of clicks.

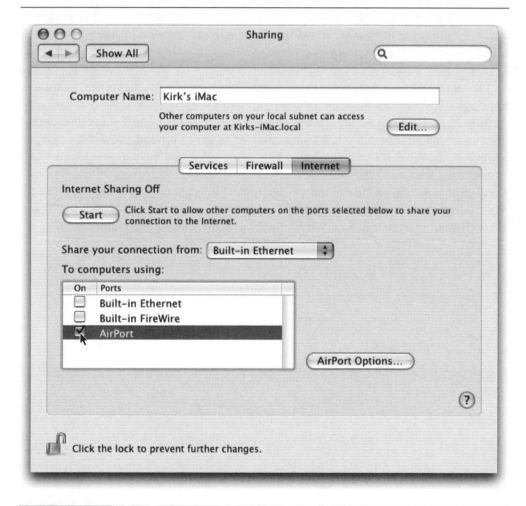

FIGURE 12-8   To turn on Internet Sharing, select the network interface in the list by clicking its check box, and then click the Start button on the Internet tab.

Select the network interface you want to use from the Share Your Connection From pop-up menu. You'll probably have Built-In Ethernet and Internal Modem, and if you have an AirPort card it will be listed here as well.

Next, check the network interfaces you want to share over: check the boxes next to the interfaces listed in the To Computers Using list. Finally, click the Start button.

CAUTION   *Sharing an Internet connection may disrupt the settings of other customers of your Internet service provider. You'll see an alert regarding this if you check the same port that is accessing the Internet. This may occur with connections such as a cable or DSL connection. If you do disrupt other customers' access, your ISP may detect this and simply turn off your Internet access. You should therefore not use the same network interface both to receive your incoming Internet connection and to share to other computers on your local network.*

To share your Internet connection, your client computers—the other computers sharing your connection—must be configured to use DHCP, as explained earlier in this chapter. Once you set this up, all your computers can share one connection. Be aware that sharing a modem connection splits very limited bandwidth among several computers; Internet sharing is only practical if you have a broadband connection, such as DSL or cable.

By the way, if you have Windows computers on your network, they can share your Internet connection as well. Just configure them to use DCHP, and they'll get their IP addresses automatically from the Mac that's sharing the connection.

Part IV

Get to Work with Your Mac

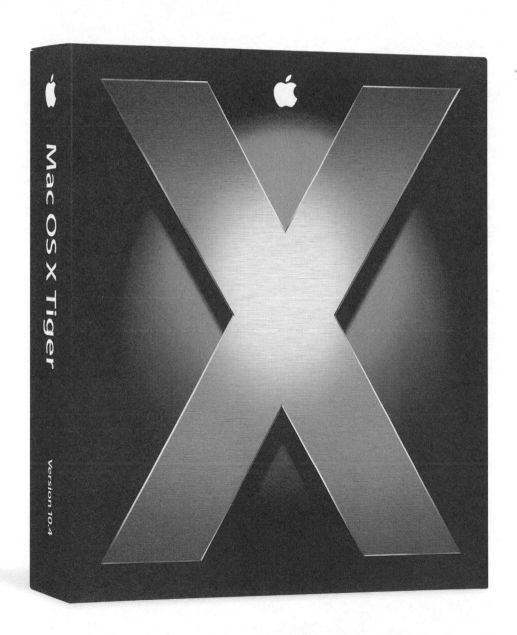

Chapter 13

Work with Applications

How to...

- Open and launch applications
- Open and save files
- Install applications
- Use the Classic environment

When you come right down to it, what you want a computer to do for you is let you run the applications you need to do your job, complete your chores, or have fun. An operating system lets the computer do this, controlling what goes on under the hood, but you spend most of your time working with different applications. In your everyday work with your Mac, you don't see the operating system much. You work with the Finder, which, while part of Mac OS X, is a separate application you use to manage your files. You also work with other parts of Mac OS X itself when you log in and out, change System Preferences, or start up and shut down your Mac; however, most of what you do is with your applications.

Mac OS X comes with a full suite of applications to surf the Web (Safari, see Chapter 10), manage e-mail (Mail, Chapter 10), and manage personal information (iCal and Address Book, Chapter 15), as well as Apple's renowned digital music program iTunes (Chapter 16). (If you've recently bought a new Mac, you'll also have Apple's iLife, which contains iPhoto, iMovie, iDVD, and GarageBand.) But you can also purchase plenty of other applications, to do everything from word processing to graphic design, from managing your budget to playing games. There are thousands of applications available for Mac OS X, ranging from the standard graphics programs (Adobe Photoshop and Illustrator) to productivity software (Microsoft Word and Excel) to games and utilities.

In this chapter, I'll look at the tasks you do with applications that are the same for all programs: I'll show you how to get your applications up and running, how to quit them, how to open and save files, and how to install new applications. I'll even tell you a bit about the Classic environment, which lets you run applications written for Mac OS 9 or earlier.

Applications Included with Mac OS X

Mac OS X is an operating system, which controls all the operations you carry out on your Mac, but which also comes with many bundled applications. Here's a list of what you get with Mac OS X and what the different programs do. (I don't include here other applications bundled with specific Mac models that are not a part of Mac OS X.) These programs are all found in the Applications folder on your Mac.

- **Address Book**   This program manages your contacts and integrates with Mail and other programs. See Chapter 15.

- **Automator**   This is a tool for creating *workflows,* or files that contain actions that you can repeat on specific files or applications.

- **Calculator**   This is a powerful calculator with advanced mathematical functions, as well as memory, and can also convert dozens of values, such as areas, lengths, weights, and even currencies by updating its exchange rates over the Internet.

- **Chess**   If you play chess, you'll find this program to be quite a challenge.

- **Dashboard**   While not strictly an application, a Dashboard icon does appear in the Applications folder. See Chapter 3.

- **Dictionary**   This is an excellent dictionary and thesaurus available as a stand-alone application or from within other programs. See later in this chapter for more on using Dictionary.

- **DVD Player**   This program controls your DVD playback if you have a built-in DVD drive in your Mac.

- **Font Book**   This program lets you install and manage fonts. See Chapter 14.

- **iCal**   Apple's calendar program lets you manage your appointments and tasks. See Chapter 15.

- **iChat**   Apple's instant messaging program lets you carry out text, audio, and video chats. See Chapter 10.

- **Image Capture**   This program lets you import images from digital cameras and scanners.

- **Internet Connect**   This tool lets you control Internet connections with certain network interfaces. See Chapter 10.

- **iSync**   This tool lets you synchronize your personal information between several Macs, or with Palm PDAs and some cell phones.

- **iTunes**   Apple's digital music program lets you create, listen to, and burn your own digital music files. You can also use iTunes to purchase music from the iTunes Music Store. See Chapter 16.

13

- **Mail**   This is Apple's e-mail program. See Chapter 10.

- **Preview**   This is Apple's tool for viewing images and PDF files.

- **QuickTime Player**   This program lets you view video files in QuickTime format, and some other formats, on your Mac.

- **Safari**   This is Apple's web browser. See Chapter 10.

- **Sherlock**   This is Apple's web services tool. See Chapter 10.

- **Stickies**   This is Apple's program for creating and managing sticky notes.

- **System Preferences**   This interface organizes all your Mac's preference panes. See Chapter 9.

- **TextEdit**   This simple text editor lets you create and read text files in plain text, RTF, and Word format.

Your Mac also includes a number of utilities, which are found in the Utilities folder inside the Applications folder. Here are a few of them:

- **Activity Monitor**   This tool lets you see your Mac's activity: its processor, which programs are running, its network activity, and much more.

- **Disk Utility**   This tool lets you manage your hard disk and create and manage disk images. See Chapter 19.

- **Installer**   Whenever you install Apple software, or most third-party software, this application handles the installation process. See later in this chapter for more on installing software. You'll never need to launch this application manually, but you will use it for installing most software.

- **Keychain Access**   This program manages your passwords and keeps them protected.

- **Network Utility**   This application provides information about network functions and advanced network diagnostic tools.

- **Terminal**   You can use this program to access the Mac OS X command line.

There are other utilities in your Utilities folder, but most users won't need to work with them. If you want to find out about any of these programs, check your Mac's online help.

How to ... Use Microsoft Office

One of the first questions Windows users ask when they consider buying a Mac is whether they can use Microsoft Office. Whether or not you think it's a good thing, Microsoft Office is the de facto standard for productivity software. Word and Excel are the most widely used word processor and spreadsheet programs in businesses and homes around the world, and PowerPoint is the most ubiquitous presentation software (although Apple's Keynote is a more intuitive program, and, frankly, makes better-looking presentations).

Many Windows users have pre-installed (or bundled) versions of Microsoft Office, which generally contain Word, Excel, Outlook, and Publisher. The Professional version contains these programs plus PowerPoint and Access. Microsoft also offers four different retail versions of Office, which contain four or five programs, plus a developer version that has additional tools.

If you purchase Microsoft Office 2004, the latest Mac OS X version of the suite, you'll quickly notice how similar its programs are to their Windows counterparts. While some functions are different, most are the same, and the Macintosh versions even have some functions that have not yet made it into the Windows versions. These programs are not just copies of the Windows programs, but were written for the Mac, taking into account the specificities of Mac OS X and its Aqua interface.

To ensure compatibility, the formats for these applications' files are exactly the same as their Windows cousins. You can create and save files on the Mac and send them to Windows users, and you can work on files Windows users send you.

The Mac version of Microsoft Office includes four programs: Word, Excel, PowerPoint, and Entourage; the Professional Edition of Microsoft Office also includes Virtual PC, a program that lets you run Windows on a Mac. Windows users are not familiar with Entourage, which is a powerful e-mail, contact, and calendar program, roughly equivalent to Outlook. However, the Macintosh version of Office does not offer Access, or any equivalent, nor does it offer Publisher. The Mac offers many comparable solutions to replace these programs. FileMaker Pro (www.filemaker.com) is a powerful cross-platform database solution, and for page layout, Adobe InDesign (www.adobe.com) and Quark XPress (www.quark.com) are industry standards.

13

Open Applications

Mac OS X uses the Dock to manage applications, and the Dock, as you saw in Chapter 3, can also serve as a launcher to open applications. There are several ways to open applications on your Mac. Here's a list of the different ways you can do this:

- **Click the application's icon in the Dock.** If an application icon is in the Dock, click it once to open the application. Apple includes icons in the Dock by default for some of the most commonly used applications, such as Safari, Mail, iTunes, iChat, iCal, and more. For more on using the Dock and placing icons there, see Chapter 3.

- **Double-click an application icon.** When you double-click an application icon, the application opens and either presents its window, if it's an application with just one window (such as iTunes), or opens a new document (Word, Excel, AppleWorks, and others). All your applications should be installed in the Applications folder, which you can open by clicking the Applications icon in the Finder window sidebar or by pressing ⌘-SHIFT-A. (See Chapter 3 for more on the sidebar.) If you want to open any utilities stored in your Utilities folder, you can open this folder by double-clicking the Utilities folder icon in the Applications folder or by pressing ⌘-SHIFT-U.

- **Double-click a file.** When you double-click a file, Mac OS X looks for the application that created it and opens the file with that application. If it cannot find an application for the file, it displays a dialog asking you to choose which application you want to open the file with.

- **Open an item from the keyboard.** You can open files, applications, or folders by selecting them and pressing ⌘-O or selecting File | Open. You can also press ⌘-DOWN ARROW to open any file or application.

- **Open an item from the contextual menu.** If you hold down the CONTROL key and click any item, or if you right-click with a multi-button mouse, a contextual menu displays. You can select Open from this menu to open the item, or, if the item is a file, you can also select Open With to choose which application you want to open the file with.

- **Drag a file onto an application's icon.** Whether the application is running or not, you can drag a file icon onto its icon in the Dock. You can also drag a file onto an application's icon in the Applications folder, or an application alias anywhere. This is especially useful when you want to open a file with an application that did not create the file. Say you want to open a plain text file in Word, or a graphics file in Photoshop; dragging the file on an application icon "forces" the application to open the file. But this only works if the application can read the file's format.

- **Select an application from the Apple Menu | Recent Items.** The Apple menu, which is always accessible in the menu bar, contains a Recent Items submenu. (See Figure 13-1.) Select a recently used application if its icon isn't in the Dock. This stores a list of the last ten applications and documents you have used, and you can change this number in the Appearance pane of the System Preferences (see Chapter 9). If you select a document from the Documents section of this submenu, the application that created that document opens. Some programs also offer similar menus or submenus: in Microsoft Word, for example, recent files are at the bottom of the File menu; AppleWorks has an Open Recent menu at the bottom of its File menu; other programs may display recent files in different locations.

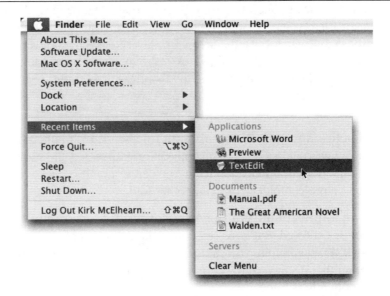

13

FIGURE 13-1   Opening an application from the Recent Items menu is just like double-clicking its icon.

Launch Bar

There are many application launchers available for Mac OS X, most as shareware, programs that you download from the Internet to try out and then pay for if you like them and want to keep using them. I'll be totally subjective and tell you about one of them, which is a program I couldn't live without: Launch Bar. This simple utility, available at www.obdev.at/products/launchbar, displays a small bar below your menu bar when you press its hotkey: by default, this is ⌘-SPACE, but you can set it to whatever you want. When this bar is visible, type the first few letters of the name of the application you want to open. Launch Bar narrows down the choices until you find the program to launch, displaying a list of all applications and files that contain the characters you typed. You can navigate with the arrow keys in its list, if your application doesn't come up at the top, and then press RETURN to launch it.

The beauty of Launch Bar is that it learns from your choices. Say I type S-A-F to open Safari. Launch Bar may, at first, display a couple of other applications or files (you can use it to open any file on your Mac, in addition to applications), but when I use the arrow keys to select Safari, it remembers this, and after a couple of times, typing S-A-F shows Safari at the top of the list. Using Launch Bar, I never have to open my Applications folder.

- **Double-click an application's alias.** In Chapter 4, I explained how to use aliases. When you double-click an application's alias, it is the same as double-clicking the original application icon. You can store aliases anywhere: on the Desktop, in project folders, or in any other folder.

- **Open an application from the Applications folder in the Dock.** In Chapter 3, I showed you how you could place your Applications folder in the Dock. If you do this, you can access all your applications with a click. The menu that displays shows you all the applications and folders inside your Applications folder.

- **Set an application as a Startup Item.** In Chapter 8, I showed you how you could set any items—files, folders, or applications—to open automatically when you log in to your Mac. If you have certain applications you use all the time, such as your e-mail program, iChat, Safari, or a word processor, you can set them to open automatically by adding them to Startup Items.

While you definitely won't use all of these methods for opening applications, you can see that you have a choice. The only reason I went into such detail in this section is because some of these methods are useful in specific situations: the best way to open an application when you have a file is to just double-click the file icon, but dragging a file onto an application icon can be useful for certain files. And when you don't have a file, but want to create a new one, it is useful to know the different ways you can open applications.

It can also save you time to create aliases for certain applications, especially if for a specific project you need to use three or four programs. Rather than going to the Applications folder to open these programs, creating aliases in your project folders can save you time.

But probably one of the best ways to work with applications you use regularly is to put their icons in the Dock so you can open them with a single click. See Chapter 3 to find out how to do this.

Quit Applications

While there are many ways to open applications, as I showed in the previous section, quitting applications is much easier. There are three ways you can do this: using the keyboard, using a menu item, and using the Dock. Try them out to find which is most practical for you:

- **From the keyboard**   I find this the quickest and easiest way to quit applications, and, in fact, rarely do it any other way. Just press ⌘-Q on the keyboard. Every Mac application quits when you press this keyboard shortcut.

- **From the application menu**   The application menu (the menu with the name of the application) of every Mac application has a Quit menu item at the end of the menu (Figure 13-2). Select this menu item to quit the active application.

- **From the Dock**   If you click and hold an active application's icon in the Dock, a small menu displays (Figure 13-3). Select Quit from this menu to quit the application. Using this method, you can also quit applications that are hidden without bringing them to the front.

When you have a file open, and have not saved it, the application will always ask you if you want to save your changes before it quits. For more on saving files, see the "Save Files" section later in this chapter.

13

FIGURE 13-2   When using iCal, the application's name is on the menu bar. Select Quit
iCal to quit the program.

Show and Hide Applications

When you work with your Mac, you often have several applications open at the same
time. In Chapter 3, I explained how to switch from one application to another using
the Dock, the keyboard, and Exposé. At times, it is useful to hide an application's
window(s) to keep them out of the way and make your screen less cluttered.
For example, you may have iCal open at all times, since you use it to record
appointments and give you reminders, but you probably don't need to have its
window visible all the time.

FIGURE 13-3   You can quit any application from the Dock by selecting Quit from
its menu.

Figure 13-4 shows a cluttered screen: in the front is Microsoft Word, behind that is a window open in Safari, then you can see the edge of an iCal window, and, finally, there is a Finder window open all the way in the back.

It is certainly easier to work in a cleaner environment (though my desk looks a lot like the window in Figure 13-4), and you can hide any of the applications you aren't using. To do this, switch to the application you want to hide by clicking its icon in the Dock, and then select the Application menu | Hide *<application name>* or press ⌘-H. If you want to hide Microsoft Word, for example, you would select the Word menu | Hide Word, as in Figure 13-5, or press ⌘-H on the keyboard.

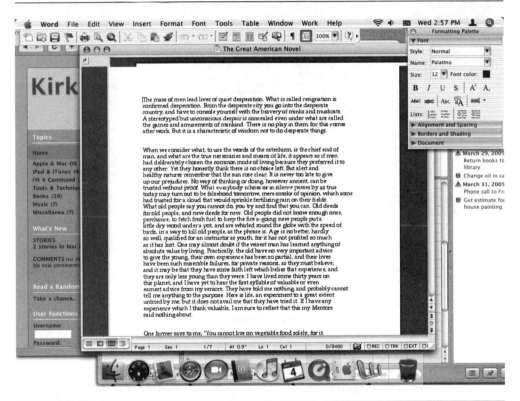

FIGURE 13-4   Four applications are open and all their windows are visible.

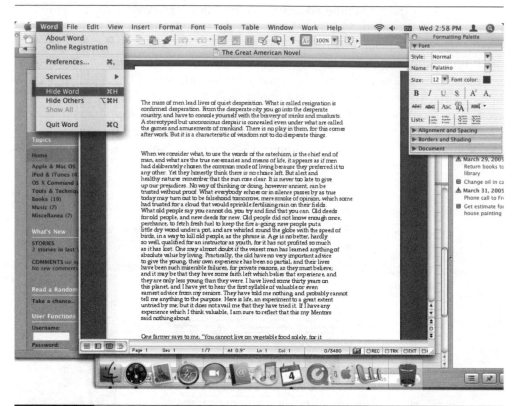

FIGURE 13-5 Hiding Word by selecting the Hide Word menu item. The application's window disappears, but the application stays open.

TIP *Learn the ⌘-H shortcut. It will save you lots of time, and you'll soon find that it becomes a reflex: when you don't need to work with an application, but don't want to quit it, just press that keyboard combination to get it out of the way. However, some applications, especially Adobe programs like Photoshop, use ⌘-CONTROL-H for Hide instead of the standard shortcut.*

When you hide an application, you make its window(s) disappear, but you don't quit it. As you can see in Figure 13-6, with all but one application visible, your screen is much cleaner.

Another way to hide applications is to choose the Hide Others menu item (see Figure 13-5), or press ⌘-OPTION-H, when working with the application you

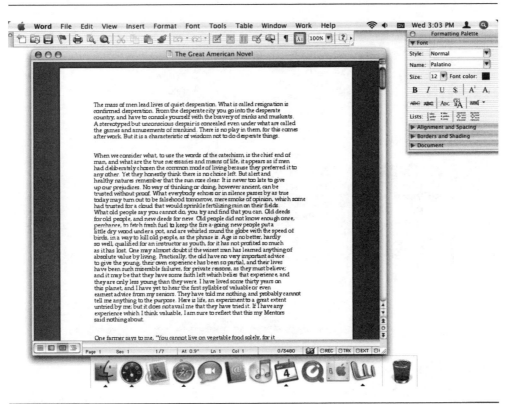

FIGURE 13-6   Four applications are open (five, if you count Dashboard), shown by the triangles beneath their Dock icons, but only Microsoft Word is visible.

13

want to remain visible. This does what it says: it hides the windows of every application except the one at the front.

To show a hidden application, just click its icon in the Dock. You can always tell which applications are running by the triangles beneath the Dock icons.

 *There is still another way to hide an application. Click and hold its Dock icon and select Hide.*

Open Files

Earlier in this chapter, when telling you the myriad ways you can open applications, I explained that when you double-click a file icon, it opens with the application that created it. But there are other ways to open files once an

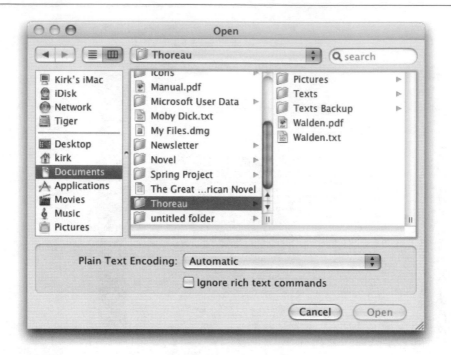

FIGURE 13-7   The standard Open dialog, shown here from Apple's TextEdit

application is running. All Mac OS X applications use a standard Open dialog, as shown in Figure 13-7.

When you select File | Open from any application, or press ⌘-O, a dialog displays, similar to the one in Figure 13-7. You use this dialog to navigate to the location of the file you want to open. In most cases, this dialog opens in your Documents folder, since this is likely to be where you store your files. If you store files in other locations, some programs open to the last-used folder. You can navigate through the folders in this dialog by clicking folders or moving the scroll bars up and down or to the right and left. This is the same as navigating in Finder windows in Column View.

The Open dialog is very similar to a Finder window: you'll find the same icons here as in the sidebar, and you can click any of the sidebar icons to display their contents. You also have Back and Forward buttons to move back and forward to folders you've visited in this dialog. In addition, you can choose List View if you'd rather navigate in this manner by clicking the List View button at the top of the dialog.

How to ...   **Work with AppleWorks**

Some Mac models include Apple's productivity suite, AppleWorks. This program integrates several modules, allowing you to create word processing documents, spreadsheets, presentations, databases, and drawing and paint documents. AppleWorks is an easy-to-use, intuitive program, whose unique way of combining these different modules lets you do everything from within a single program.

Apple includes this program for free with its consumer models: iMacs, eMacs, and iBooks. You can also purchase it from Apple. While it does not have the power and flexibility of other productivity programs, such as Microsoft Word and Excel, its price and ease-of-use make it an excellent choice for people who don't need to create professional documents. AppleWorks can, however, open and save documents in many formats, including Word and Excel, so you can share documents with Microsoft Office users if you need to.

13

FIGURE 13-8   The pop-up menu at the top of the Open dialog shows the parent folders of the current folder, and all its parents up to the highest level of your Mac. Note the keyboard shortcut to your home folder (⌘-SHIFT-H).

The pop-up menu at the top of the window (Figure 13-8) shows you the parent folder(s) of the current folder. Click this menu to display it.

You can choose any of the parent folders of the current folder, and if you are somewhere within your home folder, you'll see a keyboard shortcut to access that folder.

TIP   *Even though they don't display in the pop-up menu, you can use the following keyboard shortcuts to access certain folders from an Open dialog: ⌘-SHIFT-H displays your home folder, ⌘-SHIFT-D the Desktop, ⌘-SHIFT-A your Applications folder, ⌘-SHIFT-K your Network, ⌘-SHIFT-I your iDisk, and ⌘-SHIFT-C your Computer. These shortcuts also function in Save dialogs, which I discuss in the upcoming "Save Files" section.*

You can also choose from any Recent Places, those shown at the bottom of the menu, which are the most recent folders you have opened from an Open dialog.

TIP   *If you find that the Open dialog is too small, you can resize its window by clicking and dragging the resize box at the window's bottom-right corner. Enlarging this window gives you additional columns to view your files and folders. You can also resize the columns just as you can with Finder windows. In fact, Open dialogs (and Save dialogs, which I present in the following section) are very similar to Finder windows. See Chapter 3 for more on working with Finder windows.*

Finally, you can use Spotlight searching in Open dialogs. (See Chapter 5 for more on Spotlight.) If you don't remember where you've stored a file, or if you simply don't want to click through a hierarchy of folders, just type part of its name or contents in the Search field. The Open dialog will display the results of your search.

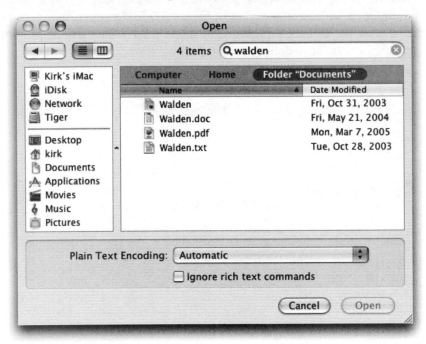

When you find the file you want to open, click to select it, and then click the Open button at the bottom of the window, or just double-click the file. If you open a document created with another application, you may need to select its type and format from the Open dialog. Some applications add their own menus and check boxes to this dialog. These can include menus to select file types or translators, check boxes for certain formatting or importing options, and more.

You can select multiple files to open (if they're in the same folder) from the Open dialog; hold down the SHIFT key and select contiguous files, or hold down the ⌘ key and select noncontiguous files.

Save Files

Almost every application lets you save files so you can use them later or send them to other people. The only exceptions are programs that use just one window, such as iCal, or programs that manage other files, such as iTunes or iPhoto. With these programs, you can usually export files, and while the task has a different name, it is done in a similar way.

All Mac OS X applications use a standard Save dialog that is very similar to the standard Open dialog, seen earlier in Figure 13-7. However, there are two different kinds of Save dialogs. Figure 13-9 shows a Save dialog in AppleWorks; in this application, the Save dialog is a separate window.

FIGURE 13-9   A Save dialog. Under AppleWorks, this is a window.

FIGURE 13-10   A Save sheet under TextEdit is attached to the window it affects.

Other applications use a Save sheet, which looks the same as the Save dialog in Figure 13-9, but is attached to the window it affects. Figure 13-10 shows a Save sheet under TextEdit.

Sometimes, you'll see a Save window or sheet that looks different; this is because you're looking at the Save dialog in its minimized version. When you see a Save dialog like this, click the triangle icon near the top of the window or sheet to expand the dialog to its full size.

13

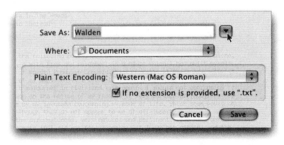

When saving a file, choose a location for the file either by navigating in the Save dialog's column list, by selecting a folder from the pop-up menu above the columns, or by searching for a folder using the Search field. Using the Save dialog is the same as using the Open dialog presented in Figure 13-7. In fact, Apple has harmonized these two dialogs so they are almost exactly the same. The same view options apply, as do the same keyboard shortcuts.

Many applications let you choose a specific format to save your file. In the following illustration, the format selected is Microsoft Word Document, but if you click the Format pop-up menu, you'll see a dozen choices, including Text Only, Rich Text Format, and others.

Some applications also offer other options, as in the preceding illustration: Microsoft Word includes an Options button in the Save dialog that gives you access to specific features of this program.

Work with Dictionary

One interesting "little" application included with Tiger is Dictionary, a combination dictionary and thesaurus that contains electronic versions of two excellent Oxford dictionaries. You can use this application on its own, by opening it from your Applications folder, or you can call it from within some applications.

To access Dictionary from within an application, select a word and press ⌘-CONTROL-D, or hold down the CONTROL key and select Look Up In Dictionary from the contextual menu. (This does not work with all applications; it works with Apple's TextEdit, but not Microsoft Word; it also works with Safari and many other programs.) This opens the Dictionary application to the selected word. You can then choose between the definition dictionary and the thesaurus.

But it gets better. Why should you have to switch to another application to see a definition or a list of synonyms? If you go to Dictionary's preferences, in the Contextual Menu section, check Open Dictionary Panel to display a small panel directly above the word in your application. It looks like this:

> though they do not appear to me at all im
> the circumstances very natural and pertin
> o ec **noun**   I wa
> hav   on o
>   **1** (usu. **circumstances**) a fact or   lies
> urpc condition connected with or relevant to ar
> . I   event or action   iders
> me   • an event or fact that causes or helps to   ier s
>   cause something to happen, typically   n, i
> . I
> inec Oxford Dictionary ▼   More...   the
> not remember that it is, after all, always

You can choose from the dictionary or thesaurus by clicking the pop-up menu at the bottom of the panel, and if you click More, you'll open the definition or list of synonyms in the Dictionary application. If you're a writer, or a reader, you'll appreciate this practical new tool.

13

Use Stationery Files

Stationery files, or templates, are a special kind of document that you can create with some applications. The idea behind this type of document is that you create a template with specific formatting that you'll reuse to create many other documents. This can be a blank document or it can contain text or graphics: you can create forms, for example, that you'll fill out with different data and save, each time, with a new name.

To create a stationery file or template, create the document in the format you want to use: this could contain specific font settings, styles, or layouts, and it may contain text, graphics, or other data. Select File | Save As, and then, in the Format pop-up menu, select Template, Document Template, or Stationery. (The terminology can differ, but all of these are the same.) Some applications offer a check box or radio button for this kind of file.

When you select this format, some applications will automatically switch the current folder in the Save dialog to its Templates folder. Others will let you save your document anywhere.

You can spot these files at a glance by their icons: they look like a pad of paper with one corner turned up. (In fact, this is why Apple originally called this type of document Stationery; it was supposed to function like a stationery pad.)

My Budget Template   My Form Template

   *Some stationery files, such as those created with TextEdit, do not display this special icon, but most of these files do show a stationery icon.*

If your application doesn't offer you the possibility of saving documents as stationery files or templates, there's another way to create them. Click a document's icon to select it, and then select File | Show Info. In the Info window, check the Stationery Pad check box. Your document is now a stationery document.

How to Use Stationery Files

Once you have set up a stationery document with its formatting or contents, just double-click it to open it. Most applications immediately create a copy of the document and then open that copy.

You can then work with your document, which uses all the characteristics of the stationery file, and when you want to save it, you'll be prompted to save a new file; the stationery file won't be altered.

Some applications, such as Microsoft Office, only create a new document from stationery files when you open them from its Project Gallery. If you open a stationery file in Word, you must select File | Save As to save your changes; if you select File | Save, your changes will be saved in the original stationery file. See your application's help for more on using these files if they do not work in the standard way.

Force-Quit Stuck Applications

While Mac OS X is a very stable operating system, individual applications may not be quite so stable. Occasionally, an application gets stuck and you need to force-quit it to close its windows. The advantage of using Mac OS X, compared to earlier versions of Mac OS and some other operating systems, is that when one application gets stuck, you can quit it without it affecting the entire operating system.

If an application doesn't respond for a while, press ⌘-OPTION-ESCAPE, or select the Apple Menu | Force Quit. This brings up the Force Quit Applications window, as shown in Figure 13-11.

If an application has really frozen, it will usually appear in red in this list. Click the name of the application you want to quit, and then click Force Quit. You can also relaunch the Finder from this window if it seems to be stuck. Click its name, and the Force Quit button changes to Relaunch. Click the Relaunch button and the Finder quits and restarts immediately.

13

SHORTCUT

To force-quit the front-most application, without even bringing up the Force Quit window, just press ⌘-SHIFT-OPTION-ESCAPE. This should kill the application immediately.

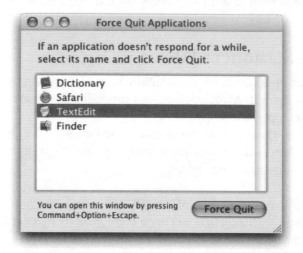

FIGURE 13-11   If you need to force-quit an application that's stuck or not responding, press ⌘-OPTION-ESCAPE to bring up the Force Quit Applications window.

Install Applications

While Mac OS X includes many applications, as I pointed out earlier in this chapter, you'll probably buy or download other software for your Mac. Installing applications on the Mac is easy, and there are two ways to do so. The first is the simplest: many applications tell you just to drag their icon or folder into your Applications folder. You don't need to run an installer, and you can launch the application immediately afterward.

Other applications use an installer, either Apple's Installer application or other installer programs. If you need to use an installer to install an application, you must usually be an administrator—the installer asks you for an administrator's password, and if you don't have this password, you can't go any further.

Many Mac applications come in disk image files. (See Chapter 4 for more on disk images.) Double-click the disk image file icon to mount its disk image, which you can then double-click to see its contents (see Figure 13-12).

In the example in Figure 13-12, the disk image contains a package file, with a .pkg extension; this is a special file used to install programs. Some disk images contain applications, and you just drag them to your Applications folder.

To install a package file, double-click it; the Apple Installer opens. Follow the steps as the installer moves you from screen to screen, reading any special information, agreeing to a user license, choosing the destination disk if you have more than one, entering your administrator password, and then finally installing the software.

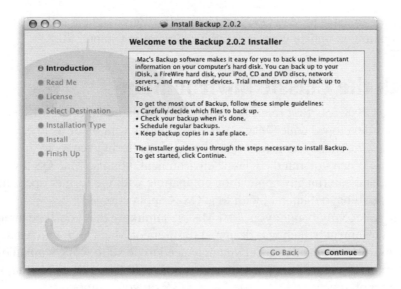

Some software installations require you to restart your Mac after they are finished. If this is the case, the installer warns you before installing. But you can install many applications without needing to restart.

FIGURE 13-12   A disk image file and a mounted disk image at the top, with the contents of the disk image in a window at the bottom

13

Installing updates to Mac OS X and its applications can be a little different, and I'll tell you how to update your Mac OS X software in Chapter 20.

Work with the Classic Environment

When Mac OS X was first released, Apple had to ensure compatibility with applications developed under Mac OS 9, the previous version of its operating system. The *Classic environment* is Apple's way of offering access to these older applications. When you run the Classic environment, you use Mac OS 9 within Mac OS X, and can run any application compatible with the former operating system, yet still have it interact with Mac OS X applications.

If you've recently bought your first Mac, it's unlikely that you'll be using the Classic environment, which was designed for users of Mac OS 9 who wanted to use their existing applications. Yet you may need to do so to work with an older Mac program. If you're sure you will never need to do this, you can both ignore the Classic preferences and not install Mac OS 9 on your computer.

The Classic preference pane (Figure 13-13) lets you choose where your Mac OS 9 System Folder is, and lets you start or stop the Classic environment. Open the System

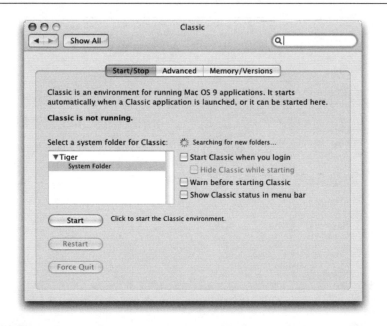

FIGURE 13-13   The Classic preference pane lets you manage the Classic environment.

Preferences application by clicking its Dock icon or by selecting the Apple Menu |
System Preferences, and then clicking the Classic icon.

Select where your Mac OS 9 System Folder is located in the Start/Stop tab.
You can start the Classic environment by clicking Start; this button changes to
Stop when Classic has started running. You can stop it by clicking the Stop button.

Check Show Classic Status In Menu Bar to display a Classic icon in your menu
bar at all times. This lets you start and stop Classic more easily and shows you
whether Classic is running or not.

This menu extra also gives you quick access to Classic preferences and lets you
launch items in your Classic Apple Menu.

The Advanced and Memory/Versions tabs let you manage advanced features of
the Classic environment and view the memory usage of Classic applications.

Using the Classic environment is just like using Mac OS 9. When you launch
Classic, you'll see a window display the startup process. If you are a former OS 9
user, you'll find this very familiar.

You can work with just about every OS 9–compatible application in the Classic environment, and working with these applications is no different than the way you did under OS 9. You can copy and paste data between OS X and Classic applications, and you'll find that working with Classic is fast—your Mac doesn't emulate anything to run Classic; it actually runs OS 9 in part of its memory. For this reason, if you use Classic a lot, you'd be advised to put additional memory (RAM) into your Mac; Classic applications use Mac OS 9's memory management and may require more memory than similar applications under Mac OS X.

Many Mac OS X features do not function with the Classic environment: Exposé, keyboard shortcuts that you set in the Keyboard & Mouse preferences, and so on. Classic can only execute functions that were available with Mac OS 9.

For more on using the Classic environment, see your Mac's online help.

Chapter 14

Print, Fax, and Work with Fonts

How to...

- Set up printers
- Manage fonts
- Print and fax with your Mac
- Save documents as PDF files

While pundits and futurologists have long been forecasting the arrival of the paperless office, you've probably noticed that the more you work with your computer, the more you print. You have many more documents and texts to work with, and it's still easier to read them on paper than it is to read them on screen. It's also easier to make notes and comments on printouts, and pass the printed documents on to others.

So you'll naturally want to print from your Mac. Mac OS X offers excellent compatibility with many models of printers, and printing from a Mac is as easy as clicking a few buttons. Mac OS X also offers integrated faxing, so you can send a fax as easily as you print documents. Your Mac can receive faxes as well, storing them for later reading, printing them automatically, or sending them by e-mail.

Your Mac also lets you create PDF files, which retain formatting, styles, and graphics that you can send to other users, even those on other platforms, so they can see your documents exactly as you want them to be seen. Finally, Mac OS X offers tools for managing fonts and working with special characters to help you find the right characters and make your documents look their best.

In this chapter, I'll tell you about using printers with Mac OS X. I'll tell you how to set up your printer, how to print documents, and how to save documents as PDF files and view PDF files. I'll show you how to send and receive faxes with your Mac, discuss how to manage fonts, and tell you how to find special characters when you're working with your documents.

Set Up Your Printer

Printers, like many other hardware devices, often use USB connections, and this is the easiest and most common way to connect a printer to a Mac. (Professional-quality printers often use Ethernet connections and work over a network.) Most of the main printer manufacturers offer Mac drivers for their printers, and Mac OS X installs drivers for dozens of printers by Apple, Brother, Canon, Epson, Hewlett-Packard, Lexmark, Ricoh, and Xerox. If you've just upgraded to Mac OS X, you should verify if your printer has a driver available: check the manufacturer's web site. If you plan to buy a printer, make sure there is a driver for Mac. The first thing you need to do to set up a printer is install its driver. To do this, check the CD-ROM that comes with the printer, or check the manufacturer's web site for the latest driver. You'll install the driver the same way you install any other software on your Mac. See Chapter 13 for more on installing software. (If your printer already has a driver installed by Mac OS X, you won't need to worry about installing one.)

NOTE *If you've already installed Mac OS X and then you get a new printer, you don't have to go through the entire installation process again to install a driver for it. If the printer doesn't come with a Mac OS X driver, but the Tiger installation disc does, just double-click the Optional Installs package on the installation disc. This opens the Mac OS X installer and lets you install anything other than the operating system: applications, printer drivers, additional fonts, and language translations. Choose the drivers for your printer and install them.*

Once you have installed the driver, plug your printer into your Mac and turn it on. (Some installers may tell you to plug your printer in and turn it on before

Gimp-Print Drivers

Mac OS X also includes a set of printer drivers called Gimp-Print. These drivers, written by open-source developers and distributed freely, allow you to use many older printer models whose manufacturers haven't bothered to write drivers for newer operating systems. You can choose to install the Gimp-Print drivers when installing Mac OS X; if you didn't do so and want to find out if an older printer is supported, check the Gimp-Print Mac OS X page first: http://gimp-print.sourceforge.net/MacOSX.php3. As of press time, Gimp-Print supports more than 500 printers.

If you haven't already installed it when you installed Tiger, do as explained in the preceding Note—double-click the Optional Installs package on the Tiger installation disc and select Gimp Printer Drivers from the Printer Drivers list.

14

FIGURE 14-1   The Printer Browser detects any printers connected to or available to your Mac.

installing its driver.) Open the System Preferences, click the Print & Fax icon, and then click the Printing tab. Click the + icon below the printer list to display the Printer Browser (Figure 14-1).

If you find your printer in this list, click it to select it, and then click Add. If not, and it's a network printer, click the IP Printer icon at the top of the Printer Browser window. If you use an IP printer, your network administrator will provide the necessary setup information. Finally, click More Printers and select AppleTalk, Bluetooth, or Windows Printing, if your printer uses one of those connection methods.

When you find your printer, click it to select it, and then click Add. The Printing preferences window reflects this addition, showing the printer you added (Figure 14-2).

If you have several printers, and you add them all, they all display in this list. To add additional printers, follow the same procedure for each one. To set one of these printers as the default printer, click the Selected Printer In Print Dialog pop-up menu and select the desired printer. This printer will always display in the Print dialog, but you'll be able to choose another printer if you wish from that dialog. (See the next section, "Print Documents," for more on choosing printers.)

FIGURE 14-2 With a printer added to the Printing preferences, you are ready to print.

Print Documents

Almost every application offers a Print menu item—to print any document, select File | Print. When you do this, the Print sheet displays (Figure 14-3). This is where you choose print settings, such as the number of copies, the pages you want to print, and more.

14

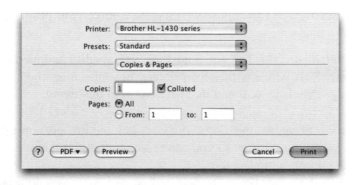

FIGURE 14-3 The Print dialog lets you choose print settings.

NOTE   *Some applications offer other ways of printing documents. Microsoft Word and Excel, for example, have a Print button in their toolbars that sends one copy of your document to the printer using default settings, without displaying the Print dialog. Other applications may offer similar shortcuts.*

If you have more than one printer, select your printer from the Printer pop-up menu. Each printer driver offers different settings, so the Copies & Pages pop-up menu will have several additional menu items:

- **Layout**   Choose your printout's layout, whether you want one page per sheet or more, whether you want borders, and the layout direction. Portrait is a vertical layout, with the shorter side of the paper at the top, and landscape is a sideways layout, with the longer side of the paper at the top.

- **Scheduler**   If you're printing to a shared printer, you might want to schedule your print job by setting a time and priority. Even if you're printing to your own printer, you might want to set long print jobs to run later when you're not at your desk, so you don't have to listen to the printer work.

- **Paper Handling**   This lets you reverse the page order (printing last page to first) or print odd- or even-numbered pages, if you want to print something on both sides of the paper. You can also scale your document to fit the paper size in your printer.

- **Color Sync**   This lets you apply color conversions and filters to your print job. See your Mac's online help for more on using Color Sync.

- **Cover Page**   This lets you print a cover page either before or after your document. This is mostly useful when sending faxes. (See later in this chapter for more on faxing.)

- **Paper Feed**   You can choose which paper source your printer uses, if it has more than one.

- **Print Settings**   This lets you adjust the print quality and media type, and use Toner Save Mode with some printers. In some cases, the application or printer you're using will add its own item(s) to this menu.

When you've chosen your settings, you can click the Presets pop-up menu and select Save to save your settings so you can reuse them without having to select each menu and choose settings again.

Click Print to send your file to the selected printer. After you do this, a printer icon opens and displays in the Dock. (See Figure 14-4.)

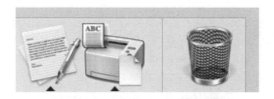

FIGURE 14-4 The printer icon in the Dock shows that a print job is in process.

To monitor the print job, click the printer icon in the Dock to open your printer's Jobs window. (See Figure 14-5.)

The toolbar in the printer's Jobs window (Figure 14-5) has six icons to manage printing. Click a job in the list at the bottom of the window; the following four icons are available to act on your selected job.

- **Delete**   Click this icon to delete the selected print job.

- **Hold**   Click this icon to pause the selected print job. Other jobs will print in the meantime.

- **Resume**   Click this icon to resume a print job that you have paused with the Hold icon.

- **Stop Jobs**   Click this icon to stop all print jobs. If you click this icon and stop printing, it changes to Start Jobs. Click Start Jobs to resume all print jobs.

Two other icons give you other functions: the Utility icon opens a third-party utility program, if your printer has one, where you can access special features, check ink levels, and more. The Supply Levels icon opens a window (for some printers) showing the amount of ink or toner remaining in your printer.

The Jobs window shows both active and completed jobs; click the Completed tab if you want to see the jobs you've run in the past, when you've printed them, and whether they were successful or, for some reason, they did not print.

Share a Printer

If you have several Macs on a network and want to share a printer among them, you can connect the printer to one of your Macs and share printing services from that computer. If you click the Sharing tab of the Print & Fax preference pane

14

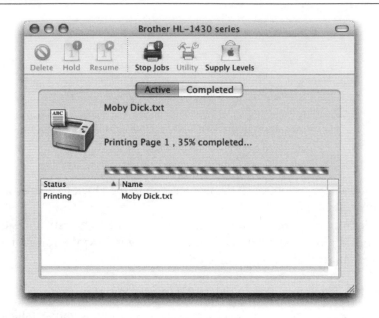

FIGURE 14-5   The Jobs window for the selected printer shows the progress of all current print jobs.

and then check Share These Printers With Other Computers, you can check any printers you want to share with other users on your network.

You must make sure to install the driver for the shared printer on each of the Macs that is going to use the printer.

When you want to print a document to a shared printer, click the Printer pop-up menu and select the printer from the Shared Printers or Bonjour Printers submenu. (See Figure 14-6.)

Shared printers are those printers that a user has chosen to share, as described above. Bonjour Printers are other printers on the network that are shared automatically (such as a network printer that is autodetected or a printer connected to an AirPort Express base station). After selecting the printer, click Print, and the print job will be sent to the shared printer. You can even share printers across an AirPort wireless network, allowing you to print from any computer connected to the network.

NOTE   *You can print to a shared Windows printer as well. You need to turn on printer sharing in Windows and install the appropriate driver in Mac OS X.*

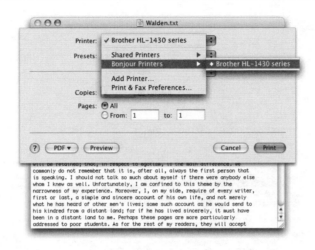

FIGURE 14-6   The Shared Printers and Bonjour Printers submenus show you all the shared printers available on your network.

Work with PDF Files

Adobe's PDF (Portable Document Format) is a file format designed so you can distribute files and ensure that they look the way you want. You can include graphics and use complex layouts, and the resulting PDF file looks the way it does in the application you used to create the file. It is also a good way to send files to people who don't have the software you used to create them (though they won't be able to make changes to the PDF files).

Mac OS X lets you create PDF files from any of your printable documents with just a click. To do this, open a document and select File | Print. The Print sheet or Print dialog displays (see Figure 14-7).

Click the PDF button, select Save As PDF, and save your file. The resulting file is a PDF file, which users can read with Apple's Preview application under Mac OS X or with Adobe Reader on Mac or other platforms. (You can use Adobe Reader with Mac OS X if you want; download it from Adobe's web site and install it.) Make sure to add the .pdf file extension if you are planning to send this file to users on other platforms.

The PDF button offers other possibilities: you can save a PDF as a PostScript file (if you need a file in that format), you can fax the PDF (we'll look at faxing later in this chapter), and you can perform several actions on PDFs, such as compressing them, encrypting them, and more.

14

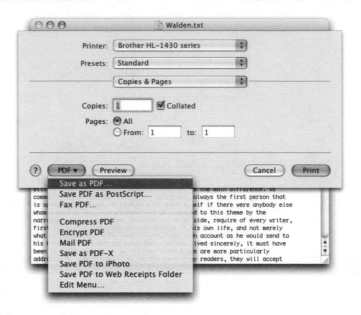

FIGURE 14-7   To create a PDF file from any document, just click PDF and select Save As PDF in the Print sheet or dialog.

View PDF Files

As I mentioned earlier, PDF files allow you to send documents with fonts, graphics, and layouts that remain the same across platforms, regardless of what program was used to create the document. Many companies use PDF files to distribute product information, since they have control over the layout and they can be sure what their customers see.

Mac OS X comes with a fast PDF viewer: Preview. This application, which also lets you view many graphics files, lets you read and print PDF files. Figure 14-8 shows you an example of a PDF file displayed in Preview.

When you open a PDF file in Preview, it displays as seen in Figure 14-8: at its actual size (100%) and, if the document has several pages, it shows thumbnails of the pages in a drawer. You can zoom in or out by clicking the Zoom In and Zoom Out buttons in the toolbar, and you can move ahead and back by clicking the Page Down and Page Up buttons or by clicking a thumbnail in the drawer. If you select View | Continuous Scrolling, you'll be able to scroll through the document more easily than if you move one page at a time.

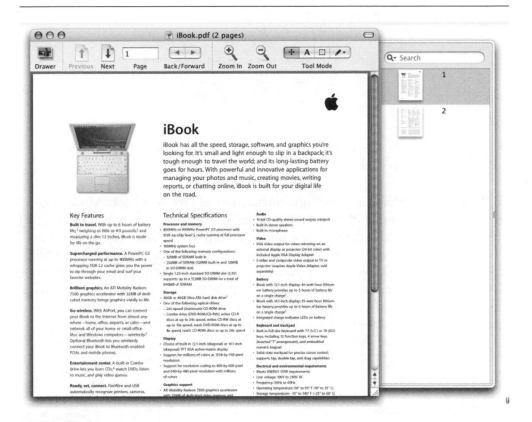

FIGURE 14-8 Many companies, including Apple, use PDF files to distribute product information.

14

NOTE *The Mac OS X Save As PDF feature is a quick way to create PDF files, but if you want to work with PDF files a lot, and especially if you want to optimize them (files created using Save As PDF can be very big), you should consider purchasing Adobe Acrobat (www.adobe.com), which gives you much more control over how you create PDF files. You can adjust your files' resolution and compression, optimize their size, and annotate them so users can see your comments. Mac OS X's built-in PDF creation is good for casual use, however, allowing you to create PDF files with a single click.*

If you want to select text in a PDF document to copy into another document, click the Text Tool (the A button) in the Tool Mode button bar in the toolbar. Select your text by clicking your cursor and dragging it over the text you want to select, and then choose Edit | Copy to copy it.

iBook

iBook has all the speed, storage, software, and graphics you're looking for. It's small and light enough to slip in a backpack; it's tough enough to travel the world; and its long-lasting battery goes for hours. With powerful and innovative applications for managing your photos and music, creating movies, writing reports, or chatting online, iBook is built for your digital life on the road.

NOTE   *In some PDF documents, which are protected, you won't be able to select and copy any text.*

You can click the Select Tool (the square, dashed box in the Tool Mode button bar), and select part of a PDF file. After doing this, you can copy it and select File | New From Clipboard to create a new image in PDF format that you can then save or use in certain graphics programs. And if you click the Annotate Tool (the pencil icon in the Tool Mode button bar), you can select from Text Annotations and Oval Annotations to make notes in PDF files. To use the former, click and drag to create a text box; to create oval annotations, click and drag to create red ovals around specific parts of the document to highlight them.

You can print PDF files just as you print other types of documents. Simply select File | Print and follow the printing instructions earlier in this chapter.

Work with Faxes

Mac OS X lets you send and receive faxes on your Mac, as long as it's connected to a phone line via a modem. (You can't send and receive faxes over DSL or cable connections without using special services.) If your Mac has an internal modem, which all new models do, or if you have an external modem connected to your Mac, you can use this fax function to save time and paper.

Send Faxes from Your Mac

One of the advantages of sending faxes with your Mac is that you don't have to print them first. When you have a document you want to fax, just select File | Print, click the PDF button, select Fax PDF, and then click Fax. This opens a new dialog (Figure 14-9) that lets you choose your recipient, a subject line, a dialing prefix and layout settings, and a cover page. You can also select a modem from the Modem pop-up menu; you'll find other modems here if other Macs on your network have chosen to share their modems for you to send faxes.

Most of the settings available in the pop-up menu in the middle of this dialog are the same as those for printing (see earlier in this chapter). There are, however, two additional choices for faxes:

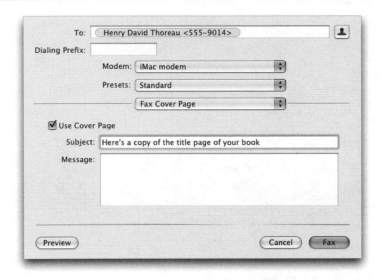

FIGURE 14-9   The Fax dialog, which lets you choose the recipient for your fax and adjust settings

- **Fax Cover Page**   This lets you set cover page text. This text, which you enter in the large text field in this dialog, is sent on a cover page before the rest of your document.

- **Modem**   This lets you choose whether your modem uses tone or pulse dialing, whether its sound is on or off, and whether it should wait for a dial tone before dialing.

After you've chosen all your settings and entered any cover page text, if you choose to use a cover page, click Fax to send your fax.

Receive Faxes on Your Mac

To receive faxes on your Mac, you must have a modem connected to a phone line, and you must turn on fax reception. Open the System Preferences application by clicking its icon in the Dock or by selecting the Apple Menu | System Preferences. Click the Print & Fax icon to display the Print & Fax preferences. (See Figure 14-10.) The Faxing tab shows the Faxing preferences.

To be able to receive faxes, check Receive Faxes On This Computer. Enter your fax number, the number of the phone line your Mac is connected to. Then select after how many rings your Mac will answer: if your Mac is connected to a line used by a telephone as well, set it to answer after several rings; if it is a dedicated line,

14

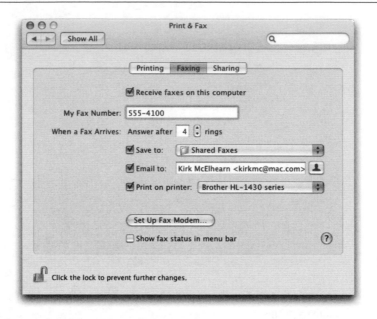

FIGURE 14-10 The Faxing tab of the Print & Fax preferences lets you set fax reception settings.

used only for faxes, set it to one. If you have an answering machine or voicemail on the same line that picks up after a certain number of rings, you'll need to set this number to one ring less than the answering machine.

There are three options you can choose for how your Mac handles incoming faxes, and you must check at least one of these, but can check any two or all three if you want:

- **Save To** You can choose from Shared Faxes, Faxes, or any other folder if you select Other Folder. Faxes received are saved as PDF files, and you can view them, using Preview, or print them out after they are saved. If you choose Shared Faxes, this creates a Faxes folder in the /Users/Shared folder, where all users can access the faxes. If you choose Faxes, this creates a Faxes folder in your home folder; only you can access the faxes received when you are logged in.

- **Email To** You can have faxes e-mailed to anyone you choose. This sends the PDF file of the fax to the selected e-mail address.

- **Print on Printer** If you want your faxes printed out immediately, select a printer here.

Work with Fonts

Anyone who works with computers, creating documents to distribute to others, knows that different fonts can help spice up your documents. As you can see in this book, different fonts are used for headers, body text, sidebars, and other elements to help them stand out and make different sections readily identifiable.

Although fonts can help you spice up your documents, too many spices make them hard to digest. It's good to use a couple of fonts, but not to mix more than a handful to make an effective document.

Mac OS X comes with dozens of fonts for you to choose from. These include the classic Mac fonts, such as Palatino and New York, standard fonts used on Windows, such as Times New Roman and Arial, and many other fonts, ranging from classical styles (Cochin and Didot) to modern sans-serif fonts (Futura and Optima), by way of specific fonts designed for onscreen reading and web use (Georgia, Trebuchet, and Verdana). Mac OS X even includes fonts for languages such as Chinese and Japanese, and, if you choose to install them, additional fonts for other languages as well.

Apple's font management tool, Font Book, lets you view all your fonts so you can see exactly what they look like and what characters they contain. This program is found in the Applications folder. When you open it (Figure 14-11), you'll see a list of collections, fonts, and a preview of the selected font.

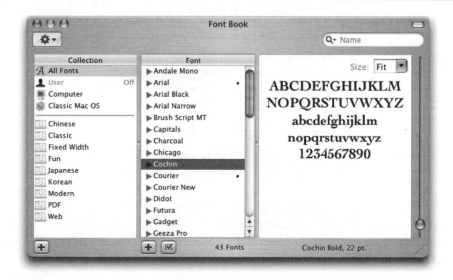

FIGURE 14-11   Looking at the Cochin font in Font Book

Font Book lets you create and manage font collections, each of which is a group of fonts. Some of these are already set up, as you can see in Figure 14-11, but you can create your own by clicking the + button beneath the Collection list. When you do this, a new collection appears. Enter a name for it and press RETURN.

To add fonts to your collection, just drag them from the Font column.

The advantage of using collections is twofold: first, you can access your favorite fonts more easily. (I'll tell you about that later, when I talk about using fonts.) The second is that you can disable collections either permanently or temporarily. These collections won't show up in Font dialogs if you disable them.

To disable a collection, click the collection to select it, and then select Edit | Disable *Collection Name*.

You can also disable individual fonts: click a font in the Font list and click the check box button below the list. If, for example, you don't need to use Chinese and Japanese fonts, you can disable them and they won't appear in any of your applications' Font menus. While you can disable a collection, this does not disable individual fonts; so if you want to limit the length of your Font menus, you need to disable fonts from the Font column.

You can reactivate any fonts or collections by selecting a disabled item (it will be dimmed to show it has been disabled) and clicking the check box button again.

Use Fonts in Your Documents

As I mentioned earlier in this chapter, fonts can spice up your documents, and Mac OS X offers dozens of fonts for you to use. Some applications offer font menus from which you can select fonts, and other menus to select sizes and styles. Microsoft Word, for example, works this way, as does AppleWorks and certain other productivity programs.

Many applications use a Font dialog that looks a lot like Font Book, which I presented earlier. (See Figure 14-12.) This dialog lets you work with collections and individual font families, as well as styles, or typefaces, and sizes.

In Figure 14-12, you can see the similarity between the Font dialog and Font Book; any collections that appear in Font Book also appear in the Font dialog, and you can also select from All Fonts, Favorites, and Recently Used fonts. To add

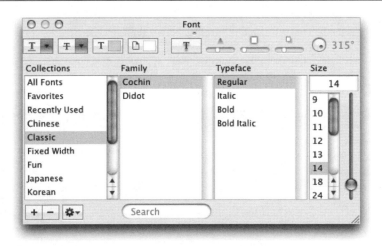

FIGURE 14-12   The Font dialog, which many Mac OS X applications use.

a font to the Favorites collection, select a Family, Typeface, and Size, and then select Add To Favorites from the Action button at the bottom of the dialog.

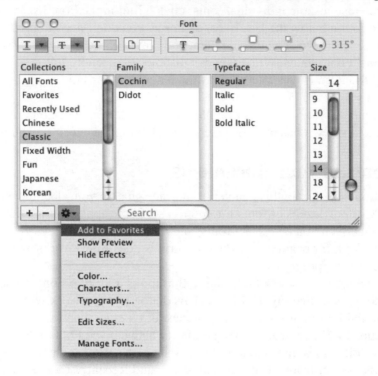

If you click Favorites, in the Collections column, your favorite fonts display in the Family column, showing their font face and style.

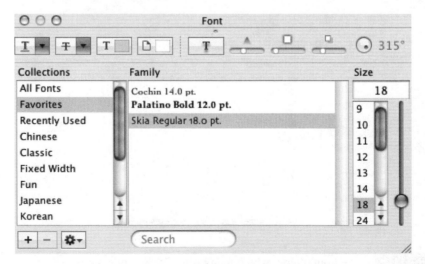

You can then select one of these fonts and apply it to text in your documents with a single click.

Work with Special Characters

Most of the time, you type standard characters in your documents: abc, 123, and so on. But occasionally you need to type *special characters*, ones that are not letters or numbers. These are either symbols or regular alphanumeric characters such as ©, ¥, Å, or ≈.

There are two ways to access these characters. Many applications offer a Special Characters menu item in their Edit menu. Select this menu item to display the Character Palette. This palette lets you choose from hundreds of special characters in several categories.

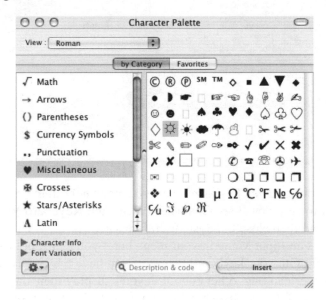

Click one of the categories to display its characters, and then click the character you want to use, in the right-hand section, to select it. Click Insert to insert this character at the current cursor location in your frontmost document.

If you click the View menu, you'll see several groups of characters: Roman, Japanese, Traditional Chinese, Korean, Simplified Chinese, Glyph, and a few others. If you need characters from these sets, explore the many categories they offer.

When you're finished using the Character Palette, click its Close button to close it.

But not all applications offer access to this character palette from their Edit menu. Because of this, it's a good idea to make this palette accessible in another way. To do this, open the System Preferences, and click the International icon and

14

then the Input Menu tab. This displays a list of keyboard layouts, input methods, and palettes that you can add to the Input Menu.

You'll see your selected keyboard checked somewhere in the bottom section of this list, and at the top you'll see Character Palette and Keyboard Viewer—check both of these, and then close the System Preferences.

This displays an Input Menu in your menu bar—you can spot this menu by the icon corresponding to your keyboard layout. If you have a U.S. keyboard layout, you'll see an American flag; other country layouts display their flags, and some keyboards, such as Dvorak, display letters (such as DV for Dvorak).

Click this icon to see the Input Menu; select Show Character Palette to display the Character Palette.

I suggested earlier that you also check Keyboard Viewer in the Input Menu preferences. Here's why. When you select Show Keyboard Viewer from the Input Menu, this palette displays:

The Keyboard Viewer is a small palette that shows the letters assigned to your keyboard layout. This can be helpful if you are working with a layout you are unfamiliar with, or if you are editing foreign-language texts and need to find how to enter certain characters. (The Character Palette may be even easier to use, though; it all depends on how often you need to use these characters.)

The Keyboard Viewer is most useful when you hold down a modifier key (such as the OPTION, CONTROL, or SHIFT key), so you can see what special characters these keys let you type. Even though you can use the Character Palette, you'll find it easier to learn where some special characters are if you need to type them often (such as the é character that I've had to type in the word Exposé throughout this book).

Hold down the different modifier keys, first one at a time and then in combination, to see what characters you can access. As you can see in the following illustration, holding down the OPTION key shows different characters than the normal layout:

14

Some of these characters are highlighted in orange—these characters work in two steps: first press the outlined key and then another key to create an accented character. For example, to type the é character, you must press OPTION-E, then E. You'll see as you do this that the accent displays in your document with highlighting and then, after typing the E alone, the é character displays.

NOTE   *The Keyboard Viewer does not display any Unicode fonts (such as Symbol, Zapf Dingbats, Chinese or Japanese fonts, and so on). To enter special characters from these fonts without memorizing the keystrokes, you must use the Character Palette. If you work with languages such as Chinese or Japanese, there are special input palettes available to help you input text. See the Mac OS X help for more on this.*

Chapter 15

Manage Personal Information

How to…

■ Manage your life with iCal

■ Subscribe to other people's calendars

■ Manage contact information

■ Synchronize your data with another Mac

Computers can do lots of things to make your life simpler: they can help you balance your checkbook; let you write letters, reports, and flyers, and print them out with professional quality; let you surf the Web; and give you tools for working with digital media, such as music, photos, and movies. But another way they can help you is by providing tools that organize your life: your appointments, your contacts, and tasks you need to do.

Mac OS X includes two powerful programs that let you manage your personal information. iCal, Apple's calendar application, enables you to create as many calendars as you need: for your personal events, your professional appointments, your family's activities, and more. By sharing your iCal calendars, your colleagues or family can know what you've got planned and can organize their events accordingly.

Address Book is a repository for your contacts: you store their names, e-mail addresses, telephone numbers, and addresses, and Apple integrates Address Book with iCal and its Mail application (see Chapter 10 for more on Mail) so you have a central storage center that you can use with all your applications.

In this chapter, I'll show you how to manage your personal information. I'll tell you how to use iCal to organize your life and share your calendars with others, and I'll show you how to use Address Book to organize your contacts. I'll also explain how Apple's iSync lets you synchronize this information between several Macs or to your .Mac account, if you have one, so you can access all this data from the Web when you're not at your home computer.

Organize Your Life with iCal

Apple's iCal, its versatile calendar program, gives you a revolutionary way to manage your events and your life, as well as the events of others: friends, family, and coworkers. Instead of just offering one calendar, as most scheduling applications do, iCal (Figure 15-1) lets you create as many calendars as you want. Each calendar

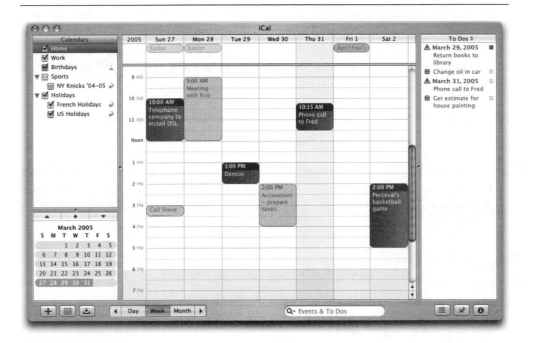

FIGURE 15-1   You can create multiple calendars with iCal: here you can see a personal calendar—one for work, one for birthdays, two showing holidays, and one for a favorite sports team.

is a group of activities, appointments, and To Do items grouped under a specific heading. All the items in a given calendar appear when that calendar is displayed, and you can hide any calendar and its items.

To open iCal, click its icon in the Dock, or double-click its icon in the Applications folder.

When you first open iCal, you'll see two calendars in the Calendars list: Home and Work. You can use these two calendars as a starting point, creating events in either or both of them. To create a new event, first choose which calendar you want to use for the event by clicking it in the Calendars list to select it. Then choose which view you want by clicking one of the buttons at the bottom of the iCal window: Day, Week, or Month.

 *You can use keyboard shortcuts to switch views: ⌘-1 for Day view, ⌘-2 for Week view, and ⌘-3 for Month view.*

Navigate to the day, week, or month you want to add an event to using the arrow buttons.

 *You can always jump to the current day, in any view, by pressing ⌘-T.*

To create an event in a calendar in Day or Week view, click at the time the event is to begin and drag until you reach its ending time. To create an event in a calendar in a Month view window, double-click anywhere on the date of the event; you'll see how to set its time later.

 *You'll find it simpler to create new events in Day or Week view since you can set their starting and ending times more easily.*

After you've created your event, you can type a name for it. Just select the New Event text and type your own name.

That's all you need to do to add events to your calendars. You can now make changes to your events, add alarms, set them to repeat, and more.

Edit Events

When you create a new event on one of your calendars, all you do is set a name and a start and end time for the event. (When you create an event in a calendar in Month view, you only set a name and date.) But you can now edit lots of details about the event. To do this, click the event to select it, and then click the Info button to display the Info Drawer (if it's not already visible).

 *You can also display the Info Drawer by pressing ⌘-I.*

The Info Drawer lets you edit any of the details about your event. This drawer displays information about the selected event; to see the information for another event, just click it in the main calendar window to select it.

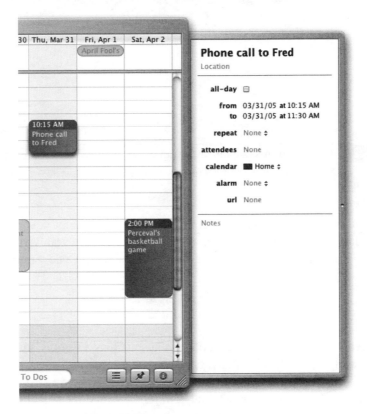

Here's what you can change for your event:

■ **All-Day**   Check this box to make the event an all-day event. If you do this, the event no longer displays at a specific time in your calendar, but appears at the top part of the calendar window, in Day or Week view, or as a solid band of color in Month view. (See Figure 15-2.)

TIP   *You can tell iCal to display times when in Month view. This is turned off by default, probably because times take up a lot of space in the small areas available for each day in this view. Select iCal | Preferences, and check Show Time in Month View in the Month section of the Preferences window.*

15

FIGURE 15-2 All-Day events display at the top of Day or Week view calendars or as solid bands in Month view.

- **From and To** Click here to set the start date and time of your event, and its end date and time. To make changes, just click the item you want to change (the month, day, or year; the hour or minutes) and type a new number.

from   03/31/05 at 10 15 AM
to   03/31/05 at 11:30 AM

- **Repeat** If the event is a repeating event—such as a weekly squash game, a monthly meeting, a birthday, or something else that occurs at a regular frequency—click the pop-up menu and select Every Day, Every Week, Every Month, or Every Year. To set a custom repeat schedule, select Custom and choose from its options. You can choose, for example, to have an event repeat on a given date each month, on the second Friday of each month, every three days, or other types of repetition. If you select a repeating schedule, another field displays below Repeat: this is End, and you can choose when you want the repetition to end by selecting Never, After, or On Date.

- **Attendees** Click here to add the names of anyone who is attending your event. This field works in conjunction with Address Book (see later in this chapter for more on using Address Book) and suggests contacts that you have entered in Address Book as you start typing. You can also select Open Address Book from the Attendees pop-up menu and manually add contacts by dragging their names from the Address Book window. After you've added attendees, you can click Attendees and then click the Send button at the bottom of the Info Drawer to open Mail and create e-mail messages to the attendees inviting them to the event. If the attendees are using Mac OS X, they can easily add the event to their own calendar, while allowing you to keep track of who is planning to attend.

- **Calendar**   You can switch events from one calendar to another, but only among calendars that you have created. (You can't move events to calendars you have subscribed to; see the next section for more on subscribing to, and sharing, calendars.) Just click the pop-up menu and select a different calendar.

- **Alarm**   One of iCal's powerful features is its ability to remind you of upcoming events. You don't have to keep checking iCal's windows to see what's on your schedule; you can set alarms so it tells you automatically. Click the pop-up menu and select Message (this displays a message onscreen), Message With Sound (this displays a message and plays a sound), Email (this sends an e-mail message with Apple Mail), Open File (this opens the file or application of your choice), or Run Script (this runs an AppleScript that you select). You can also set multiple alarms; after setting one alarm, click the word Alarm and select Add Alarm from the pop-up menu.

15

NOTE   *iCal activates alarms even when it's not running, so if you want to use alarms you don't have to have the program open.*

- **URL**   You can set a URL for any event by typing it in the URL field or by pasting a URL you have copied from another location (Safari, an e-mail message, and so on). To go to that URL, just click URL and select Go To Location.

- **Notes**   You can enter notes about the event by clicking Notes and typing at the bottom of the Info Drawer.

Hide and Display Calendars

With iCal, your calendars are all independent, but you can view as many of them as you want on its screen. You can hide and display them by clicking the check boxes next to your calendars in the Calendars list.

Turning off calendars can make it much easier to view your events, especially since some events may overlap, making it more difficult to see what they are. When events overlap, you can focus on one event by clicking its calendar in the Calendars list—the events in that calendar come to the front and partially hide events in other calendars.

Group Calendars

Since your life may be complex, and you may use calendars for work, for family commitments, and for other interests, you'll probably find that you have several calendars. In addition to being able to hide and display individual calendars, you can create groups for your calendars, using these to hide and display several calendars with a single click.

To create a group, select File | New Calendar Group. Give the group a name, and then drag several calendars into the group. The group will show a disclosure triangle allowing you to view the individual calendars or simply the name of the group, and if you uncheck the group name, all the calendars in the group are hidden.

Share Calendars

iCal is great for managing your life, but it's also designed to display other people's calendars. In fact, the real power of iCal comes from its ability to share calendars so you can see what your family, your coworkers, or your friends are doing and organize your life accordingly.

You can share your calendars in two ways: you can export them or you can publish them to .Mac. (The latter option is only available if you have a .Mac account; see Chapter 11 for more on .Mac.) If you publish a calendar on .Mac, others can view it in two ways: they can see the calendar on a web page, or they can subscribe to the calendar and view it in their copy of iCal.

Export Calendars

If you export calendars, you save them as files that you can send to others. To do this, select a calendar in the Calendars list, and then select File | Export. This saves the calendar as a file with an .ics extension. Send this file to someone else, either over a network or by e-mail, and all they have to do is double-click the file to add the calendar to their copy of iCal.

This is a good way to share calendars for fixed events, such as a school schedule, a sports schedule, or other calendars that won't change. But even if the events do change, you can make changes on your calendar and re-export it, or the other person can add or edit events, export the calendar, and send it back to you.

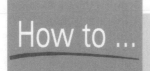 **Change Calendar Characteristics**

As you've seen, when you open iCal and add new calendars, iCal automatically chooses colors for your calendars. However, you can change these colors and their names, and add a description for them. Click a calendar in the Calendars list to select it, and then click the Info button to display the Info Drawer. You can change the calendar's name by clicking the name in the Info Drawer and typing a new name; you can change the calendar's color by selecting a color from the pop-up menu at the top right of the drawer; and you can enter a description by clicking Description and typing any text you want.

Publish Calendars on the Web

If you have a .Mac account, you can publish calendars on the Web. Other users can view them on a web page, whether they have iCal or not, or they can subscribe to them (see the next section) and view them in their copy of iCal. Click the calendar in the Calendars list to select it, and then select Calendar | Publish. A Publish sheet displays.

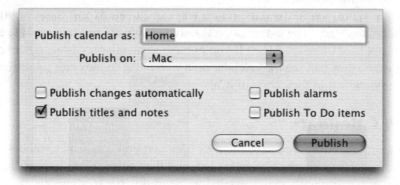

There are several options available on this sheet:

■ **Publish On**   You can choose from publishing on .Mac or on a private server. The latter is usually only available on corporate networks.

- ■ **Publish Changes Automatically**   If you check this, iCal updates the published calendar whenever you make any changes, as long as you have an active Internet connection.

- ■ **Publish Titles and Notes**   This publishes titles, or the names of your events, along with any notes you have added in the Info Drawer. If you uncheck this, your published calendar will show others when you are busy, but not what you are doing.

- ■ **Publish Alarms**   This also publishes alarms. These alarms are only accessible if other users subscribe to them with iCal. (See the upcoming "Subscribe to Calendars" section.)

- ■ **Publish To Do Items**   This also publishes a list of To Do items (see the "Manage To Do Lists with iCal" section).

After you publish a calendar, you'll see a Calendar Published dialog confirming that the publication was successful. (If you don't have an active Internet connection, or if there are other network problems, you'll see an error message.)

This dialog shows the URLs that can be used to view or subscribe to the calendar; you can select these URLs and save them. The dialog also has three buttons:

- ■ **Visit Page**   This takes you to a web page where anyone can view your calendar, from any web browser on any platform. This web page displays like the following illustration.

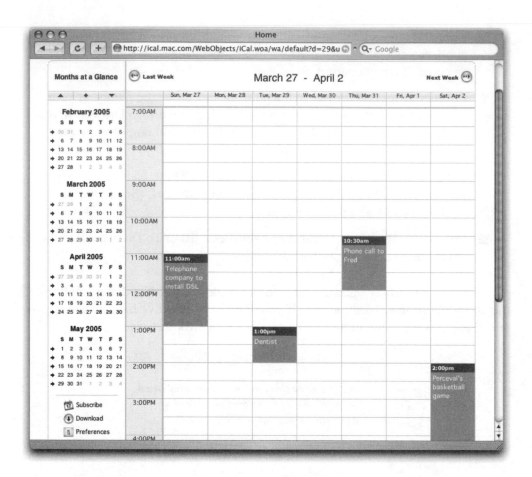

TIP
As you can see in the preceding illustration, there are Subscribe and Download links in the left-hand column of the calendar's web page. If users who have iCal click one of these links, they'll be able to subscribe to, or download, the calendar.

■ **Send Mail**   This sends an e-mail message, containing the URLs for the calendar, using Apple Mail. Add the recipients you want to this message and send it so others can access your calendar.

■ **OK**   Click this to close the dialog.

TIP
To unpublish a calendar, or stop sharing it, select Calendar | Unpublish.

Subscribe to Calendars

You saw earlier how you can share your calendars and allow others to view them on a web page. Your friends, family, and coworkers who have iCal can also subscribe to your calendars so they can always have your latest schedule visible in their copy of iCal.

To subscribe to a calendar, you need to know its URL, which you saw earlier in the Calendar Published dialog. Either send this URL to the people you want to access your calendar, or direct them to its web page, where they can click the Subscribe link. Or, if they received an e-mail message inviting them to share your calendar, they merely have to click its link to activate iCal and subscribe to your calendar.

If not, you can subscribe to a calendar by selecting Calendar | Subscribe. The Subscribe sheet displays. Enter the URL of the calendar in the Calendar URL field; this is the URL that begins with *webcal*. Click Subscribe, and iCal checks the .Mac server to find the calendar; it then displays a sheet containing subscription options.

Check Refresh, and select a frequency if you want iCal to check regularly and update the calendar. This is a good idea if you have a permanent Internet connection and need to stay up-to-date with the latest changes.

Check Remove Alarms so the calendar doesn't alert you to its events; however, uncheck this if you want alarms to activate. Check Remove To Do Items if you don't want to see the To Do items on the calendar.

After you have done this, click OK, and the calendar will be added to your Calendars list.

Subscribe to Other Calendars

Since you can subscribe to calendars, you can imagine that you're not just limited to those made by your friends, family, or coworkers. You can subscribe to many other calendars, containing holidays, sports schedules, entertainment events,

15

school test dates, and more. If you select Calendar | Find Shared Calendars, you'll go to Apple's iCal Library web page where you'll find plenty of calendars to subscribe to. This site lets you subscribe to calendars for sporting events, holidays, entertainment, and more.

You can start by subscribing to a holiday calendar. Subscribe to US Holidays, for example, and each holiday displays as an all-day event.

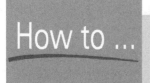 **Create a Birthday Calendar**

iCal's latest version, included in Tiger, adds a useful feature that can help ensure that you never forget a birthday again. No more worrying about getting a birthday present for that family member, friend, or coworker at the last minute. If you have added a birthday to your contact information in Address Book, iCal can read that information and automatically create a birthday calendar for you. Just select iCal | Preferences, and then click the General icon. Check Show Birthdays Calendar, and all the birthdays you've entered in Address Book show in their own, special calendar.

If you live in a different country, or work with people in other countries, you can subscribe to holiday calendars for those countries as well. And, if you're an iCal junkie, you can find hundreds of calendars to subscribe to at iCalShare (www.icalshare.com). As of press time, this site contains more than 2,000 calendars, for sports teams, birthdays, academic schedules, TV, movies, and much more.

> **TIP** *To remove any calendar you've subscribed to, just click it in the Calendars list to select it, and then press DELETE.*

Manage To Do Lists with iCal

Since the things you have to do in everyday life don't only involve appointments and events, iCal lets you manage tasks you need to do as well. You can create a To Do list in iCal, set priorities, choose due dates, add notes and URLs to the item's info, and move your items from one calendar to another.

To display the To Do list, click the pushpin button of the iCal window. This adds a To Dos column at the right side of the window, shrinking the calendar display accordingly.

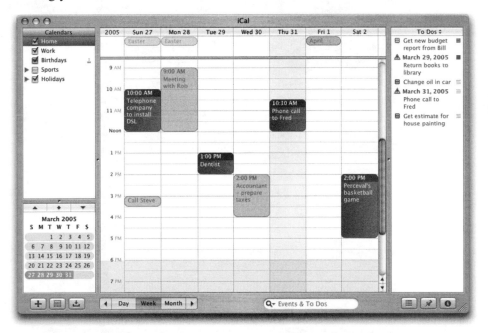

To Do items are linked to individual calendars, so to create a new To Do item, click the appropriate calendar in the Calendars list, and then double-click anywhere in the To Do Items list. This displays a new To Do item, with the text New To Do.

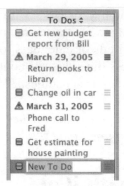

Type the text you want for the To Do item, and then press RETURN. You can edit info about your To Do items by selecting one of them and clicking the Info button to display the Info Drawer.

You can edit the following items in the Info Drawer:

■ **Completed**   Check this when you have completed the event. iCal's preferences let you decide how long completed To Do items are displayed. Select iCal | Preferences, click the Advanced tab, and enter a number of days in the Hide To Do Items *n* Days After They Have Been Completed field.

■ **Priority**   This lets you choose a priority for your To Do item; choose from Very Important, Important, Not Important, or None. The priority displays to the right of the To Do item as a number of horizontal lines; one line means Not Important, two lines means Important, and three lines means Very Important. If you don't set a priority, these lines display as dimmed.

■ **Due Date**   If your To Do item must be completed by a certain date, set that date by checking this box and selecting a date. When you set a due date, the check box to the left of your To Do item becomes a triangle if the To Do item is overdue.

■ **Alarm**   If you check Due Date, the Alarm field displays. Click the pop-up menu and select Message (this displays a message on screen only if iCal is running), Message With Sound (this displays a message and plays a sound), Email (this sends an e-mail message with Apple Mail), Open File (this opens the file or application of your choice), or Run Script (this runs an AppleScript).

■ **Calendar**   You can switch To Do items from one calendar to another, but only among calendars that you have created. (You can't move To Do items from calendars you have subscribed to, nor can you move your To Do items to a calendar you have subscribed to; see the earlier "Subscribe to Calendars" section for more on subscribing to, and sharing, calendars.) Just click the pop-up menu and select a different calendar.

■ **URL**   You can set a URL for any To Do item by typing it in the URL field or by pasting a URL you have copied from another location (Safari, an e-mail message, and so on). To go to that URL, just click URL and select Go To Location.

■ **Notes**   You can enter notes about this To Do item by clicking Notes and typing at the bottom of the Info Drawer.

Some of the choices you make in the Info Drawer display in the To Dos Items list:

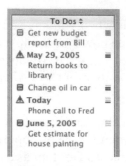

In this illustration, the first item is set to Very Important priority, the next two to Important, the next to last item to Not Important, and the last item has no priority set. The second, fourth, and fifth items in the list have due dates set, which can be seen by dates that display in bold above the tasks. Two To Do items are due, which is seen by the triangular icons to the left of them; one, the second item, is overdue. The fourth item, marked Today, is due today.

You can make some changes to To Do items by CONTROL-clicking the To Do item and selecting commands from the contextual menu that displays. You can change the calendar or the priority, you can mail the To Do item to someone, and you can change the sort order.

By default, your To Do items display in the order in which you created them. You can change this order by dragging any of them to a different location in the list, or you can sort the list by Due Date, Priority, Title, or Calendar; click the

To Dos header to display a menu where you can make this choice. You can also choose, from this menu, whether you want to hide items outside of the calendar view (not see To Do items for days that are not displayed) and whether you want to show completed To Do items.When you've completed any of the items in your To Do list, just check the boxes to the left of them. Depending on the preferences (set in iCal | Preferences | Advanced), they'll remain visible for one or more days.

Manage Contacts with Address Book

Apple's Address Book is your central repository for contacts under Mac OS X. Many Mac applications use this program: it contains names and e-mail addresses for use with Mail, holds information on your buddies for use with iChat, and even works with iCal when you want to add attendees to events or send invitations. You can store all kinds of information for your contacts, from their phone numbers and e-mail addresses to their home page URLs, their birthdays, and their .Mac public folder addresses. You can even add pictures to your contact cards.

To open Address Book, click its icon in the Dock or double-click its icon in the Applications folder.

Address Book has a simple interface (see Figure 15-3), and is fast and efficient. You can enter individual contacts and create groups or drag vCards

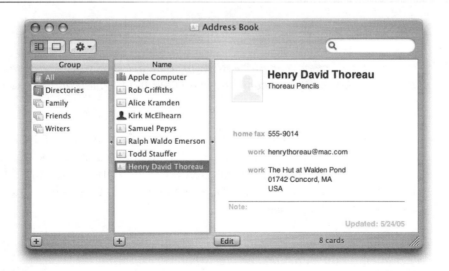

FIGURE 15-3   Address Book organizes your contacts.

(virtual address cards) sent with e-mail messages or saved by other programs. Better yet, Address Book acts as your little black book of e-mail addresses when working with Mail. All the addresses you add from messages you receive in Mail are entered in Address Book.

To create a new contact, click the + button at the bottom of the Name column. Enter as little or as much information as you want: you can enter a name or address, a telephone, fax, or cell phone number, an e-mail address, an instant messaging name, and more.

TIP   *Your contacts can have multiple items in some fields. If you see a green + icon, click this to add a second phone number field, e-mail address, and other items.*

Some of the fields you can use don't display by default; you can add them by selecting Card | Add Field and selecting one of about a dozen fields in its submenu.

When you've finished entering information for your contact, click the Edit button; you can see that it's depressed in the preceding illustration. When you click it again, you turn off editing mode.

TIP   *To change any of your contact's information, just enter editing mode by clicking the Edit button and change whatever you want.*

To create a new group, click the + button at the bottom of the Group column. Type a name for the group, and you can then drag contacts from the Name column onto each group you create.

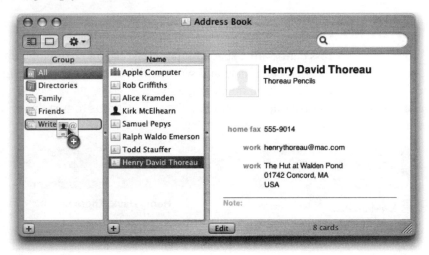

You can search for contacts by entering a few letters of their name in the Search field at the top of the window. Just start typing, and Address Book whittles down your contacts to those containing the letters you type immediately. You probably won't even need to type a full name to find the person you're looking for, unless you have lots of contacts.

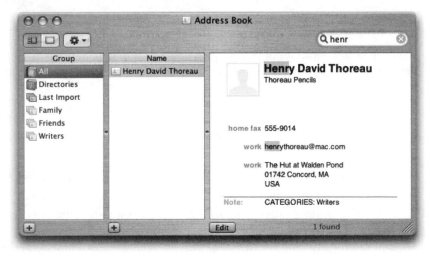

15

You can change any of the labels in a contact card. Just click the label name (in bold type) and select a different label from the choices available, or select Custom and type your own custom label name.

Work with vCards

vCards, or virtual address cards, are a special kind of file used to exchange data about contacts. Address Book can create and work with vCards, making adding and exchanging contact information quick and easy.

The simplest way to save one of your contacts as a vCard is to just drag it to the Desktop or to another Finder window.

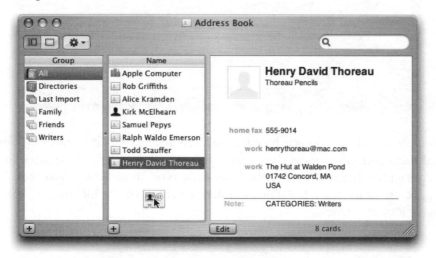

As you drag your contact, your pointer picks up a vCard icon, and when you place it on the Desktop or in a Finder window, it shows as a file with the contact's name.

You can save your own contact information as a vCard and send it to someone, say by e-mail, as an attachment. To import a vCard sent by someone else, just double-click the vCard file. Address Book displays a dialog informing you that it's adding a new card. Click OK to accept or Cancel if you don't want to import it. If you've already got information for the same person, Address Book tells you there's a duplicate of this contact and offers to let you review the duplicate:

You can choose to keep the old card or the new card, update the existing card, or keep both. This is a good way to update contact information—just have your contacts send you their vCards when they change their addresses, phone numbers, or e-mail addresses, and click Update in this dialog; any different information in the new card gets added to the old card.

Synchronize Your Personal Data

Many people work with two computers: perhaps a desktop Mac at home and an iBook or PowerBook for working on the road, or one computer at work and another at home. One of the biggest problems with this is making sure that your personal data is up-to-date on both computers.

If you have a .Mac account, you can use its Sync function to synchronize certain personal data to your .Mac account (if you have one; see Chapter 11 for more on .Mac) and to another Mac, if you want. You can synchronize your Safari bookmarks, your Address Book contacts, and your iCal calendars and To Do items. When you synchronize data to your .Mac account, this data is available both online and on other computers you own.

15

NOTE *You can use iSync to synchronize data with other devices, such as Palm PDAs, certain cell phones, and more. (See www.apple.com/isync/devices .html for a full list of compatible devices.) Check iSync's online help for more on using the program with these devices. You don't need a .Mac account to use iSync with these devices.*

To turn on syncing and set your sync options, open the System Preferences and click the .Mac tab. Click Sync to see the .Mac sync settings screen.

Check Synchronize with .Mac, and choose Manually, Automatically, Every Hour, Every Day, or Every Week. Your Mac connects to the .Mac sync server, and checks to see if it has been synchronized before. It also checks with the .Mac server and looks for other computers registered with your account with which you can sync your data. You can either sync your data to the .Mac server, so you can access it from any web browser using the .Mac web site (see Chapter 11), or sync it with another Mac you own.

Choose which type of data you want to synchronize:

- **Bookmarks**   These are your Safari bookmarks.

- **Calendars**   These are the calendars you have created in iCal, not calendars you have subscribed to.

- **Contacts**   This is the contents of your Address Book contact list.

- **Keychains**   This syncs your passwords and other keychain items.

- **Mail Accounts** These are your e-mail accounts as set in Mail. This allows you to easily access your e-mail from another Mac.

- **Mail Rules, Signatures, and Smart Mailboxes** These items are synced so you can have the same Mail environment on another Mac.

If you've chosen to sync your Mac manually, click Sync Now to start the sync. If you've selected Automatically, the sync will begin on its own. The first time you sync, if this is the only computer registered with the sync server, all your data will be sent to the server. If you register another Mac—say you want to sync a desktop and a laptop—the sync server will display an alert the first time you sync the second Mac, asking whether you want to merge data (keep what's on the second Mac and add the data from the first one), replace the data on .Mac (with the data from the second Mac), or replace the data on the second computer. Think carefully as you decide which computer has the valid data for this first sync. Afterwards, if the sync server detects that both computers have updated their data, it will ask you the same question. In most cases, if you work with two computers, you'll want to merge data after the first sync.

You can check Show Status In Menu Bar to display a menu extra that shows you the sync status and lets you sync your Mac manually, as well as open the .Mac Sync preferences.

TIP *If you want to make sure your data is always up-to-date, select Automatically. Any time you change the data you've selected to sync, your Mac will upload the changes to the .Mac server. This ensures that both computers always have the latest data and that the .Mac server always has a backup of your data. If you ever lose the data on your Mac, you can always retrieve this data from the .Mac server by syncing again.*

15

Chapter 16

Work with iTunes and the iPod

Mac OS X Tiger

Version 10.4

How to…

- Listen to CDs and digital music files
- Manage playlists
- Burn music CDs
- Listen to audio books
- Manage your iPod

When Apple first released iTunes, no one realized just how far the company would go with digital music. This simple jukebox application later spawned Apple's successful iPod, which lets you carry your digital music with you, and more recently, the iTunes Music Store, which you can use to purchase and download digital music files. The iPod's now-legendary success is such that many people see Apple more as a purveyor of digital music players than a computer manufacturer. And the vast market for iPod accessories contributes to that image.

Apple has provided regular innovations to the iPod, increasing the number of ways it can be used. The first iPod was a mere music player, but recent iPods can display photos on its color screen and even on a TV using a special cable; and the iPod shuffle, a screenless ultra-mini iPod, doubles as a USB key drive. Digital music files, such as MP3 files, which compress music to about one-tenth of its size, have changed the way music is listened to and stored. You can put the equivalent of ten CDs on just one compact disc by creating digital music files from your music. If you have an iPod, you can store thousands of songs and listen to them wherever you want. The amount of music you can put on your iPod is not measured in hours like for other digital music players, but in days.

iTunes is the Mac OS X digital music nerve center. It lets you *rip*, or create, your own digital music files from CDs you own; it lets you organize and play back these files; it lets you burn CDs from your digital music files; and it transfers your music to your iPod. Apple has been one of the most important players in the digital music revolution, not only by providing the most successful listening device, but also by making available the iTunes Music Store, where you can also use iTunes to purchase music, listen to audio books and Internet radio stations, and even share your music with other users on your network.

In this chapter, I'll tell you all about iTunes: how to rip digital music files, create playlists, burn music CDs from your files, listen to audio books, access Internet radio stations, and purchase digital music from the iTunes Music Store. I'll also tell you how to use your iPod, managing your music with iTunes and syncing it to your iPod.

Work with iTunes

iTunes is Apple's application to manage, organize, and play digital music files, create digital music files from your CDs, and burn CDs in either MP3 or standard music format. To open iTunes, click the iTunes icon in the Dock, or double-click the iTunes icon in your Applications folder. When you first launch iTunes, the program asks you to agree to

iTunes

its license terms; then an assistant asks you a few questions about how iTunes will use the Internet and whether it should look for MP3 files you already have on your hard disk. The first screen of the assistant welcomes you to iTunes; click Next to continue.

On the Internet Audio screen, it's probably a good idea to select Yes, Use iTunes For Internet Audio Content. This tells your Mac that iTunes is the default music player. Let iTunes automatically connect to the Internet only if you have a permanent Internet connection; if you connect via a modem, iTunes will open a connection each time it needs to do so, which can be annoying. Click Next after choosing options on this screen.

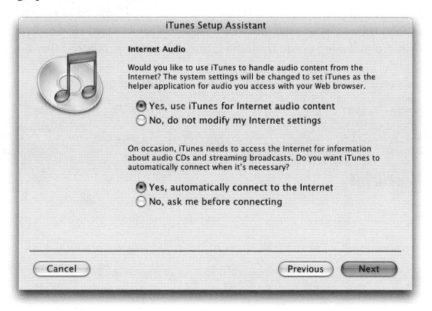

 iTunes connects to the Internet (if you have set this option) when you insert a prerecorded music CD. It does so to query a database to find the exact name for the CD and the titles of its tracks.

16

The next screen is the Find Music Files screen. iTunes offers to find MP3 and AAC files in your home folder or lets you choose to add them later. If you want iTunes to add any digital music files it finds, select the first option. If not, you can add your music later; I'll show you how to do that later on, in the section "Import Digital Music Files into iTunes." Click Next to go to the next screen.

NOTE   *iTunes can play back music files in five formats: AAC, MP3, WAV, AIFF, and Apple Lossless. You've probably heard a lot about MP3 files, since people sharing music illegally commonly use them. The MP3 format is used to compress music, making the files much smaller than the original sound files on CDs. AAC is a different format that offers better quality and smaller file sizes at the same bit rate; iTunes uses AAC by default. WAV and AIFF are uncompressed formats, and Apple Lossless is a compression format that retains all of the music yet compresses it to about half the original size.*

The last screen offers to take you to the iTunes Music Store right away, or to your iTunes Library. Your iTunes Library will be empty if you have no existing digital music files on your Mac, but that's a good place to start. However, if you want to start purchasing music from the iTunes Music store, choose that option. Click Done.

After you answer these questions, the main iTunes window displays.

Listen to CDs with iTunes

While you can use iTunes to rip, or import, music from CDs, you can also use it when you want to listen to a CD on your Mac. When you insert a music CD in your Mac's CD-ROM drive, iTunes opens automatically. (You can change this setting in the CDs & DVDs preference pane; see Chapter 9.) If you have told iTunes to connect to the Internet automatically, it queries the CD Database (CDDB) to find the name of the CD and the names of its tracks. If the CD is listed in this database, iTunes displays this information (Figure 16-1); if not, it just displays Track 1, Track 2, and so on.

To listen to the CD from the beginning, just click the Play button at the top left of the iTunes window. To listen beginning at a specific track, double-click that track in the list. You can fast-forward or rewind using the buttons on either side of the Play button, and you can pause the music by clicking the Pause button (see Figure 16-2).

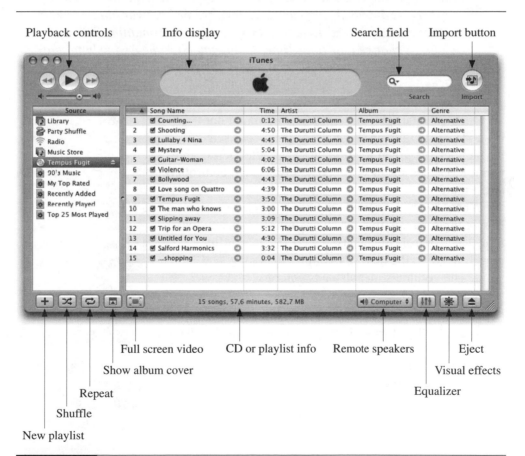

FIGURE 16-1 When you insert a music CD in your Mac, iTunes opens and displays the name of the CD and its tracks, if possible.

Click the Play button (left) to start playing music. Click the Pause button (right) to pause, or the Fast-Forward or Rewind buttons to move through the track.

TIP *The info display at the top of the iTunes window cycles between the name of the CD you're listening to, the artist, and the name of the song. Below this info is the elapsed time of the song. If you click the time indicator, or drag its diamond, you can move forward or backward in a song. If you click the Elapsed Time text, this changes to Remaining Time; click again to change it to Total Time. And if you click the Arrow button at the left of the display, this changes the display to a kind of frequency display.*

Once you start playing your CD, you might not want iTunes to take up so much space on your screen. If you click the green Resize button at the top left of the window, iTunes shrinks to become just a small controller (see Figure 16-3).

When iTunes is in miniature mode, click the green Resize button again to return the window to its previous size. The Controls menu lets you choose to shuffle, repeat, move to the next song or previous song, and more. The volume slider also lets you raise and lower volume.

Another way to control iTunes is from the Dock. Click this icon and hold down your mouse button. This displays an iTunes menu, as shown at the right. You can control many of iTunes' functions from this menu without bringing the application to the front.

FIGURE 16-3   iTunes in miniature mode. You can pause and play, fast-forward and rewind, and see what's playing. You can also enlarge this window by dragging its bottom-right corner.

TIP   *Whenever you're listening to music and want to pause, bring iTunes to the front and press the SPACEBAR on your keyboard. To resume playing, just press the SPACEBAR again.*

Rip Digital Music Files from Your CDs

iTunes can rip, or import, music files from a CD with a single click, allowing you to convert your entire CD library into digital music files. Insert a CD in your CD-ROM drive. iTunes searches the Internet to find the title of the album and tracks,

How to ...   Listen to Music with AirTunes

As you saw in Figure 16-1, iTunes has a button at the bottom of its window that allows you to choose remote speakers through which you can listen to your music. This button only displays if you have an Apple AirPort Express on your network; this device, which is a miniature wireless base station, has an audio jack you can use to connect it to a stereo or self-powered speakers. If you have a wireless network (see Chapter 12 for more on wireless networking) and an AirPort Express, you can use this AirTunes function to stream music to your stereo. The AirPort Express can be anywhere in your home or office, as long as it is within range of your base station. This is a great way to use your Mac as a music center and stream music to a different room in your home.

16

and displays the results. To import this disc into your iTunes library, just click the Import button at the top right of the iTunes window. iTunes begins converting the CD into digital music files and shows its progress in the display at the top of the window.

The time it takes to import music depends on the speed of your Mac and the quality you use for your digital music files. By default, iTunes imports music in AAC format at 128 Kbps, which is very good quality, and you can change this in the iTunes preferences. Select iTunes | Preferences and click the Importing tab, and then select a different bit rate from the Configuration pop-up menu.

Import Digital Music Files into iTunes

If you already have digital music files on your Mac, you can import them into iTunes by selecting File | Add To Library. Select the folder containing your music files from the Import dialog, and then click Open. This adds all the digital music files in the selected folder to your iTunes library.

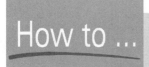 **Choose the Right Music File Import Format**

iTunes offers you five formats for importing digital music files from your CDs: AAC, MP3, AIFF, WAV, and Apple Lossless. AAC is a format that offers a good compromise between quality and file size; but many digital music devices, such as home CD and DVD players, cannot play these files. If you are only importing your files to play them back on your Mac, or to use with an iPod, AAC is probably the best choice. Use MP3 if you want compatibility with other devices.

AIFF and WAV formats do not compress the music, and if you want the highest quality, choose AIFF. If you're importing music from your CDs to make compilation CDs, AIFF is the best choice, since there is no compression and you won't lose any quality. Choose WAV if you want the highest quality files to use on a Windows computer. (However, both of these formats take up a lot of disk space—about 600MB per hour.)

Apple Lossless is, as its name suggests, a lossless compression format, one that loses none of the data in the original music files. These files take up about half as much disk space as noncompressed files (or about 300MB per hour) and provide the same quality as CDs. If you're an audiophile and have lots of disk space, this is a great way to get perfect quality yet stuff more music on your hard disk.

You can also choose a bit rate for your digital music files. By default, iTunes use 128 Kbps for AAC files and 160 Kbps for MP3 files. If you're planning to listen to your music on a portable device, or don't have much disk space, these settings are acceptable. But if you're a classical or jazz music fan, or connect your Mac to a stereo, you might be disappointed by these imported files. Select Custom in the Setting menu, and select a higher bit rate—at least 160 Kbps for AAC or 192 Kbps for MP3 files. If you find the music doesn't sound as good as you want, experiment with higher bit rates—but remember that the higher the quality, the larger the files.

16

Another way to import digital music files is to click the Library icon in the Source column of the iTunes window, and then locate the folder containing the files on the Desktop or in a Finder window. Drag the folder into the Library section of the iTunes window, and iTunes will add them to your library.

If you drag a folder containing digital music files into the Source section of the iTunes window, this adds the files as a playlist; you'll see a new playlist added to this part of the window. (I'll tell you more about playlists shortly.)

Listen to Digital Music Files

When you import MP3 files into iTunes, they are added to your Library. You can see the contents of this library by clicking the Library icon in the Source list (see Figure 16-4).

FIGURE 16-4   A Library of digital music files in iTunes

Another way to view the Library—and one that is more flexible—is in Browse mode. To view your music like this, click the Browse button at the top right of the iTunes window. This displays the contents of your Library sorted by genre, artist, and album at the top, and the contents of the selected item at the bottom. For example, if you select a genre, then an artist, and then an album, you'll only see the tracks on that album.

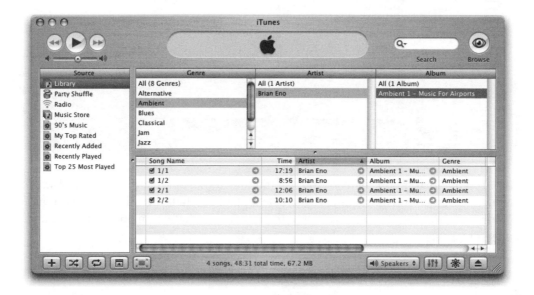

You can listen to any of the songs in your Library by double-clicking one of them. iTunes starts playing your Library at the song you double-click, and then continues playing the rest of the Library in order. Or if you are in Browse mode, just click the Play button to start playing the tracks that are visible at the bottom of the iTunes window. The speaker icon next to the track name indicates which track is currently playing.

16

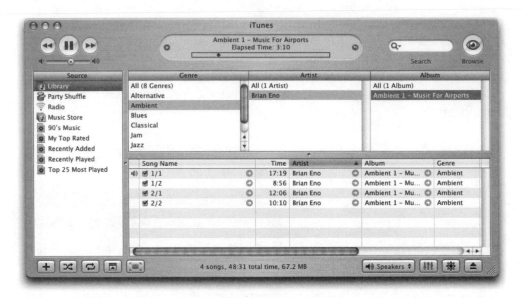

To have better control over your digital music files, you can create *playlists,* which are custom lists of songs. To create a playlist, click the + icon beneath the Source list. A new playlist is added to this list. Type whatever name you want, and then press ENTER.

TIP   *To find songs to add to your playlists, use the Search field at the top of the iTunes window. Type a few letters of a song, album, or artist, and iTunes displays the corresponding tracks almost instantly. You can then drag these tracks to your playlist.*

Now, in your Library, find the songs you want to add to the playlist and drag them onto the playlist's name; you can drag one song at a time or several. This doesn't make copies of the files on your disk; it just adds them to the playlist.

When you have finished dragging songs onto your playlist, click the playlist in the Source list to display its contents.

You can drag the songs up and down in the list to change their order. (Make sure the leftmost column header is clicked, which allows you to sort songs.) At the bottom of the iTunes window, a summary text shows the number of songs, the time, and the amount of disk space used by the songs in the playlist.

16

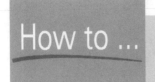**Rate Your Favorite Songs**

In addition to maintaining information about your music—the artist, album, song name, and more—iTunes allows you to add some custom information about your songs, such as ratings for your favorite songs. You can rate a song on a scale of one to five; this can be useful if you want to create a smart playlist containing only your favorite songs.

To rate a song, hold down the CONTROL key and click its name. From the contextual menu, select My Rating, and then a number of stars from one to five (or select None to remove a rating you applied previously).

To listen to one of the songs, just double-click it. To listen to the entire playlist, click the Play button. You can also burn the playlist to a CD; see "Burn Music CDs with iTunes" later in this chapter.

Create Smart Playlists

In addition to basic playlists, which I explained earlier, iTunes lets you create *smart playlists,* which are dynamic and work like searches with multiple criteria. A smart playlist can contain music that belongs to a specific genre or is performed by a specific artist, or it can contain only songs with certain ratings you've given them or songs that you haven't listened to since a certain time.

You've seen the concept behind smart playlists elsewhere in this book; the Finder uses Smart Folders (you saw them in Chapter 5), and Mail uses smart mailboxes (Chapter 10). Smart playlists work the same way as other smart items.

iTunes comes with some sample smart playlists—you can see them in the Source column of its window; they have gear icons.

To create a new smart playlist, select File | New Smart Playlist, or hold down the OPTION key and click the + button beneath the Source list. This displays the Smart Playlist window.

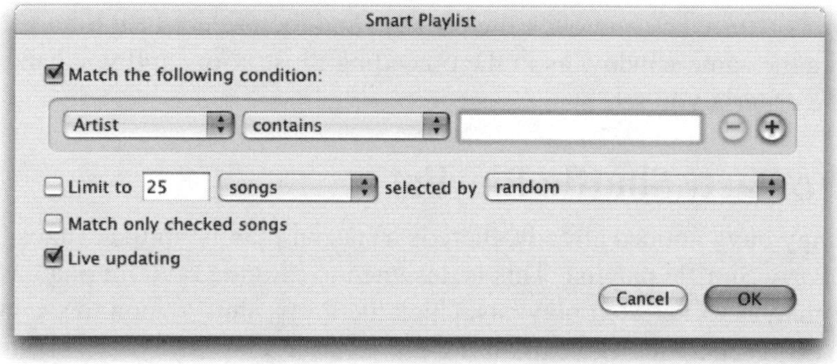

As you can see here, you have several choices for how you set up a smart playlist. In the top section are criteria—you can choose from more than a dozen of them in the first pop-up menu, including Artist, Genre, Last Played, Year, Play Count, My Rating, and many more. In the second pop-up menu, select Contains, Does Not Contain, Is, Is Not, Starts With, or Ends With. Finally, enter the appropriate data in the field—this could be the name of an artist or song, a play count, a rating, or something else.

You can then limit your playlist to a certain number of Songs, Minutes, Hours, MB, or GB, and choose how the songs are selected: Random, by Album, Artist, Rating, or more.

To add criteria, click the + icon at the right of a criterion line. You can create smart playlists that sort your music in many ways. Here's one example:

16

The smart playlist shown in the preceding illustration includes up to 25 songs, all of which are by the Grateful Dead, are longer than 15 minutes, and haven't been played in the last two weeks.

To change any smart playlist, just select File | Edit Smart Playlist, or hold down the CONTROL key and click the playlist, and then select Edit Smart Playlist. You'll see the same window as in the preceding illustration, and you can change any of the criteria you set.

Use the Party Shuffle Playlist

As you may have noticed already, there is a special playlist in the iTunes Source list: the Party Shuffle playlist. This is designed to provide random playback of your Library, or of selected playlists. Click the Party Shuffle icon to see how it works. You'll see a message explaining this in brief, and then you'll see the special Party Shuffle display.

By default, the Party Shuffle displays the last five songs it has played and the next 15 that are queued up. (In the preceding illustration, only five upcoming songs are shown.) As you play songs, the "recently played" songs go up above the blue "current song indicator," and new songs get added to the upcoming song list. At the bottom of the window, you can choose the source (your entire Library or a specific playlist), the number of songs to display, and whether iTunes should choose higher-rated songs more often.

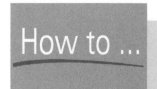 **Share Your Music on a Local Network**

If your Mac is connected to other Macs across a local network, such as at home or at work, you can share your music so other users can access your playlists. Select iTunes | Preferences and click the Sharing tab. Check Share My Music if you want to share your music, and check Look For Shared Music to share other users' music. You can choose to share your entire music library or only selected playlists.

When you launch iTunes, it searches the network for shared music (if you have told it to look for shared music). You'll see, in the Source column, an icon for each user on your network. (If several shared libraries are available, you'll see a Shared Music icon, which shows below it the different libraries available.) Click a user's icon to see that user's music, and listen to it the same way you listen to playlists on your Mac.

The advantage to using this feature is that you can have one Mac with all your music on it, say at home, and anyone on your network (even Windows users with iTunes 4.1 or later) can access your music. You can centralize all your music files on one computer this way. However, iTunes must be running on that computer for others to access its music.

If you don't like the choices the Party Shuffle offers, just click the Refresh button at the top right of the iTunes window. This gives you a whole new selection. You can also add songs manually to the Party Shuffle from your Library or from a playlist. CONTROL-click a song (or several songs, or an entire album) and select Add To Party Shuffle to add the song at the end of the Party Shuffle list, or Play Next In Party Shuffle to queue that song up after the current song.

Listen to Audio Books with iTunes

In addition to playing music, iTunes can play audio-book files you download from Audible.com (www.audible.com) or purchase from the iTunes Music Store. When you buy books from Audible.com, you get a user name and password that you must enter when iTunes requests it. You can download audio books in a special format and play them back in iTunes.

16

After you download an audio-book file from Audible.com, just double-click the file and iTunes will begin importing it into your Library. The first time you do this, you'll be prompted to enter your Audible.com user name and password. You can listen to the file the same way you listen to music files.

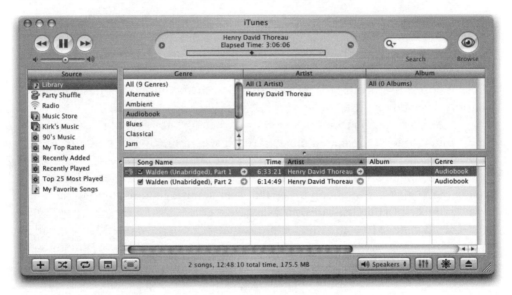

Note that when you quit iTunes, it remembers your location in the audio-book file, and when you next start playing it again, it picks up where you left off. If you synchronize your audio books to your iPod, you can pick up listening at the same point. When you next connect your iPod, iTunes picks up bookmarks in your audio books and updates the files on your Mac. With this feature, you can listen to your favorite books on your Mac and on your iPod without ever losing your place.

Burn Music CDs with iTunes

iTunes can burn music CDs from your digital audio files: you can burn audio CDs, which you can play in any CD player, or MP3 CDs, which you can use either to back up your MP3 files or to play in compatible CD or DVD players. You can also burn data CDs, which simply copy your music files; these are good for backing up your music files. By default, iTunes burns audio CDs, but you can change this by selecting iTunes | Preferences and clicking the Burning tab. Check MP3 CD in the Disc Format section if you want to burn MP3 CDs, or click Data CD if you want to burn CDs but save your files in their original format.

To burn a CD with iTunes, start by creating a playlist with the songs you want to burn. You can use an existing playlist or create a new one, but it's best to make sure it is no longer than the amount of time available on your blank CD. You can burn a playlist that is longer than one CD; iTunes will ask for additional CDs as necessary.

Click the Burn Disc button at the top right of the iTunes window. Insert a blank CD-R or CD-RW in your CD writer when iTunes asks you to. iTunes checks your CD and then asks you to confirm by clicking Burn Disc again.

When iTunes has finished burning the CD, it will eject it from your CD burner and you're ready to listen to the CD or to archive it as a backup of your digital music files.

Listen to Internet Radio with iTunes

When you run out of music, you can use another of iTunes' great features to hear new tunes: you can listen to Internet radio stations. These radio stations "broadcast" their music and talk programs over the Internet; some are regular AM or FM radio stations that offer Internet broadcasting in addition to their regular broadcasting, and others are Internet-only radio stations.

To listen to Internet radio with iTunes, click the Radio icon in the Source list in the iTunes window. This displays a list of categories in the list window.

To see the different Internet radio stations available, click the disclosure triangle next to one of the categories. Double-click a radio station to listen to it.

16

Some Internet radio stations send song information with their broadcasts. If this is the case, the artist and song title show in the status display at the top of the iTunes window, as shown in the preceding illustration.

If you connect to the Internet with a modem, make sure you don't try to listen to any radio stations with bit rates over 56 Kbps; you'll just get music that starts and stops as iTunes tries to get enough data to play the stream. If you have a broadband connection, you can listen to any of the stations.

Buy Music from the iTunes Music Store

The iTunes Music Store is Apple's online music purchase service, where you can choose from hundreds of thousands of songs and buy them individually (for 99¢ each at press time) or buy entire albums. You can also buy audio books from the iTunes Music Store, whose content is provided by Audible.com.

NOTE   *The Audible.com site offers more purchase options for audio books than the iTunes Music Store. You can get low-priced monthly subscriptions, and you can also choose from several formats that allow you to more easily listen to your audio books on different digital music devices. However, some individual books are cheaper from the iTunes Music Store, so if you are only interested in buying one or two books, compare prices to get the best deal.*

The iTunes Music Store lets you use iTunes to search for, preview, and purchase music. You then download your purchases and listen to them or burn them to CDs using iTunes, or sync them to your iPod to listen to on the move. Listening to your purchased music, and burning it to CDs, works exactly as I explained earlier in this chapter.

To access the iTunes Music Store, click Music Store in the Source list of the iTunes window. You'll see a window that looks something like this:

The iTunes Music Store interface works like a web site: you click different links or graphics to access different pages, or you select items from pop-up menus. Type song, artist, or album names into the Search field to search the contents of the store, and use the navigation bar at the top of the window to move through the Music Store:

In this example, I'm viewing the Grateful Dead's album "Wake of the Flood." You can go back to the Grateful Dead section by clicking that part of the navigation bar; you can go to the Rock section by clicking that part of the bar; and you can go to the iTunes Music Store's main page by clicking the home icon. You can also click the Back and Forward buttons to go back and forth between pages you've already seen.

16

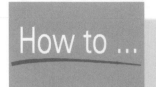

How to ... Buy Music from Other Online Vendors

You can buy music from other online vendors, but not all of them are compatible with iTunes and your iPod. Many online music vendors use Windows Media Player files, which iTunes cannot read. (iTunes for Windows can convert unprotected Windows Media Player files, but not those purchased from most online vendors.) Depending on your musical tastes, you'll find some niche vendors who not only sell great music but do so without DRM (digital rights management) in the files, meaning you can use them and burn them to CD, or copy them to your iPod, with no restriction.

Two of my favorite sites for music are Magnatune (www.magnatune.com), which sells music in a variety of genres—ambient, classical, jazz, and more—directly from the artists. Working much like a cooperative, Magnatune even lets you choose the price you pay for albums. Disclogic (www.disclogic.com) sells live concerts from some of today's hottest jam bands, including moe., Ratdog, The Disco Biscuits, Umphrey's McGee, and others. You can buy these concerts in a variety of formats, and some bands sell dozens of their concerts at really nice prices.

The iTunes Music Store lets you listen to a 30-second sample of any of its songs or audio books. Just double-click a song to hear this preview. If you want to buy something, click Buy Song or Buy Album. If you haven't yet set up an account, you'll be prompted to do so.

After you purchase songs, you'll be able to download them and use them like any other digital music files. You can listen to them, burn them to CDs, and transfer them to your iPod or other digital music device.

Use an iPod

Apple's iPod is a unique combination of excellent design and faultless functionality. In its sleek plastic and metal case is a hard disk, ranging from 4GB for the smallest capacity iPod mini to 60GB (at press time, 60GB is the largest model available), which stores your digital music files and lets you listen to them on the move.

NOTE   *The iPod shuffle, with capacity of 512MB or 1GB, is a small, simple music player. With no screen, the iPod shuffle, as its name suggests, is best for people who want to listen to music at random, though you can also listen to music sequentially. A great iPod for those who want music while they work out, run, or cycle, the iPod shuffle is light and sturdy.*

The iPod is designed to interface seamlessly with iTunes. In fact, to update your music on your iPod, just plug it into your Mac's FireWire port and launch iTunes (if it doesn't launch automatically when you plug in your iPod), and your music transfers automatically. To turn off automatic transfer and manually manage your music, select your iPod in the Source list, and then click the iPod Options button at the bottom of the iTunes window.

You can choose from the iPod preference pane whether you want all songs and playlists updated automatically, or only selected items updated. You can also choose to manually manage songs and playlists.

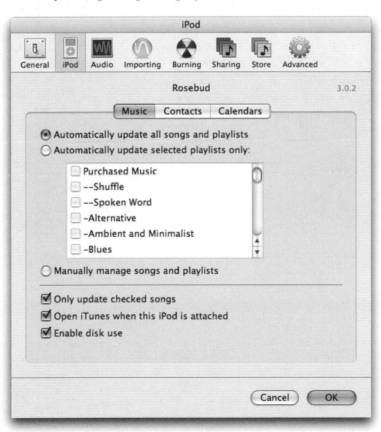

16

You have three ways of updating your iPod:

- **Automatically Update All Songs and Playlists**   This is the easiest way to sync your iPod, and probably the best for most people. When you connect your iPod, iTunes syncs its library to the iPod—every song, every playlist. As long as you don't have more music than your iPod will hold, this is a snap.

- **Automatically Update Selected Playlists Only**   This is great when you have too much music to put on your iPod, for instance, if it is an iPod mini with limited disk space. Check the playlists you want to update. No music is copied if it is not in a selected playlist, so you may want to create playlists containing many artists and albums.

- **Manually Manage Songs and Playlists**   With this setting, you drag the songs, albums, and playlists you want from your iTunes library to the iPod's icon in the Source list. Only those songs you copy manually are added to the iPod.

Two other tabs on the iPod preference pane may be useful: on the Contacts and Calendars tabs, you can choose to sync your Address Book contacts and your iCal calendars to your iPod.

For more on using your iPod, see its documentation or check out my book *iPod & iTunes Garage* (Prentice Hall, 2004).

Part V

Go Further with Your Mac

Chapter 17

Keep Your Mac Secure

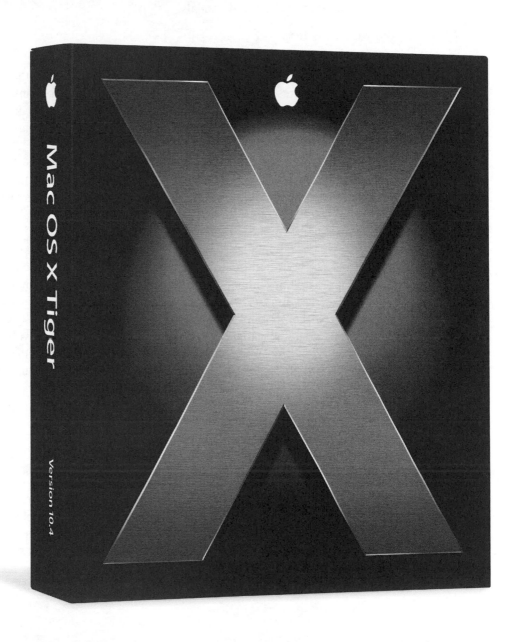

How to…

- Protect your sensitive files and data
- Permanently delete files
- Protect your Mac from hackers and vandals
- Keep your Mac virus-free

Computer security, once a concern only of corporations, universities, or other centers with large computers and sensitive data, has in recent years become an issue that affects every computer user. Now that most personal computers are connected to the Internet, the possibility of attack or infection has been increased substantially.

Computer security is a serious issue, especially given the widespread use of the Internet and the frequency at which users download and exchange files. The main threats are viruses and hacker attacks. While Windows users suffer from these attacks frequently, Mac users are much less bothered by them. But you owe it to yourself and your files to protect your Mac from the people who want to harm your data.

Security covers several areas, but begins, as do many things, at home. You need to control physical access to your computer to protect your personal files. Next comes your network access: if your computer is connected to the Internet or another network, there's a risk that malicious users may attack your Mac to try to get at your data, or simply to harm your computer. Finally, viruses are a serious threat. They can damage your files, and potentially incapacitate your operating system as well.

In this chapter, I'll tell you how you can protect your Mac from these security threats. I'll explain how to protect your Mac from physical access, how to protect it against hackers and vandals, and how to stop viruses from damaging your system. I'll also show you how to safeguard your most sensitive files with encryption and how to use Mac OS X's security features, such as FileVault.

Control Physical Access to Your Mac

One of the first ways to protect the security of your Mac and its files is to ensure that no one can access it. While it's easy to prevent anyone from accessing a computer over a network—just unplug its Ethernet cable, or turn off AirPort wireless networking—physical access to your Mac is another story. It has been said that the only truly safe computer is one locked in a vault and protected by armed guards, but that defeats the purpose of having a computer.

Your Mac is already protected so others cannot access your files: you have an individual user name and password, which allow you to access your account and the files in your home folder. If you are the administrator of your Mac, which is the case if you are its only user (see Chapter 8 for a discussion of the administrator account), you can eventually access any user's files on your Mac.

If you use your Mac in an environment where others can approach your Mac—your home, office, school, or lab—there's little you can do to prevent these people from accessing your Mac, but you can do several things to prevent them from accessing your files. Some of these are settings in the Security pane of the System Preferences. (See Figure 17-1.) To access these settings, open the System Preferences by clicking its icon in the Dock, or select the Apple Menu | System Preferences. Click the Security icon to display this preference pane.

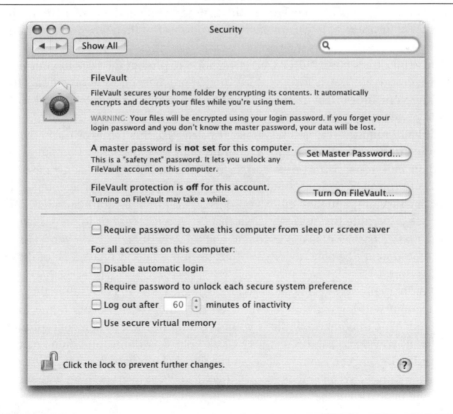

FIGURE 17-1   The Security preference pane is where you turn on settings that can protect your Mac.

17

To access many of the settings on this preference pane, you must be an administrator, and if the lock icon shows a closed padlock, click it and enter your user name and password to make changes. If you are not an administrator, you can access FileVault settings for your account and turn on password protection after waking from sleep or a screen saver.

If your Mac is in an office or school, or even if you work in a store or any other location where a lot of people pass through, you might want to consider a Kensington MicroSaver security cable (www.microsaver.com) to lock your Mac and prevent anyone from walking off with it.

Use FileVault

Mac OS X 10.4 includes a security feature called FileVault, which automatically encrypts the contents of your home folder. When you need to use a file in this folder or its subfolders, FileVault decrypts it on-the-fly; then when you've finished working with it, it encrypts it again.

FileVault offers powerful 128-bit encryption to protect the files in your home folder in case your Mac is lost or stolen. It also prevents hackers or vandals from accessing your files if they manage to enter your computer over a network and you are not logged in to your account.

FileVault requires that you set a master password; this password, which only an administrator can set, can unlock any FileVault account on the computer. Users need their individual password to access their account; this is the same password they use to log in to their account. To turn on FileVault for your account, click Turn On FileVault, and then enter your password at the prompt and click OK. You'll see a warning that makes it clear that "if you forget your login password and the master password is not available, your data will be lost forever." This is no joke; you won't be able to get your files back if you don't have one of these two passwords.

If you're really sure you want to go ahead, click Turn On FileVault in this dialog. Your account will log out and you'll see a FileVault screen as your home folder is encrypted. This may take a while if you have a lot of files. When encryption has completed, you'll see a login window. Click your user name, and then enter your password to log in. You can now access your files as before, with the difference being that they are protected and other users will not be able to decrypt them without either your login password or the master password.

You can tell that your home folder is encrypted by its icon, visible either in the Finder window sidebar or in the Users folder.

kirk

If you ever want to turn off FileVault protection, open the Security pane of the System Preferences and click Turn Off FileVault. You'll be prompted to enter your password; do this, and then click OK. A dialog asks you to confirm that you want to turn off FileVault. Click Turn Off FileVault to do this. As when you turned on FileVault, your Mac logs out your account. It then decrypts your home folder and displays a login screen for you to log in again.

> NOTE   *Before deciding to use FileVault, you should be aware of its advantages and disadvantages, and decide whether it is worth using. FileVault offers no choice in what you encrypt. It encrypts your entire home folder, and if you store digital music files, photos, and video there, it can be very slow and take a long time to encrypt or decrypt. If you do use FileVault to protect your files, make sure to back up these files often. (See Chapter 19 for more on backing up files.) If you only have a handful of files that are sensitive enough to warrant encryption, there are other solutions available. I'll tell you about them later in this chapter in the "Other Encryption Solutions" section.*

Other Security Settings

The Security preference pane offers other security settings as well.

☐ Require password to wake this computer from sleep or screen saver

For all accounts on this computer:

☐ Disable automatic login

☐ Require password to unlock each secure system preference

☐ Log out after 60 ⬍ minutes of inactivity

☐ Use secure virtual memory

You can choose to activate the following functions for your account:

- **Require Password to Wake This Computer from Sleep or Screen Saver**   If you check this, your Mac will ask you to enter your password when you wake it from sleep or when a screen saver has become active. This applies only to the active account, and each user can access this setting. This is useful to protect physical access to your Mac if you go away from your desk and put your Mac to sleep or if you turn on its screen saver using a hot corner when you step away.

17

The remaining settings on the Security preference pane affect all accounts, and only an administrator can change them.

- **Disable Automatic Login**   If you check this, your Mac will ask users to log in by entering their password each time it starts up. If you use automatic login—which is convenient if you're the only user of your Mac—this password request is bypassed, and your Mac starts up in the user account selected for automatic login. Turning off automatic login means that a user with an account must be present when the computer is turned on for any files to be accessible. Otherwise, anyone can turn on your Mac and access the files belonging to the user who logs in automatically.

NOTE   *You can also turn on automatic login from the Login Options screen of the Accounts preference pane. This is a bit confusing, though. The Accounts pane lets you turn automatic login on and choose which users log in automatically. The Security pane lets you turn it off—in spite of it saying "Disable Automatic Login," it doesn't disable this feature or turn it off permanently. Checking this option on the Security pane is the same as turning off automatic login from the Accounts pane. If you do this and then turn automatic login back on in the Accounts pane, you'll see that Disable Automatic Login is no longer checked in the Security pane.*

- **Require Password to Unlock Each Secure System Preference**   Checking this means that even administrators, logged in to an administrator account, must enter their password each time they want to access secure system preferences. These are preference panes where you see a lock icon at the bottom left. They include the Startup Disk, Network, Sharing panes, some items on the Security and Accounts panes, and others.

- **Log Out After *n* Minutes of Inactivity**   This tells the Mac to log out if its user is inactive for the number of minutes you select. This restricts physical access to the Mac if the user leaves his or her computer and doesn't log out. However, it doesn't protect that same Mac for the number of minutes *before* it logs out. If you set this to a low number, users who are in front of their Macs and not using them—maybe they are on the phone or doing other work—will be annoyed by having to log in often. If you set it to a high number, it won't protect the computer much, since users can be away from their desks for several minutes before it activates. If you're really worried about such access, turn on Fast User Switching (see Chapter 8) and instruct your users to select Login Window from the user menu whenever they leave their desks. This displays a login window without logging out the current user. When they return to their desks, they can just click their user name, enter their password, and get back to work right away.

■   **Use Secure Virtual Memory**   This encrypts your virtual memory files—files that are created on your Mac and used by the system and applications—which may contain sensitive data. Since they are outside your home folder, if you use FileVault, these files could potentially leave traces of sensitive files on your hard disk. Only use this if you *really* have top-secret files on your Mac.

Other Encryption Solutions

In the section on FileVault earlier in this chapter, I pointed out that there are advantages and disadvantages to using FileVault. There are other solutions for protecting selected files by encrypting them—some are commercial, but one is built into Mac OS X.

Among the commercial solutions is software called PGP (Pretty Good Privacy; www.pgp.com). PGP offers a full range of encryption solutions, from e-mail to files, and its product line includes software for everyone from home users to large companies. Most Mac users will find that PGP Personal Desktop meets their needs. This offers e-mail encryption and includes PGP Disk, which creates volumes that are encrypted when not in use and offers excellent security for portable computers in case they are lost or stolen.

Work with an Encrypted Disk Image

One of the best ways to protect sensitive files is built into Mac OS X. You can create an encrypted disk image, in which you can copy any sensitive files you have on your Mac. When you mount the disk image, you are asked for its password, and when you unmount it, it is protected. Here's how you go about creating an encrypted disk image:

1.   Open Disk Utility, which is in the Utilities folder of your Applications folder.

2.   Click the New Image button it the toolbar. The new blank image sheet displays.

17

3. Enter a name for your disk image, and then select a location to save it in. (For more on using Save dialogs, see Chapter 13.) You'll probably want to save it in your Documents folder or somewhere else in your home folder.

4. Select a size from the Size pop-up menu. By default, this displays 40MB. If you want to protect a lot of files, calculate how much space they will take up, and then add about 25 percent to make sure that you can add other files. If you only have a few files to protect, select a smaller size, such as 5MB. If you think you'll be adding many files to this disk, plan accordingly and choose a larger size.

5. Click the Encryption pop-up menu and select AES-128.

6. Leave the format as Read/Write Disk Image, so you can add files to it later.

7. When you've made all these selections, click Create.

8. A dialog displays asking you to enter a password for this disk image. Enter a password, and then enter it again in the Verify field. If you want to add it to your keychain, check Remember Password (Add To Keychain). (I'll talk about the keychain later in the "Work with Keychains" section of this chapter.)

9. Click OK to record this password.

10. Disk Utility creates your encrypted disk image and then mounts it on the Desktop. (See Figure 17-2.)

To add files to the disk image, just copy them into the mounted disk image, the icon on the right in Figure 17-2. This works like a virtual disk; you can double-click this icon to display its contents, add files to it, and remove files by dragging them to the Trash. When you're finished adding files to the disk image, drag it to the Trash (or click it and select File | Eject) to eject it. (Make sure not to drag the disk image file to the Trash. This is the file with the .dmg extension.)

My Files.dmg   My Files

FIGURE 17-2   A disk image file, at the left, and its disk image mounted on the Desktop

When you want to access your files, double-click the disk image file to mount the encrypted disk image. If you chose to add your password to your keychain, you may not need to enter your password; if you've already entered your keychain password in the current session, your keychain will be unlocked. If not, you'll be prompted to enter your password to access the disk image's files.

As long as your files remain inside this disk image, they are encrypted, but if you copy them to another location on your Mac, the encryption is removed. You can delete any of the files in the disk image by dragging them to the Trash and then emptying it.

Delete Your Files Securely

When you place files into the Trash and then empty the Trash, your files are not actually deleted. This may surprise you, but what actually happens is the operating system merely deletes pointers to the files in your hard disk's directory, a catalog file that records the locations of individual files.

For this reason, disk recovery software (see Chapter 19) can sometimes recover files that you have accidentally deleted or that have been lost to hard disk corruption. The files remain on the disk, but Mac OS X can't find them.

Sometimes, however, you want to *really* delete your files, erasing them in such a way that no one can get them back. This may be the case for sensitive files, but you may also want to securely delete files on a hard disk you are going to remove or on a Mac you are going to sell or give away.

To securely delete files in the Trash, select Finder | Secure Empty Trash. An alert displays asking if you're sure you want to do this; after all, you won't be able to recover these files in any way. If you're sure, click OK. This writes zeros over the files' locations on your hard disk, instead of just deleting their directory records. However, since most applications rewrite files each time they save them, this only really deletes the latest versions of the files; it's entirely possible that there are dozens of older versions of the files on your disk.

17

TIP

You can also permanently delete the free space on your hard disk using Disk Utility, which you saw earlier in this chapter in the section "Work with an Encrypted Disk Image." Open Disk Utility, select your hard disk, click the Erase tab, and then click Erase Free Space. Choose one of the three methods available for erasing your hard disk's free space. See the next section, "Reformat Your Hard Disk Securely," for more on these erasing options.

Reformat Your Hard Disk Securely

The only way to fully delete the files on your hard disk, especially if you are changing your disk, or selling or giving away your Mac, is to reformat your hard disk. Yet, again, simple formatting is not enough; you must totally erase the disk when you reformat it.

To do this, you'll need to restart from a Mac OS X Install disc or from a different hard disk (such as a second internal hard disk or an external disk). In the first case, insert the installation disc, and then double-click the Install Mac OS X icon; you can also insert the disc and restart your Mac while holding down the C key on your keyboard. Then select Installer | Open Disk Utility to access Disk Utility. (If you are working from a second hard disk, just launch Disk Utility from this disk.)

Select your hard disk in the disk list at the left of the window, and then click the Erase tab. Click the Security Options button to display Erase Options:

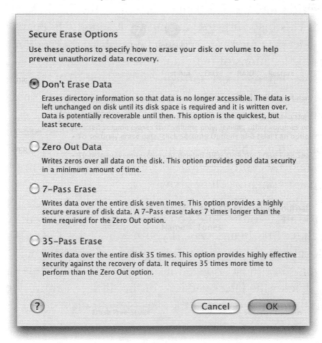

You can choose from two options. If you choose Zero Out Data, Disk Utility writes zeros to all the disk's sectors. If you choose 7-Pass Erase, Disk Utility reformats the disk writing random data seven times. And if you choose 35-Pass Erase, Disk Utility writes data 35 times on your disk. Either of these choices greatly increases the time it takes to reformat your disk, but they are the only way to truly delete all the remnants of your files. If you choose the 35-Pass Erase, this will take a very long time. . .

Work with Keychains

Keychains record passwords you use for applications, network servers, or web sites, and they store these passwords globally in a single, strongly encrypted file. The advantage of using keychains is that you can record your individual passwords and access them with a single keychain password. The advantage of this is that you only need to remember one password—your keychain password—instead of dozens of individual passwords.

You'll see a check box in a password dialog whenever you can add a password to your keychain. Check this to add the password to your keychain so you won't have to enter it again.

The preceding illustration shows this in a dialog, but you'll also see this in many e-mail programs, where you can choose to record your e-mail account password in the keychain, and in some programs' preferences if passwords are required.

When you create an account, an initial keychain, called *login*, is created for you. Unless you create additional keychains, all your passwords will be added to this one. This keychain uses your login password; you can change the password—but in that case, you'll have to enter the keychain password the first time, in each session, when an application requests information from the keychain.

17

Changing the keychain password makes your Mac a bit more secure since, if you use automatic login, your keychain is automatically unlocked if it has the same password. Also, while an administrator may need to know your login password, you can have a different keychain password that you don't need to share.

To do this, open Keychain Access, which is in the Utilities folder in the Applications folder.

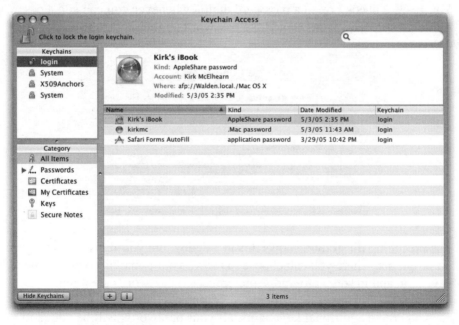

If your keychain is locked, click the lock icon, and then enter your password to unlock it. Next, select Edit | Change Password For Keychain "login". (If your keychain has a different name, this name will appear in quotes.) Enter your password in the first dialog, enter it again in the second dialog, and enter the new password twice. Click OK to change the password.

Store Sensitive Data in Keychain Notes

Your keychain can hold more than just passwords. A useful feature available in Keychain Access is its Note feature. If you select File | New Secure Note Item, you can add a secure note to your keychain.

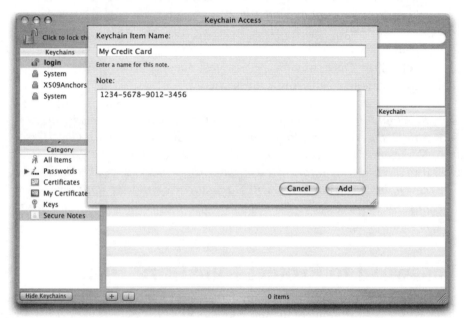

Enter a name for your note, enter the text you want to add, and click the Add button. Only you can read this note after entering your keychain password. When you add a note, it displays in the list of items in the keychain window. Click that item, and then check Show Note to see its contents. You can copy the contents of the note by clicking Copy Note To Clipboard.

Even if your keychain is unlocked, you'll need to enter your password to access the contents of the note.

NOTE

You'll see the preceding dialog on many occasions, whenever you need to enter your keychain password to allow a specific application, server, or web site to access your password. You always have the same three options: Deny, Allow Once, and Always Allow. However, you'll find that Always Allow doesn't always stick, and you'll occasionally find places where you need to enter your password no matter how many times you click Always Allow.

Enter your password in this dialog or click Deny. If you enter your password, you can click Allow Once, to view the note just once, or Always Allow, to view the note again without re-entering your password.

NOTE

Keychain also stores passwords you enter in web site forms if you use Safari. Select Safari | Preferences, and then click AutoFill. Check User Names and Passwords to turn this on. When you enter a user name and a password, Safari will ask you if you want to store this data in the keychain. If you do, Safari will automatically enter the data for you the next time you return to the web page. If you haven't yet unlocked your keychain, Safari will ask you to do so.

Set a Password to Protect Your Hard Disk

As you've seen throughout this book and when working with Mac OS X, you need a password for your user account, and you also need passwords to access certain services or web sites. Password protection is at the heart of computer security, but one thing that's not protected, by default, is your hard disk.

In Chapter 18, I tell you how to start up your Mac in FireWire target mode. This lets you connect your Mac to another Mac and start it up as if it were an external hard disk. If the other Mac is using Mac OS X, permissions are respected, but if it's running Mac OS 9, the other Mac can access any of your files. The same is true if anyone starts up your Mac from an installation CD or from some disk repair CDs—anyone can access your files since your hard disk is not password-protected.

Apple offers a utility called Open Firmware Password that allows you to provide more solid protection. You can download this free program here: http://www.apple.com/support/downloads/openfirmwarepassword.html. Open Firmware Password is a simple program; it sets a password in the boot software of your computer, and no one can do *anything* with your computer without this password. Other users cannot change your startup disk (which you set in the Startup Disk preference pane), nor can they start up your Mac from an external FireWire disk, a CD-ROM, or another partition or disk in your Mac.

To set this password, download Open Firmware Password from the preceding URL, and then follow its instructions. Make sure you don't lose this password; you'll need it if you want to make any changes or start your Mac up from a different disk.

Protect Your Mac from Network Intrusions

So far in this chapter, I've been talking about controlling physical access to your Mac—about keeping unwanted people from accessing your files by sitting down in front of your Mac and opening your files and folders. This section is about the other main security problems that affect computers: intruders, vandals, and hackers attacking your Mac over a network, either to disable it or to get copies of your files.

Unless you work for the CIA or the FBI, your files don't interest that many people. Or do they? As surprising as it seems, industrial espionage is very common, and you may have competitors or even coworkers who would be interested in seeing some of your files. Some people might want to steal your *identity,* or personal information, so they can masquerade as you and use your credit card or other personal information for financial gain. Also, hackers may want to use your Mac as a *relay* to attack other computers. Finally, some hackers are just malicious and get a kick out of doing damage to other people's computers.

If you have a permanent connection to the Internet—a cable or DSL connection or other "always-on" connection—you should protect your Mac with a firewall application. This type of software keeps hackers out of your Mac and protects you from damaging attacks.

Your Mac comes with a built-in firewall, which is limited but efficient. Open the Sharing preference pane in the System Preferences and click the Firewall tab to access it. (See Figure 17-3.)

This firewall lets you block incoming traffic to all services other than the ones you enable. To activate this firewall, just click the Start button. Incoming network traffic to any services other than those you have turned on in the Services tab of this preference pane will be blocked. This is good protection, but it does not keep you safe from all kinds of hacker attacks.

You can start protecting yourself by not turning on any unneeded network services. I talk about sharing and network services in Chapter 12. If you don't

17

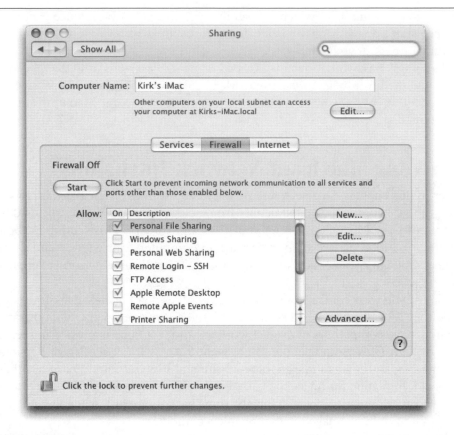

FIGURE 17-3 The Firewall tab of the Sharing preference pane lets you access the Mac OS X built-in firewall.

need to share files at all, don't turn any of these services on. See Chapter 12 for an explanation of each of them.

In addition to the Mac OS X built-in firewall, several third-party programs offer additional protection. Beyond simply blocking network traffic, these programs can prevent many kinds of attacks and intrusions, let you set your own firewall rules, and offer monitoring functions as well.

The two main third-party firewall programs for Mac are Intego NetBarrier X3 (www.intego.com) and Norton Personal Firewall (www.symantec.com). Both these programs offer protection against the main types of attacks, but NetBarrier goes further, offering more than just firewall protection.

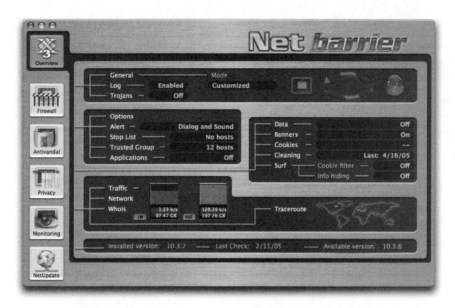

No matter which firewall you choose—whether you use the Mac OS X built-in firewall or a third-party product—remember that this type of application is only useful if it is correctly configured. If you configure it incorrectly, you may open your Mac up to possible intrusions, but you may also make it more difficult for you to use the Internet or another network.

Protect Your Mac from Viruses

If you're used to working with Windows, you're also used to worrying about viruses. Viruses are a different story on the Mac. Not only are there very few viruses for the Mac, but since Mac OS X is based on a Unix operating system, viruses can only affect files the current user has the right to change. You don't have to worry about viruses or worms like I Love You, Melissa, or Klez. When the evening news talks about the latest virus spreading across the Internet, you can feel safe and secure. This said, the virus threat is real, and while you have a much smaller chance of catching a virus on your Mac, that chance still exists.

The most common kind of viruses seen on the Mac are macro viruses that affect Microsoft Word or Excel. While you can protect yourself from these viruses by turning off macros in Word and Excel (see the programs' online help for instructions on how to do this), you may need to use the macros contained in a file you receive,

17

exposing yourself to risk. If you ever do receive files with macros, check with your correspondents to make sure they added the macros. They might not even be aware that they are infected.

There are several antivirus programs available for Mac OS X. Intego VirusBarrier X3 (www.intego.com) and Norton Antivirus (www.symantec.com) can both catch and kill all known viruses on the Mac, including those insidious macro viruses. Think about protecting yourself, even if the risk is limited; the day a serious virus hits Mac OS X, you'll be happy you did.

Chapter 18

Use Peripherals to Extend Your Mac

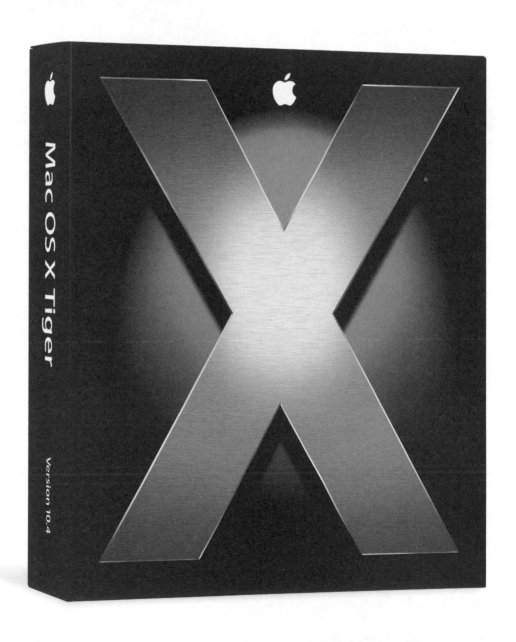

How to...

- Learn about all the connectors and plugs on your Mac
- Use different mice and keyboards with your Mac
- Use external hard disks
- Work with removable media

When Apple introduced the first iMac in 1998, the company heralded two revolutions that have since changed the personal computer industry. The first was the death of the floppy disk. Apple realized that the floppy disk was becoming useless, since files were increasing in size as users added graphics and other multimedia content to them. Try putting any digital music file more than a minute long (at decent quality) on a floppy disk and you'll see what I mean. Other PC manufacturers have since decided to abandon the floppy disk; it only took the PC industry five years to realize that Apple was right.

The second revolution was the introduction of USB as a standard interface for connecting peripherals. Apple certainly didn't invent USB, nor were they the first to offer it on computers, but they were the first to offer working support for USB devices. It took Microsoft until Windows 98 Second Edition to provide the same level of functionality.

Before Apple added USB to its computers, you couldn't find more than a handful of peripherals that connected using this system. After the introduction of the iMac, hardware makers began developing more devices that used USB, and this is now the industry standard for connecting hardware devices to personal computers.

Since all Macs include USB, as well as FireWire and other means of connecting peripherals, you have a wide choice of hardware you can connect to your Mac. In addition, you may be able to use peripherals designed to work on Windows PCs. In this chapter, I'll talk about the different hardware devices you can use, from mice (with two or more buttons!) to keyboards, and from scanners to hard drives. You'll see just how much you can connect to your Mac, and how much you can extend its functions and features. And if you're a gadget freak, you'll see that you can fulfill your desire with dozens of interesting peripherals for your Mac.

How to Connect Peripherals to Your Mac

There are many ways you can connect hardware devices to your Mac. Here's a brief overview of the different types of connectors available on new and recent Macs (see Figure 18-1):

■ **USB**   Universal Serial Bus is a technology that allows many types of devices to interface with computers. You can connect your mouse and keyboard via a USB port, but you can also connect hard drives, CD/DVD drives, and other storage devices, digital cameras, music players such as iPods, and more. You can connect up to 127 USB devices via a single port using hubs. USB is the most versatile way of connecting hardware devices to your Mac, but it's not the fastest; limited to 12 Mbps, it wasn't designed for high data throughput devices. For this reason, storage devices, such as hard drives or CD/DVD drives, cannot work at their maximal speeds. USB 2.0 is a much faster version of this technology that allows data transfer rates of up to 480 Mbps, making it possible to fully exploit storage devices. As of press time, most new Macs include USB 2.0 ports, and these are backward compatible with the older USB specifications, so you can use any USB device on your Mac.

NOTE   *While you can physically connect any USB device to your Mac, in many cases you need drivers, or special software that allows Mac OS X to communicate with the device. The same is true for some other types of hardware devices as well. Your Mac can generally work with any storage devices without requiring special software, but some input devices need their own drivers to function correctly. Other devices work without drivers, but offer additional features with them.*

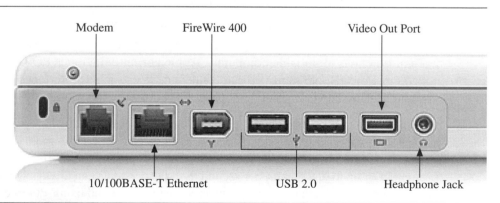

FIGURE 18-1   These are the ports and connectors available on an iBook as of mid 2005.

18

■ **FireWire**   The FireWire standard, which Apple invented in the 1990s, is also known by the more prosaic name, IEEE 1394. This is a high-speed data transfer protocol that is used for external hard drives, CD/DVD drives, and digital video devices, such as video cameras. You can connect up to 63 devices to a FireWire port, either through hubs or by daisy-chaining them. While the original FireWire 400 standard has been surpassed by USB 2.0 (which offers slightly faster throughput), a new FireWire 800 standard is now available. Many new Macs include FireWire 800 ports, but these are not compatible with FireWire 400 devices, which use a different type of plug. For this reason, current Macs offering FireWire 800 also have a FireWire 400 port.

■ **SCSI**   Long the dominant standard for connecting hard disks, scanners, and other devices that require high data throughput, SCSI (Small Computer System Interface) has lost ground to USB and FireWire in recent years. Several SCSI standards exist, with different data throughput speeds, but FireWire is easier to use and allows you to connect more devices in a chain. You can buy a SCSI card for any Mac that has PCI connectors (see the following), and you can use this with older devices; some high-end scanners still use a fast version of SCSI, but FireWire is the way of the future.

■ **PCI**   The PCI (Peripheral Component Interconnect) system uses *slots* or special connectors inside a computer to add cards that extend the functionality of the computer. Apple's tower models all include PCI slots, and you can use these to add special sound, video, or data transfer connectors. PCI is a versatile technology that is widely used on PCs to add functions (for example, many PCs do not come with FireWire ports, but you can add a PCI card that has one or several such connectors). You can use PCI cards to add internal devices, such as extra hard disks, or even to add processor upgrade cards to older Macs.

■ **PC-Card**   Once called PCMCIA (Personal Computer Memory Card International Association) cards, PC-Cards are credit card–sized devices that add functions to portable computers. Apple currently includes PC-Card slots on its PowerBooks, and you can connect devices such as interfaces and adapters for networks, mobile phones, GPS devices, and more.

■ **Ethernet**   This is the standard for networking, and all Macs made in recent years include Ethernet ports. Ethernet comes in a variety of speeds, and many new Macs include Gigabit Ethernet (or 1000Base-T) ports, which offer data throughput of up to one gigabit per second, but these models can always work with slower devices on a network. I talk about networking and using Ethernet in Chapter 12.

- **AirPort**   All Macs currently sold include an AirPort card or connector, but you'll never see these. Hidden inside your Mac is an AirPort card, or a slot where you can add one, which lets your Mac use wireless networking. Some Mac models, such as the G5 tower models available at press time, include a connector for an external AirPort antenna. This antenna is built into such models as iMacs and portable Macs. (I talk about wireless networking in Chapter 12.)

- **Bluetooth**   Like AirPort, Bluetooth is a wireless technology. Designed to interface with devices whose data transfer requirements are limited, and which are not far from your computer, Bluetooth lets you use such devices as wireless keyboards and mice, or allows you to connect to PDAs and cell phones and print to Bluetooth-capable printers. Some Mac models feature an internal Bluetooth module, and you can use a USB Bluetooth adapter on others.

- **Modem**   Most Macs sold today include built-in modems (and you can add them to some build-to-order models purchased from the Apple Store if the Mac you want doesn't come with one); you simply connect the modem port to your phone jack using a phone cable. You use your modem to connect to the Internet, send faxes, or connect to some remote networks with your modem port.

- **Video ports**   All Macs include at least one type of video port. For some Macs, this offers video mirroring (projecting the same image on an external monitor), and for others, this allows you to connect an external monitor to extend your display. Depending on your Mac, you'll have one of several types of video ports. Some current models, such as the eMac or iBook, have a mini-VGA port, which, when used with an adapter, can connect to standard VGA monitors. The Mac mini has a DVI port and also includes a DVI-VGA adapter. PowerBooks include a DVI (digital video interface) or mini-DVI port. Some models also have S-Video, which you can connect to a TV or video projector. DVI is a digital technology, designed to interface with digital monitors, such as LCD screens. If you want to connect your Mac to a VGA monitor, you need an adapter. Some Macs have ADC (Apple display connector) ports, which connect directly to Apple monitors but can also connect to VGA monitors using an adapter.

- **Audio ports**   All Macs have at least a headphone jack that you can use for headphones or external speakers, and some Macs include a separate speaker jack. In addition, some models, such as all portable Macs, the iMac, and the eMac, include built-in speakers. However, some Mac models do not offer any audio input (or line in) jacks. For these models, you can use

18

USB devices. Apple's current G5 tower models also include optical audio input and output (see Figure 18-2). This allows you to work directly with digital audio via special ports, using optical (fiber optic) cables. FireWire and PCI-based audio input devices are also available.

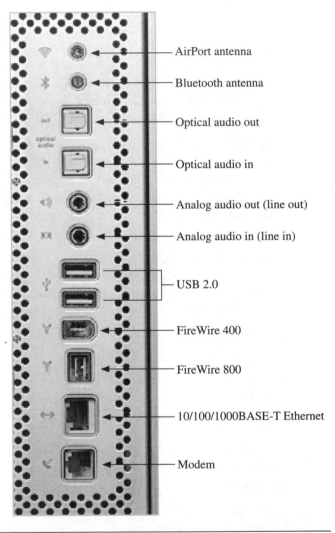

AirPort antenna

Bluetooth antenna

Optical audio out

Optical audio in

Analog audio out (line out)

Analog audio in (line in)

USB 2.0

FireWire 400

FireWire 800

10/100/1000BASE-T Ethernet

Modem

FIGURE 18-2 Apple's G5 tower models include a wide array of input and output ports and connectors.

Use Different Input Devices

Since your Mac has one or more USB ports, you can use various kinds of *input devices*. An input device is something that lets you send data to your computer or control it. This includes keyboards and mice, but also trackpads and trackballs, graphics tablets, and more.

Let's face it: there's one thing wrong with the Mac, and that's its one-button mouse. While you can use the CONTROL key and click to access contextual menus, Apple's mice just don't do the trick. Many Mac users get by with the standard mouse provided with their Mac, but lots more can't stand it. Not only is that second button missing, but Apple mice don't have scroll wheels. So the first thing you'll probably want to buy for your Mac is a replacement mouse.

Just about every mouse you can buy will work on your Mac, as long as it connects to the USB port. While many mice come with special drivers to program certain actions, a standard two-button mouse works fine on your Mac, and the right button does what you expect. Mac OS X supports scroll wheels as well. I use a generic two-button mouse with a scroll wheel on one of my Macs, and it works perfectly.

Many vendors sell mice, ranging from the basic two-button mouse to more complex devices with multiple buttons, scroll wheels, and more. Let me suggest two manufacturers who not only make quality hardware but also provide versatile drivers for the Mac: Kensington (www.kensington.com) and Logitech (www.logitech.com). I especially like the Kensington Expert Mouse, which is a large trackball with four programmable buttons and a scroll ring. While it may look strange and is very large, you get used to it quickly, and it is easier on your arm, since you don't have to keep moving your hand from side to side.

Scroll wheels are great things once you get used to them. You can use them to scroll pages in your web browser, your word processor, or just about any other application that has scrolling windows. They are especially useful if you edit digital video and want to go forward and back a few frames at a time. If you don't have a scroll wheel on your mouse, you might want to look at one of the following devices, which give you a great deal of control over scrolling: Griffin's PowerMate (www.griffintechnology.com) and Contour Design's ShuttleXpress (www.contourdesign.com). The PowerMate is a cool device that looks like a volume control from a stereo amplifier (see Figure 18-3). It turns, so you can scroll, and you can press the button to perform preset actions. The ShuttleXpress is similar but has both jog and shuttle wheels, as well as five programmable buttons. You can set different actions for individual applications with both of these devices. I've found them invaluable, providing both excellent scrolling functions and quick ways of performing common actions, and I use them in addition to mice or trackballs. If you use an iBook or PowerBook, one of these devices can give you scrolling functions that your portable does not offer.

18

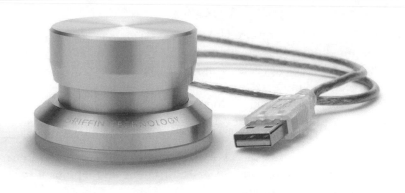

FIGURE 18-3   The Griffin PowerMate: nothing but a button that turns and clicks, but it is immensely flexible.

Mac keyboards are generally very good, but if you type a lot, you may want to look at some alternatives. All USB keyboards work on the Mac, so you have a fair amount of choice. The problem is that some keyboards send different modifier keys to the Mac; the OPTION and COMMAND keys are switched around. If the keyboard has a driver for the Mac, this will solve the problem. Kensington and Logitech, which I mentioned earlier, make keyboards as well as mice. I have long been a fan of Microsoft's Natural Keyboard family of ergonomic keyboards (www.microsoft.com). The latest models come with additional USB ports—making it easy to plug even more devices into your Mac—and Microsoft provides an excellent driver for their keyboard.

TIP   *If you use an iBook or PowerBook, you're probably used to working on its built-in keyboard and trackpad. This is great when you're on the road, but if you're planning to use a portable at home or at the office for a long time, think about getting an external mouse and keyboard. It makes it easier to work with a portable, and it lets you move the iBook or PowerBook away from you for a more ergonomic working position. You can also get a stand for your portable, such as the Griffin iCurve (www.griffintechnology.com), which raises your portable to eye-level, protecting your posture, and keeps it from overheating by allowing air to pass below it.*

If you type a lot, you owe it to yourself to use an ergonomic keyboard, which may prevent repetitive stress injury. There are other types of ergonomic keyboards, and one of the most interesting is the Kinesis Contoured keyboard (www.kinesis-ergo.com). While it looks strange, it is probably the most comfortable keyboard you can find.

Wireless Input Devices

While Apple released their own wireless mouse and keyboard in 2003, other vendors have been offering these devices for several years. Wireless input devices give you more freedom of movement and get rid of some of those cables that get tangled on your desk.

Some wireless devices, such as Apple's, use Bluetooth technology, which requires that you either have a built-in Bluetooth module in your Mac or connect a USB Bluetooth adapter. Other input devices use a different type of radio frequency technology and have their own receivers. In both cases, however, the main drawback is batteries. If you use wireless input devices, think of getting rechargeable batteries. Not only does it save you money, but it's better for the

You Can Get a USB Hub to Use More Peripherals

If you start using different peripherals for your Mac, you'll soon find that you run out of USB ports. Keyboards, mice, and other input devices connect via USB. If you have a digital camera or a Palm PDA, for example, they too connect via USB, and most printers and scanners use USB connections as well. It's possible to unplug the devices you're not using and then plug them in when needed, but it's a headache.

Think of buying a USB hub, which is a device that plugs into one USB port and provides additional ports. Most USB hubs have four ports, though you can buy some with more and others with fewer ports.

There are two types of USB hubs: bus-powered hubs, which get the power they need to function from the USB port they are connected to, and self-powered hubs, which have AC adapters. Some USB devices need more power to function than what is available from a bus-powered hub. If you have an iPod that you want to charge from your Mac's USB hub, you'll need a powered hub.

Beware of buying the cheapest USB hubs, however. Mac OS X doesn't always like them, and many problems affecting the operating system have been solved by unplugging USB devices.

18

environment; you won't be throwing away old batteries. However, you'll need to change them more often than alkaline batteries. Some wireless input devices come with docking stations that charge the device, so you won't need batteries for those.

Use External Disk Drives

Okay, the floppy disk is dead, but what if you have PC-using colleagues who haven't found out yet? What if you have years of archives on old floppy disks? You can still use an external floppy disk drive that connects to your Mac by USB if you have no other way of moving files. Several vendors make these, including Imation (www.imation.com), Iomega (www.iomega.com), and LaCie (www.lacie.com). Your Mac can even read floppy disks formatted on a PC, and you can copy files to these disks to share with Windows users.

A much better solution is to use an Iomega Zip drive (www.iomega.com). These devices, which use disks with a capacity of 100, 250, or 750 megabytes, are easy to use on a Mac, since the drivers are built into Mac OS X. And if you want to transfer files to Windows computers, you can do that easily as well, as long as you use PC-formatted Zip disks. Your Mac can read these, but Windows computers can't read the disks if they're formatted for the Mac. Some desktop Macs come with internal Zip drives, and you can buy external USB models. Just insert a cartridge and it mounts on your desktop. Iomega also has other drives with removable cartridges, such as the REV, which holds 35GB on each cartridge.

To go even further, when you need external storage, think of getting either a FireWire or USB 2.0 hard drive. All Macs sold in the past few years include FireWire connectors, and recent Macs include USB 2.0. You can plug a FireWire hard drive into your Mac and back up your files easily. Hard disks have become very cheap, and you can get a relatively large disk for backing up your files for a reasonable price. Get a hard disk that's bigger than your internal hard disk, and make sure you eject it when you are finished working with it, before turning it off. To do this, click the Eject button in a Finder window sidebar, or drag the disk's icon to the Trash.

Other Types of Storage Devices

USB key drives are very cool devices, and they are a great way to store and transfer files. These tiny devices, usually with from 256MB to 512MB of memory, are the size of a keychain, and plug into your USB port. They mount as external disks, allowing you to copy files to and from them. They're a great way to carry files between home and the office, or to make backups of your work. You can also buy an iPod shuffle, which you can use for both music playback and file storage. With sizes of 512MB or 1GB, you can put a lot of files on the shuffle.

Connect a Mac via FireWire Target Mode

Macs with FireWire ports allow you to connect them with a FireWire cable, using one of them as if it were an external hard disk in *target mode*. This lets the Mac running in target mode mount on the other Mac, making it easy to transfer files quickly without needing to be connected over a network. Here's how you connect two Macs in this way:

1. Shut down the computer that you want to mount as an external hard disk.

2. Connect the two Macs with a FireWire cable. You must connect them both to the same type of port; if only one Mac has a FireWire 800 port, you'll need to use the FireWire 400 port.

3. Start up the target computer while holding down the T key. When it starts up, you'll see a FireWire icon moving across the screen like a screen saver. This Mac's hard disk will mount on the other Mac's Desktop, or in the Finder window sidebar. You can now access any files that you have permission to access on the target Mac's hard disk. (Note: If you mount an OS X Mac in target mode, permissions are ignored.)

4. When you're finished, eject the FireWire hard disk by clicking the Eject icon in the Finder window sidebar, or by dragging the FireWire disk icon from the Desktop to the Trash.

5. Shut down the target Mac and unplug the cables. You can now start up the target Mac normally.

These drives have no moving parts: they use *flash memory,* a special type of memory that can be overwritten easily. In addition to these key drives, flash memory is used in memory cards that you may be familiar with if you have a digital camera or a PDA.

You can use any kind of flash memory card as a storage device on your Mac as long as you have something to read it with. You can buy memory card readers for specific types of memory cards, or universal readers that can handle most or all types of cards.

18

Use a Scanner

Most scanners available today plug into your USB port. Many scanners are available with Mac drivers, and some of them are self-powered, which means you can just plug them into your Mac's USB port without needing a power cable or transformer. You should make sure that the manufacturer offers Mac drivers for the scanner you want to buy. If so, just plug it into your Mac's USB port and install the drivers.

Many scanners use TWAIN drivers; TWAIN is a protocol used for imaging devices. If your scanner offers a TWAIN-compatible driver, you'll be able to use it with applications such as Photoshop or Photoshop Elements, importing images directly into those applications.

If you have an older scanner, or one for which there are no Mac drivers, there is another solution: VueScan, available from Hamrick Software (www.hamrick.com), is compatible with an extraordinary number of scanners. If you already have a scanner, and the manufacturer does not provide a driver for your Mac, check out this software to see if it supports your scanner.

High-end scanners use SCSI or FireWire interfaces. If you get a FireWire scanner, you'll have no problem plugging it into your Mac. For SCSI (Small Computer System Interface) scanners, you'll need a SCSI card, and you can only use these on Apple's desktop models with PCI slots. (You can buy a USB-SCSI adapter, but the throughput is limited to that available via the USB port, meaning that your scanner will not be able to work at its optimal speed. This is a good solution if you want to use an old scanner, but in many cases you can buy a new one for the cost of such an adapter.)

Other Peripherals

There are dozens of other peripherals available for your Mac, and if you're a gadget freak, you'll certainly find plenty to entice you. I've mentioned earlier in this chapter most of the common devices you'll want to consider buying, but here are a few more. You may not need them as much, but they will provide interesting functions.

Monitors

No computer is complete without a monitor. While many Mac models—the eMac, iMac, iBook, and PowerBook—include built-in monitors, you still may want to get an external monitor. This is especially useful if you have a 12-inch portable and need to use it at home or in the office for extended periods. Getting a bigger monitor makes it easier to work and lets you see much more on your screen.

You can use standard VGA monitors with all Macs, either directly by plugging them into the VGA ports, or with an adapter. Some Macs require special connectors, such as ADC or DVI connectors; you can get adapters that let you use different monitors with these Macs.

The ultimate monitor these days is Apple's 30-inch LCD cinema display, which will overwhelm you with its size and quality. This quality is not cheap, but you certainly get what you pay for. (Note that you need a special video card to drive this monitor.) Other Apple monitors, all flat screens, currently include 20-inch and 23-inch models. But you can buy monitors from other vendors, and you should certainly shop around.

If your Mac lets you use two monitors side by side, adding a monitor to a portable or a Mac with a built-in monitor extends your desktop and gives you two screens to work on. You can have, for example, your web browser on one screen and your word processor on another, or your graphic design program on one screen and all its palettes and toolbars on the other. You'll need more desk space, but you'll certainly be more productive.

If you work with both a Mac and a PC, you'll find that some monitors have two input plugs, so you can connect both computers to it and change easily with a front-mounted switch. Also, many monitors come with USB plugs built in. This is the case with a Sony monitor I have: it has four USB plugs, allowing me to use it as a USB hub.

Video Devices

Apple's iSight is the most impressive video device you can get for your Mac. Together with iChat, you can use the iSight to carry out videoconferences with friends, family, or colleagues. Amazingly easy to use—just plug it into a FireWire port—the iSight is a model of design and functionality. It's small, light, and efficient, and with its built-in mike, you don't need anything else to use iChat's video chat function.

Other webcams are available, some that connect via USB and others via FireWire. Make sure that any such device you purchase has drivers for your Mac.

If you want to record video from your TV, the EyeTV digital video recorder (www.elgato.com) lets you use your Mac to record TV shows, which you can later archive on CD or DVD, or watch on your TV whenever you want. Several other vendors make similar devices.

Audio Devices

There are lots of audio devices you can get to improve the way your Mac works with sound. You can get many types of external speakers, some that connect to the headphone or speaker jack, and others that connect via USB. You can also get noise-canceling headsets, including headsets with microphones that are great for audio chats with iChat.

18

Gaming Devices

If you play games on your Mac, you'll want to get a joystick, gamepad, or perhaps a force-feedback steering wheel. While Mac OS X supports many game devices without drivers, some that don't come with Mac drivers may not work correctly. There's a solution to this, though: a shareware program called USB Overdrive (www.usboverdrive.com) supports just about any mouse, trackball, joystick, or gamepad.

Chapter 19

Keep Your Mac in Tip-Top Shape

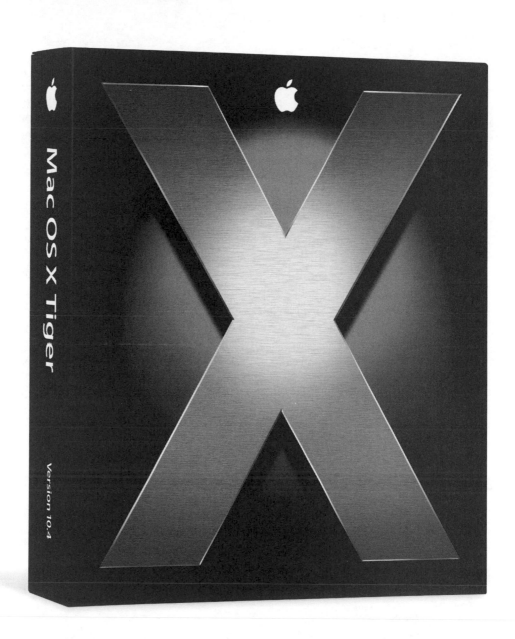

How to...

- Keep Mac OS X and your applications up-to-date
- Use Disk Utility
- Choose disk maintenance software
- Back up your files

A computer is like a car—it needs to be maintained to run smoothly. You change the oil in your car, check your tire pressure, and refill its fluids regularly, and to make sure your computer works correctly, you need to do similar actions. Fortunately, Mac OS X is built on a proven Unix foundation, providing the most stable operating system available in a personal computer. Nevertheless, both software and hardware glitches can occur, causing problems with your Mac.

There are two ways to maintain your Mac: the first is to make sure your operating system is always up-to-date. Apple regularly issues updates and bug fixes for Mac OS X and its applications, and it's easy to do this: the operating system has a built-in software update function that can check automatically, at regular intervals, to see if there are any new updates available.

The second thing you should do is to carry out certain maintenance routines, and make sure your data is backed up, just in case. There are several tools designed to check and repair problems with your hard disk, which is the most fragile component of your computer, and there are many programs that help you back up your files for protection.

In this chapter, I'll tell you how to update your software—both Mac OS X and your applications. I'll explain some of Apple's utility software included with Mac OS X, and I'll discuss the most common problems that may plague your hardware. I'll also tell you how to back up your files, just in case something happens and you lose data.

Make Sure Mac OS X Is Always Up-to-Date

When you buy a new Mac, it comes with the latest version of Mac OS X, the operating system that runs your computer. But as time goes by, the engineers and developers at Apple release updates to the system, which correct problems and add new features.

Mac OS X, like any operating system, is a work in progress. When Mac OS X 10.4, or Tiger, was released, thousands of users and developers had used it in *beta* or prerelease versions, submitting bug reports and feedback to Apple when they came across problems. While this squashed many of the bugs that were present—and there are *always* bugs, no matter how good a job programmers do—releasing an operating system to the public subjects it to more rigorous conditions. There's no way prerelease testing can cover the multitude of software and hardware combinations available, and bugs are always discovered, in many cases in the first few days. (In fact, the first update to Mac OS X 10.4 was released less than a month after Tiger reached the stores.)

Apple fixes its operating system and other software quickly when bugs are discovered, and the first update to Panther came shortly after its initial release. Whenever more bugs are resolved, Apple issues additional updates: some of these may be to specific parts of the operating system or to individual applications, while others are more general.

Ensuring that your Mac is always using the latest version of its operating system not only prevents problems, since each update includes corrections and enhancements, but also allows you to block any security threats that were discovered since your installation or last update. Apple sometimes issues *security updates* on their own to correct problems that can affect the security of your computer whenever new threats arise. Security is an issue on any operating system, but there are far fewer security holes found on Mac OS X—again, because of its industrial-strength Unix underpinnings—than on Windows. (I talk about securing your Mac in Chapter 17.)

These updates occur at a varying frequency, and your Mac comes with software to check for new updates and install them automatically. The Software Update application, which you control from the Software Update preference pane (see Figure 19-1), manages this process. (See Chapter 9 for more on opening and using the System Preferences application.)

The Software Update preference pane is set, by default, to check for updates once a week, and only when you have a network connection. If at the scheduled update time you are not connected to the Internet, the check will occur the next time you have a network connection. You can change this frequency to daily or monthly by selecting a frequency from the pop-up menu, but weekly is probably best.

If you don't want the Software Update preference pane to check for updates automatically, uncheck this option on this preference pane. You can still run manual checks at any time by clicking Check Now. If you disable automatic checking, you should still think of checking for updates regularly, say, at least once a month. In the first month after Apple released Panther, more than ten updates

19

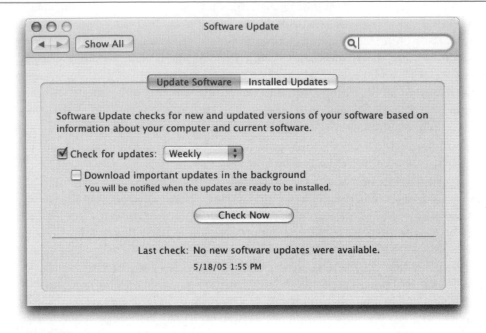

FIGURE 19-1   The Software Update preference pane controls automatic or manual
updates to Mac OS X.

were issued. Some of these updates were to the operating system itself, and others, to individual applications, including iSync, iTunes, and software for AirPort and the iPod. There were also two security updates in the first two weeks after Panther was released.

When Software Update finds new software, it comes to the front and displays a window showing the updates available (see Figure 19-2). This window asks you if you want to install the updates, and gives you information about them.

Any new essential updates displayed in the Software Update window (see Figure 19-2) are checked automatically for download. (If updates are available to software that you may not need, such as updates for specific hardware like the iPod, AirPort, or Bluetooth, they are not checked by default.) If you don't want to update certain programs—say you don't have an iPod and don't need to update its software—uncheck them in the update list and install only those updates you need, or, if there are no other updates available, click Quit.

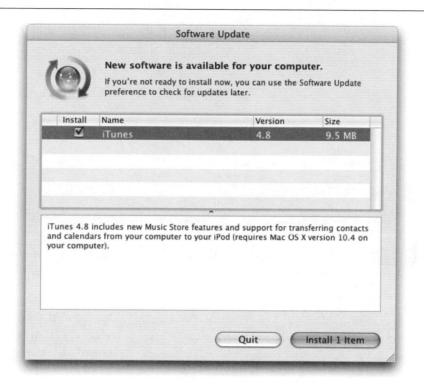

FIGURE 19-2   Software Update shows which updates are available. Click one of them to display information about the update at the bottom of a window.

To install software using Software Update, click the Install button. Software Update asks for your password: only users with an administrator account can make updates. If you don't have an administrator account, you need to enter an administrator's user name and password, or have your Mac's administrator take care of the updates.

After you enter an administrator password, Software Update handles everything. It downloads the update and installs it. The Software Update window (Figure 19-3) shows the progress of the download and installation.

When the download and installation process have completed, Software Update may tell you that you need to restart your Mac. You need to do this for system updates, and for updates to some applications. Make sure you have saved all your open files, and then click Restart in this dialog to restart your Mac.

19

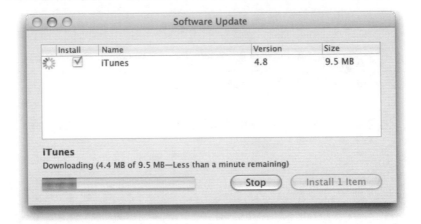

FIGURE 19-3   The Software Update window shows you the progress as downloading and installation occur.

NOTE   *Software Update lets you download and install minor updates. Major system upgrades (such as Tiger) must be purchased on DVD. Also, updates to some Apple applications are only available by download from Apple's web site.*

While the Mac OS X Software Update application is practical and easy to use, by default it only installs updates and does not save them. If you have more than one Mac and only want to download the updates once, or if you just want to save them in case you need to reinstall them later, there is a way to save updates if you want.

If you click the Update menu, you'll see four options:

■ **Ignore Update**   Select this to tell Software Update that you don't want to install this update, and that you don't want to be reminded later. You can select this for updates that you don't need: this could be AirPort software, which you don't need if you don't use wireless networking, or iPod software, which you only need if you have an iPod.

■ **Download Only**   This downloads a *package* file, a special file that works with the Mac OS X Installer application. If you select this, you are prompted for a location where the package will be saved. You can install the update by double-clicking this file and following the Installer's instructions. This is a good way to download updates for multiple Macs, or if you want to save the update, in case you need to reinstall it at another time.

■ **Install**   This does the same as clicking the Install button in the Software Update window. It installs the update immediately.

■ **Install and Keep Package**   This installs the update immediately and saves the package to use on other Macs or to use again if you need to. You are prompted for a location where the package file is saved.

If you've chosen Ignore Update for any updates and then realize that you need to install the software—if, for instance, you later buy an AirPort card or an iPod—you can reset your updates by selecting Software Update | Reset Ignored Updates. This resets any ignored updates and performs a check to see which updates are available.

NOTE   *You can check to see which updates have been installed by clicking the Installed Updates tab of the Software Update preference pane. This lists all the updates you've made to your Mac, showing the name, date, and version number of each update.*

Keep Your Applications Up-to-Date

While keeping your operating system up-to-date is the best way to keep your Mac running smoothly, you should also make sure your applications are up-to-date. Mac OS X system updates take care of the applications included with Mac OS X, but for other software updates, you need to check in many different places.

Some applications check automatically for updates when you use them. In most cases, you can turn this function on or off from the application's preferences. But for other applications, it's up to you to do the legwork—or the finger work—to find if updates are available. Updates to applications are useful for the same reasons that updates to Mac OS X are: they provide fixes to problems and offer new features. It is especially important to check for updates to an application if you have problems with it, since these updates may resolve your problems.

There are two ways to do this. The first is to check the vendors' web sites for the applications you use often. Most software companies have support or download pages that give links to updates, if they are available. The other way is to check web sites that list Macintosh software and tell you which is the latest version of a program. Two such sites are Mac Update (www.macupdate.com) and Version Tracker (www.versiontracker.com). They both contain information and links for thousands of programs, and you can check the version number of your application and compare it with the latest available version.

To find out the version of one of your applications, check the About window for the application. Just about every Mac application has a window like this. Select the Application menu (the one with the name of the application), and then select About *Application Name*. For example, when using AppleWorks, select AppleWorks | About AppleWorks. (See Figure 19-4.)

As you can see in Figure 19-4, the About AppleWorks window shows the application's version number in the text just before the copyright notice:

FIGURE 19-4   The About AppleWorks window shows its version number. Here, it is version 6.2.7.

Did you know?

About Disk Journaling

Since Mac OS X 10.3, Apple uses *journaling* by default when formatting hard disks. Journaling keeps a record of changes made to the directory, protecting against some types of corruption if you have a system crash or if you lose power. When this occurs, journaling allows your hard disk to recover its directory, as much as possible, and can prevent serious disk problems. Journaling is on by default when you format a new volume or partition, but if you upgraded from a previous Mac OS X or Mac OS 9 system, journaling won't be on. You can turn it on by using Disk Utility, which I talk about in the section "Work with Apple's Disk Utility" later in this chapter.

AppleWorks 6.2.7. When checking for updates, compare this version number with the one you find available on the vendor's web site, or an update web site. If the version you find on the Internet is later, download an update and install it.

Note that small updates are generally free. Updating AppleWorks 6.2 to version 6.2.4 is free, but updating to, say, version 7 (when this is released) may not be.

NOTE *When you install application updates, you may use the Apple Installer application, which you've seen when installing Mac OS X and other Apple software, or you may use one of various third-party installers. In some cases, you won't even need to run an installer; you may simply be able to copy a new version of an application from a disk image or compressed archive into your Applications folder.*

Maintenance for Your Mac

Computer maintenance covers many areas. I told you earlier how to keep your Mac up-to-date by regularly checking for system and application updates; that's one of the most important parts of maintaining your Mac. But proper maintenance goes beyond just ensuring that you have the latest versions of your software. While you can do little to check or repair your hardware, there is one item you need to keep an eye on: your hard disk.

The weakest hardware link in any computer is the hard disk, because this is where your data is written, stored, and read. While hard disks are very reliable and don't break down often, the way data is written to the disk can lead to problems.

A hard disk contains several magnetic *platters* and *heads.* The heads read and write to the platters, storing data in *blocks,* which are predetermined sectors on the hard disk. As data is written, the disk's driver—the software that controls the read-write process—updates a *directory,* or catalog, which keeps records of where each piece of data is stored. The main problem that can occur with hard disks is that the directory gets *corrupted,* or damaged, making it impossible to find some or all of your files.

Corruption can be minor, affecting just one or several files, or it can be more serious, affecting the integrity of the entire disk. Unfortunately, only in a perfect world would hard disk corruption not exist. If a program incorrectly writes data to the disk, crashes when doing so, or if you have a power interruption, corruption can occur. In the most serious cases, your Mac will not be able to restart, because it cannot read the system files it needs. In other cases, you might not be able to open certain files, and your applications may say that files are corrupted.

Each time you start up your Mac, the system runs a check on your hard disk. If any errors are found, and the built-in disk maintenance software can correct them, it does so. But sometimes disk corruption is more serious.

Fortunately, you can use disk maintenance software to check your disk, find out if there is corruption, and, in many cases, repair it. Several companies make such software for the Mac, and it comes either as programs designed only to repair disk problems or as part of larger packages that include other maintenance and security software. One such program is TechTool Deluxe, which is included in Apple's AppleCare package, an extended guarantee program that covers your Mac for three years. TechTool Deluxe, shown in Figure 19-5, performs a variety of maintenance tasks, from checking your hardware for problems to checking your hard disk for irregularities and correcting them if possible.

TechTool Deluxe goes further than many other maintenance programs by checking internal hardware, such as your processor, RAM, and USB system. If you do have hardware problems, it should find most of them. A similar tool, called TechTool Pro, is available on its own, without an AppleCare contract, from Micromat (www.micromat.com), which also makes another hard disk maintenance program, Drive 10.

One of the most popular and powerful disk repair tools is DiskWarrior, by Alsoft (www.alsoft.com). With a unique approach, DiskWarrior rebuilds a damaged directory. This is a tool to use when you have problems; it doesn't do anything but repair corrupted disks. It is very effective, and many Mac users have saved themselves from losing data with DiskWarrior.

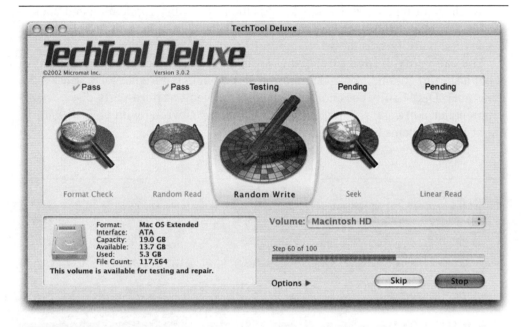

FIGURE 19-5 TechTool Deluxe checking a hard disk for problems

Another third-party application is Norton Utilities (www.symantec.com). This includes Norton Disk Doctor, which diagnoses and repairs many hard disk problems, and also contains Norton Speed Disk, which defragments your hard disk. This package contains other programs as well: Norton File Saver, Volume Recover, and UnErase all are powerful tools for protecting your hard disk and restoring its contents if you erase files by accident or have severe corruption.

It's a good idea to run one of these programs occasionally, just in case your hard disk has minor problems. All these programs can correct such problems before they become major problems, protecting you from serious corruption. Once a month is a good frequency to run hard disk checks.

Work with Apple's Disk Utility

Mac OS X includes an application called Disk Utility, which is located in the Utilities folder of your Applications folder. This program is not a full-fledged disk repair application, but it allows you to format and partition hard disks and to create and work with *disk images*. It also offers some verification and repair functions.

19

To check or repair your hard disk, open the Disk Utility application and click the First Aid tab. Click your hard disk in the left-hand column, or if your hard disk has several partitions, as shown in Figure 19-6, click one of the partitions.

You can verify the disk by clicking Verify Disk, and if the selected volume is not a startup volume, you can repair the disk by clicking Repair Disk. But remember, Disk Utility does not find as many problems as third-party disk maintenance software, so it might show that nothing is wrong with your disk, or it might find problems that it cannot repair.

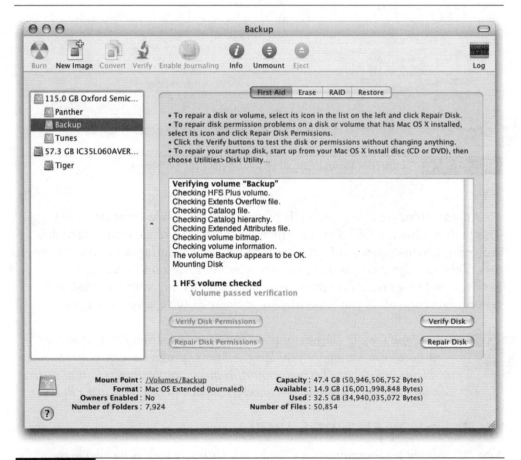

FIGURE 19-6   Disk Utility's First Aid tab, where you can perform some verifications and repairs

Repair Your Startup Disk

I mentioned earlier that Disk Utility can only repair a disk or partition that is not the startup disk. This is the case when you run Disk Utility from your startup disk, but there is a way to run the program to check and repair your startup disk if you have problems with it.

To do this, insert the first Mac OS X installation disc in your Mac, and then restart. Hold down the C key on your keyboard so your Mac starts up from the disc. This launches the Mac OS X Installer. (Don't worry; you're not going to reinstall your Mac. This is the only way you can get access to the copy of Disk Utility that's on the disc.)

Select Installer | Open Disk Utility to launch Disk Utility, and then follow the instructions I presented earlier to repair your startup disk. Since it's no longer your startup disk—the installation disc is—you can run repair operations on it.

Disk Utility can also repair disk permissions on your startup volume. Since Mac OS X is based on a Unix system, it uses permissions, or privileges, for all its files. If some of these permissions are incorrect, certain system functions may not work properly. It is a good idea to repair these permissions if you have problems, or repair them each time you make a major system update.

To do this, select your Mac OS X startup volume, then click Repair Disk Permissions to begin repair. This takes about 10 to 15 minutes, depending on your installation. Disk Utility displays corrected permissions in the window as it goes on, and when the repair procedure is finished, this window displays a message saying that permissions have been repaired.

Keep Tabs on Your Hard Disk

Note that Disk Utility can tell you the S.M.A.R.T. status of your hard disk, which can warn you if your disk is likely to have problems. S.M.A.R.T. is a technology, developed by IBM, that lets hard disks test themselves for potential problems. If you have problems with your Mac, it's a good idea to check this.

Open Disk Utility and click your hard disk at the top of the list. Look at the info section at the bottom of the Disk Utility window:

Disk Description : IC35L060AVER07-0   **Total Capacity** : 57.3 GB (61,492,838,400 Bytes)
Connection Bus : ATA   **Write Status** : Read/Write
Connection Type : Internal   **S.M.A.R.T. Status** : Verified
Connection ID : Device 0

If the S.M.A.R.T. Status is Verified, there's nothing wrong with your disk, but if it says About To Fail, you should back up your data immediately and replace

19

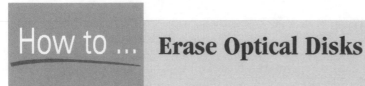

How to ...   Erase Optical Disks

If your Mac has a CD or DVD writer, you can choose from two types of media: CD-Rs and DVD-Rs. These are writable discs that you can only write to once, while CD-RWs and DVD-RWs are rewritable discs, that you can use many times.

But to record again to a CD-RW or DVD-RW, you first must erase it. To do this in Mac OS X, use Disk Utility.

Insert your CD-RW or DVD-RW and open Disk Utility. Select the optical disc in the left column, and then click the Erase tab. Click Erase to erase the disc. If you check Quick Erase, only the disc's directory is erased. Though this process is much faster, it doesn't write zeros to the disc, meaning that someone could eventually recover your previous files with special software. But for most uses, Quick Erase is fine.

the disk. This means that the disk will fail very soon. S.M.A.R.T. is only available for internal drives; external FireWire and USB hard drives will show S.M.A.R.T. status as "Not Supported."

Back Up Your Files

When it comes to maintenance, nothing is more important than regularly backing up your files. One should not ask the question: Will I lose data? The question you should ask is this: When will I lose data? Because, no matter what you do, or how careful you are, this will happen to you some day.

There are many ways you can lose data:

- Programs crash occasionally, and this can corrupt files, making it impossible for you to access their data.

- You can have a power outage or lightning can strike your home or its surroundings causing a power surge. You may lose the files you were working on at the time, and this may also damage your hard disk (not to mention some or all of your files).

TIP *One of the best investments you can make to protect your Mac is
a surge protector, or, even better, a UPS, or uninterruptible power supply.
A surge protector acts as a filter, keeping electrical current steady if there
is too much; this protects against lightning and shorts. A UPS is like a big
battery that gives you extra time in the case of a power outage. In most
cases, a UPS gives you 10 to 15 minutes of power, which is enough to save
your files and shut down your Mac correctly. Most UPS devices also have
surge protectors built in.*

- Hard disk crashes or other hardware problems can affect your files.

- If you get a virus, your files could be damaged. (See Chapter 17 for more
  on antivirus software.)

- You may lose your Mac, or it may get stolen. If you don't have a backup,
  you'll lose all your files.

- You may accidentally erase one or more files. While some of the disk
  maintenance programs presented in this chapter can help recover deleted
  files, you still may not be able to retrieve everything.

I may sound paranoid, but I have lost data. Since that happened—about ten
years ago—I have never lost data again, because I regularly back up my data in
several locations.

What to Back Up

With Mac OS X, it's pretty easy to know what to back up. If you follow Apple's
"guidelines" and use the subfolders within your home folder (see Chapter 7), all
you need to do is back up your home folder. However, if you store music, pictures,
and movies there, this folder may contain a lot of data. One way to back up your
files is to regularly back up your Documents folder, which contains files that you
create and save, and also back up any other folders that contain irreplaceable data.
But if you have digital music files in your Music folder, you don't need to back
that up often; you can always make the music files again from your original CDs.

CAUTION   *If you purchase digital music files from the iTunes Music Store, you should
make a backup immediately because you cannot download the files again
if you lose them. However, if you purchase audio books from Audible.com,
you can download any files you have purchased again at a later date.*

19

Your Pictures folder may contain huge amounts of data, but it's very possible that you don't have any other copies of your photos. If you take a lot of digital photos, think of backing them up often, and even to multiple destinations. If you back up your photos to CDs or DVDs, you could lose these discs, or they could get scratched.

CAUTION *CDs and DVDs are not permanent storage media, as librarians and archivists have discovered. Originally touted as being long-term storage solutions, it has turned out that this is not the case. The life span of optical discs depends on many factors: their type, manufacture, storage conditions, and more; but it is safe to assume that they will degrade over time. Think of dating any backups you make, especially photos that are irreplaceable, and making copies of these backups every few years.*

Your Movies folder, if you work with digital video, offers the same problems, except their size is much bigger. You'll find that you can't store much digital video on CD-ROMs, and DVDs are the best solution.

The Library folder in your home folder is relatively important, because it contains preference and setting files for all your applications, as well as your mailboxes if you're using Apple's Mail. If you lose data or have to reformat your hard disk, restoring this folder can save you a lot of time and prevent you from having to reset all your preferences.

Where to Back Up Your Files

Depending on the amount of files you have to back up, you can use a variety of different media. Here's a list of what you can use, with the pros and cons for each type of media:

- **CD-ROMs**   CD-ROMs are easy to use and let you back up 650 or 700 megabytes of data. The advantage is that they are relatively cheap, but you can only use them once (unless you use CD-RWs, or rewritable CD-ROMs).

- **DVD-ROMs**   These are like CDs, only bigger. If your Mac has a built-in SuperDrive, which is a DVD writer, you can use DVD-R or rewritable DVD-RW discs. These give you more than 4GB of storage, and new dual-layer DVDs give you twice that.

■ **External hard disks**   These are very convenient for regular and frequent backups. You can quickly copy data to a FireWire hard disk and carry it from home to office. They are more expensive than using CD-ROMs, though, but offer much more space and are faster to work with. This is the best solution for everyday backups.

■ **Your iPod**   If you have an iPod, you can copy files to it for temporary backups. The iPod is not designed to be a backup device, but it is nothing more than a small, portable hard disk, with a digital music decoder, amplifier, display, and operating system.

■ **Your iDisk**   If you have a .Mac subscription, you can back up files to your iDisk. Apple's Backup application (see the next section) can handle this automatically. But copying to an iDisk can be slow, and if you don't have an active Internet connection, you can neither back up your files nor access your backups. iDisks are good for backing up small amounts of data, but with only 100MB included with your .Mac subscription, you'll quickly run out of space.

■ **Zip disks**   If you have small amounts of data you need to back up regularly, Zip disks and a Zip drive are a good solution. With capacities of 100, 250, or 750 megabytes, they are great for small backups, but it is pretty slow to copy to them. Other types of removable media exist as well, in a variety of sizes and forms.

■ **USB key drives**   These small devices, about the size of a keychain, generally have capacities ranging from 256MB to 1GB; larger models are also available, though they are expensive. They are easy to use—just plug them into a USB port—and easy to carry around. But their limited capacity makes them practical only for small backups. An iPod shuffle can also work like a USB key drive.

■ **Another computer**   If your Mac is on a network, or if you have a portable and a desktop Mac, you can back up your data from one computer to another. Using network backups is common in companies, but you can do it if you have a home network as well.

One of the best solutions is to regularly back up important files every day to smaller media— a Zip cartridge or USB key drive—and do less frequent backups to larger media, such as CD-ROMs or an external hard disk. Your iDisk, if you have one, is an excellent solution for daily backups as well, especially since Mac OS X can automatically copy your files from your Mac to your iDisk. (See Chapter 11 for more on using your iDisk.)

19

Did I remind you to back up your files?

Backup Software

There are several applications you can use to back up your files, and the one you choose depends on how many files you have to back up, how often you back them up, and what type of media you use. Backup applications range from simple programs designed to back up a single user's files to powerful programs that can back up data from several computers over a network.

If you have a .Mac subscription, you can download Apple's Backup application. (See Figure 19-7.) This program lets you select different types of files and back them up to your iDisk, or to a CD or DVD, as well as to an external FireWire hard disk, an iPod, or a network volume.

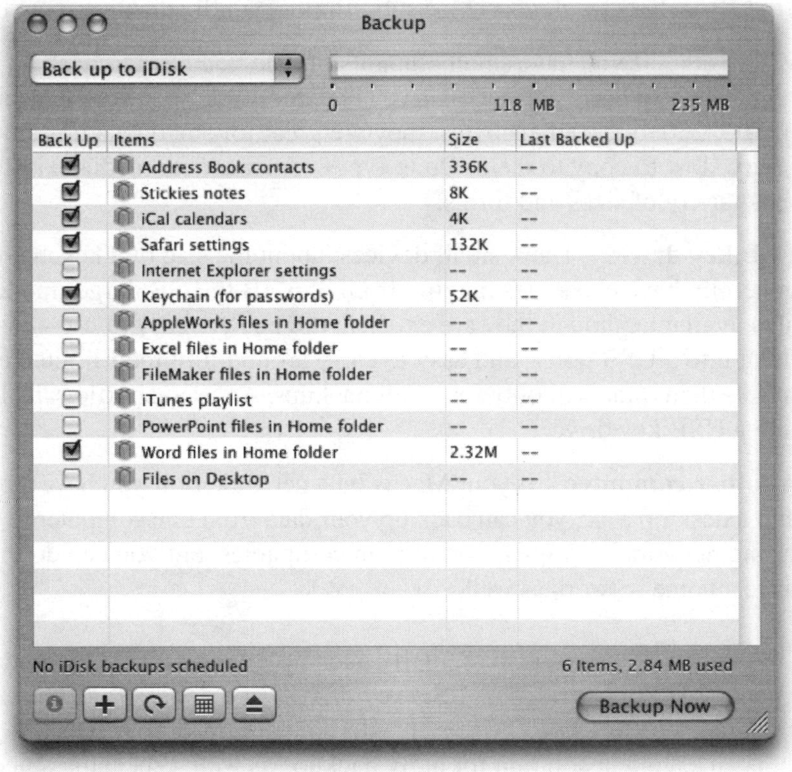

Back Up	Items	Size	Last Backed Up
☑	Address Book contacts	336K	--
☑	Stickies notes	8K	--
☑	iCal calendars	4K	--
☑	Safari settings	132K	--
☐	Internet Explorer settings	--	--
☑	Keychain (for passwords)	52K	--
☐	AppleWorks files in Home folder	--	--
☐	Excel files in Home folder	--	--
☐	FileMaker files in Home folder	--	--
☐	iTunes playlist	--	--
☐	PowerPoint files in Home folder	--	--
☑	Word files in Home folder	2.32M	--
☐	Files on Desktop	--	--

Back up to iDisk — 0 — 118 MB — 235 MB

No iDisk backups scheduled   6 Items, 2.84 MB used   Backup Now

FIGURE 19-7   Apple's Backup application lets you choose specific types of files to back up.

Backup displays sets of specific types of files that you can select for backing up by checking their check boxes. In Figure 19-7, you can see that six items are checked: these include Address Book Contacts, Safari Settings, Keychain, Word Files In Home Folder, and more. You can add items to this list by clicking the plus (+) button and selecting them, and if you choose an item in the list and click the info button, a drawer displays showing the item's contents, where you can check and uncheck individual files.

Select the type of backup you want to run from the pop-up menu at the top of the Backup window: you can choose from your iDisk (as long as you have enough room to back up your selected data), a CD or DVD, or a Drive (an external FireWire hard disk or a partition on your internal drive). To back up data to an iPod or a network volume, select Back Up To Drive and select the iPod or network volume you want to use.

To back up your files, click Backup Now. This will take a few minutes, depending on where you are backing up your data (your iDisk is generally slower than any other location) and how much data you are backing up. If you back up to a CD or DVD, you'll be prompted to insert a blank disc in your drive.

Backup can also run automatically. Click the Schedule button to see the Schedule sheet.

You can choose to back up your files automatically either daily, at a given time, or weekly, on a given day and time.

Make sure your Mac is on and logged in at the time you set for your automatic backup, and, if you are backing up to an external drive or network volume, that it is mounted. If your Mac is not on, or you're not logged in, the backup won't run until the next scheduled time.

Another excellent backup program is Intego's Personal Backup (www.intego.com). This program not only backs up and restores files, but it also synchronizes files with another volume (such as a desktop Mac and an iBook or PowerBook) and clones your Mac OS X startup volume. Cloning makes a mirror-image backup of your startup volume on another disk or partition. If you have problems or disk corruption, you can start up from this volume without having to reinstall Mac OS X. Once you clone your startup volume, you can update this clone by running the same backup script again; any new or changed files are copied to the backup.

Intego Personal Backup is easy to use. Just drag a source and a destination to the program's window and click Backup. (See Figure 19-8.)

The first time you run the backup, all your files are copied. The next time you back up your files, only new or changed items are copied, so subsequent backups are much quicker. You can also create backup scripts to run backups automatically, and the application offers many options for filtering and excluding files. One advantage over Apple's Backup is that if your Mac is off when you had set a backup script to run, Personal Backup runs the script the next time you turn your Mac on.

One other backup program is Retrospect (www.dantz.com). With several versions available for single computers, small businesses, and larger networks, as well as Windows versions, this program offers the widest range of backup possibilities for users working on a network. You can back up all the computers on a network—Macs, or computers running Windows or Linux—manually or automatically, to a single server or volume.

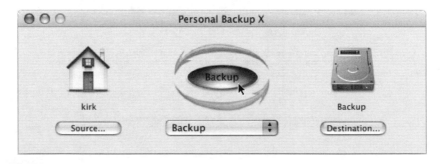

FIGURE 19-8   Making a simple backup with Intego Personal Backup

How to ...   **Back Up Your Digital Music Files**

In Chapter 16, you saw how to work with iTunes, which is your main program for organizing and controlling digital music files. While you may not need to back up all your digital music files—especially since you can always encode your CDs again if you ever lose their digital files—you'll need to back up any music you purchase from the iTunes Music Store.

It's easy to back up your entire library, or any selected playlist, by burning the music files to CDs or DVDs. You can create a playlist from your entire library by selecting all its songs and then choosing File | New Playlist From Selection. To burn these digital music files to a CD or DVD, make sure you have checked Data CD in the Burning pane of the iTunes preferences. Click the Burn button, and your Mac will ask you to insert a CD or DVD. After the first disc is burned, it will eject and you'll be asked to enter as many more discs as necessary to back up all your files.

You can continue in this manner, making incremental backups of any files you have added after this date. Right after you burn your backup, change the date to the current date; then, on your next backup, the same smart playlist only shows songs added after that date. Select the smart playlist, click the Burn button, and proceed with your backup. This time, only those files that you didn't back up the first time are burned to CDs. You can repeat this procedure for each backup, and each time the playlist will only contain songs you haven't yet backed up.

If you ever lose the data on your Mac, just copy these files back into your iTunes Music folder.

Chapter 20

Get More Help for Mac OS X

How to...

- Get help with your Mac's online help
- Get help with Sherlock
- Use Apple's web site to get help
- Use great web sites and magazines to learn more about your Mac

While you can get up and running with Mac OS X quickly, thanks to the intuitive nature of its interface, no operating system is simple. You'll need to get help to delve deeper into Mac OS X. This book covers much of what you'll need to do, but your Mac has an astounding range of functions and possibilities. It is important to know where and how to get help when you have a question or a problem.

In addition to using Mac OS X, you'll work with a variety of third-party applications. Most of these applications come with built-in help systems or work with Apple's help system. In addition, many software vendors offer comprehensive support pages and knowledge bases on their web sites.

You can get additional help in many places: from the Mac OS X online help, built into the operating system; from help systems in other applications; using Sherlock, Apple's web services application; from Apple's web site; and from other web sites dedicated to Mac OS X.

In this chapter, I'll show you how to use the Mac OS X online help, how to use help in different applications, how to use Sherlock to get help, and how to use Apple's support pages on its web site. I'll also tell you about some of my favorite web sites, where you can learn more about your Mac and keep up-to-date on the latest news surrounding it.

Use the Mac OS X Online Help

Mac OS X comes with an extensive online help system that offers assistance for both Mac OS X and its included applications. This help system uses an open architecture, so other programs can add their own help files. When this is the case, you can use the Mac OS X Help Viewer to get help for these applications.

You can access Mac OS X help by choosing Help | Mac Help from the Finder, or by pressing ⌘-?. If you are working in an application, the same

Help menu is always visible, but selecting it gives you access to help for that application, via either the Help Viewer or a special help tool included with the application.

NOTE   *While many third-party software vendors create help files that work with Apple's Help Viewer, some of the largest companies do not: this is the case for Microsoft, Adobe, and many others. When you want to get help for these applications, you need to use these companies' proprietary help systems, which work differently than the Mac OS X Help Viewer. I'll look at a couple of these later in this chapter.*

The Mac OS X help system uses an application called Help Viewer (see Figure 20-1). This application works like a web browser, displaying pages with text and links. Just click a link to go to another page.

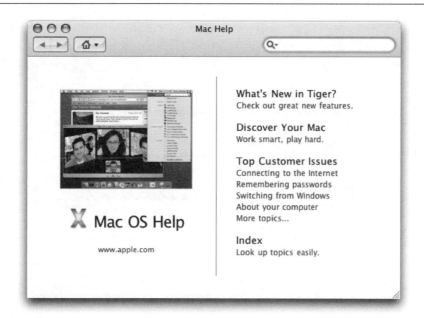

FIGURE 20-1   The Help Viewer application showing the main page for Mac OS X help

The main page the Help Viewer displays (shown in Figure 20-1) contains two sections. At the left is a logo with a clickable link to the Apple web site. At the right are several main headings:

■ **What's New in Tiger?**   This gives you an overview of new features in Mac OS X 10.4 as compared to the previous version, 10.3, or Panther.

■ **Discover Your Mac**   This takes you to a section where some basic Mac OS X tasks are explained.

■ **Top Customer Issues**   This section, and its subsections, focuses on the main questions users have about Mac OS X.

■ **Index**   You can click this link to go to an index, and then click a letter to see the terms that are indexed.

When you click any of these links, you'll find a page with further links to different sections.

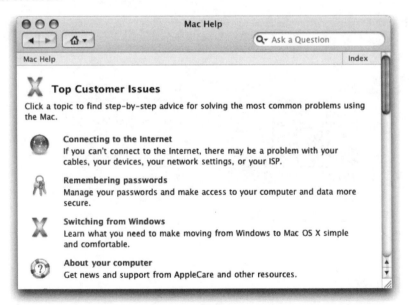

These pages lead you to other information. Some of them have general topics, such as in the preceding example, where you can find out how to connect to the Internet or get some tips if you've switched to Mac OS X from Windows. Other pages go to information on carrying out a specific task.

If you click one of these links, you'll see further information. For example, click the Connecting To The Internet link shown in the preceding image and you'll see a page that tells you how to use Network Diagnostics to check your connection, how to verify that your cables are connected, and more.

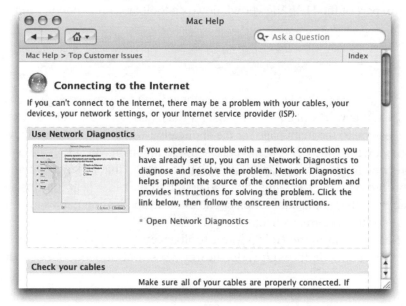

Clicking one of these links takes you to information on carrying out a specific task or, in some cases, opens a program for you. You'll find both instructions and troubleshooting information.

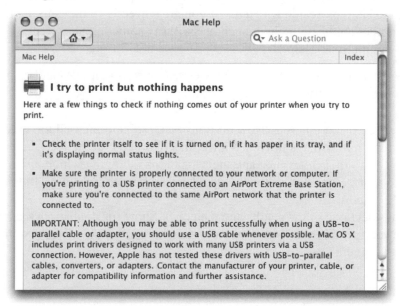

In the preceding illustration, you can see a help page telling you how to check your printer if you are having trouble printing files.

The top part of the Help Viewer window is a toolbar with two icons and a Search field.

The two arrow buttons let you move backward and forward through pages you've already seen; this works like a web browser's Back and Forward buttons. The Home button takes you to the main page for the application whose help you are viewing. If you are viewing Mac OS X help, it takes you to the main Mac OS X help page. If you are viewing help for an application, it takes you to that program's main help page. This button is also a menu; click and hold it to see other help files installed on your Mac, for other applications. Select one of these application names to go to the main page for that program's help.

The Search field in the Help Viewer toolbar lets you look for keywords in all the help files available through Help Viewer. To search in Help Viewer, do the following:

1. Click in the field that says Ask A Question.

2. Enter a question or a couple of keywords.

3. Click the magnifying glass to access its pop-up menu and select Search Mac Help or Search All Help. (If you are currently in the help file for another application, the first choice will say something different, such as Search iTunes Help.)

4. Press RETURN or ENTER. Help Viewer searches its help files and displays a list of responses. (See Figure 20-2.)

In Figure 20-2, I entered "How do I burn a CD?" and pressed RETURN. The window that displays in Help Viewer has two parts: at the top is a list of responses, with their relevance and their locations (showing which application they are about). Click one of these responses and help text displays in the bottom part of the window.

If you select one of the results and then click Show (or double-click a result), Help Viewer opens a page in its window giving more information about your search, as shown in Figure 20-3.

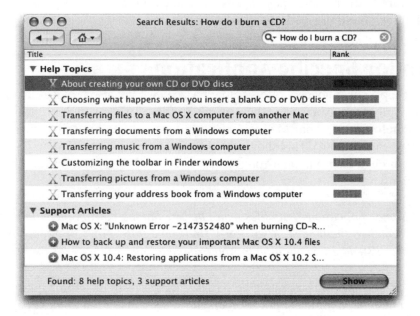

FIGURE 20-2   Help Viewer provides answers to questions you enter in its Search field.

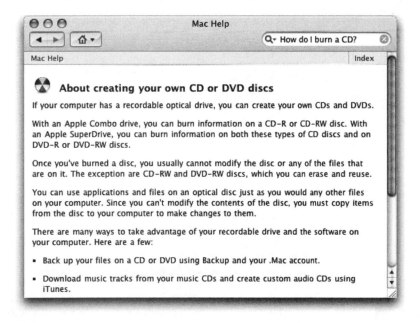

FIGURE 20-3   You can print out any of the help pages by selecting File | Print.

20

To return to the previous page at any time and see the results of your search, click the Back button in the Help Viewer toolbar.

Get Help for Specific Applications

Apple's Help Viewer not only offers help for Mac OS X but also provides an interface that other programs can use for their own help files. To see which programs have installed help files on your Mac, click and hold the Home button, as mentioned earlier (see Figure 20-4). This shows the different help files installed on your Mac, available through Help Viewer. (You can also select the Library menu to see the same information.)

NOTE   *Some applications' help files won't be listed in the Library menu until you've launched them once. Also, you'll find some third-party applications' help files listed here in addition to Apple applications.*

To look at a specific program's help files, select it from the Home button menu. The main help page for the application displays (see illustration on next page).

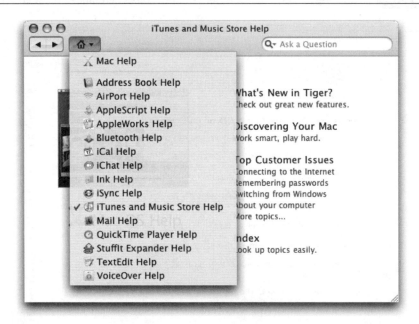

FIGURE 20-4   Help Viewer's Home button menu shows the help files available for other applications.

In this example, the iTunes and Music Store Help page offers four links: Contents (a table of contents with clickable links), What's New in iTunes? (new features in the latest version), Learn About iTunes (an overview of the program's main functions), and Solving Problems (troubleshooting information). There is also a link below the title, to the left; this takes you to the iTunes web site in your browser. Most of Apple's applications have help files that are set up like this, though many of them don't have a specific web site link.

Some applications use their own help systems, and these are always accessible from their Help menus. For example, if you select Help | Word Help Contents when in Microsoft Word, this application's help opens.

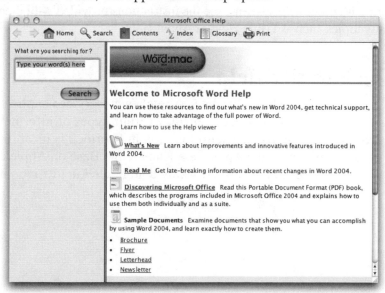

20

Most third-party applications' help systems work similar to Apple's, with a main page and clickable links to go to specific topics. In addition, they generally offer a search function. In the Word help shown in the preceding illustration, click the Search button and then type the text you want to search for in the search field. Click Search, and several topics display in the left-hand column below the search field.

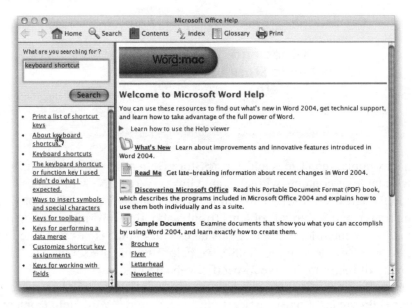

Click one of these links to display its help page.

To work with other help systems, see the instructions provided with them. These are generally topics such as Using Help or About Help.

Use Sherlock to Get Help

In Chapter 10, I told you about Sherlock, Apple's web services application. This program serves as an interface to display certain types of information available from web servers. One useful function in Sherlock is its ability to search for information in the AppleCare Knowledge Base on Apple's support web site. You can launch Sherlock by double-clicking its icon in the Applications folder.

To get help using Sherlock, click the AppleCare icon on the Sherlock toolbar.

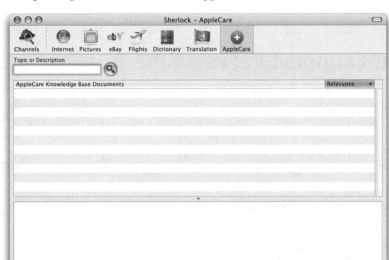

The AppleCare search page opens. Enter a question or a few keywords in the search field at the top of the window, and then press RETURN or ENTER, or click the green magnifying glass icon. Sherlock displays results in the top part of its window.

Click the name of one of the Knowledge Base documents in the top part of the window; the document displays in the bottom section.

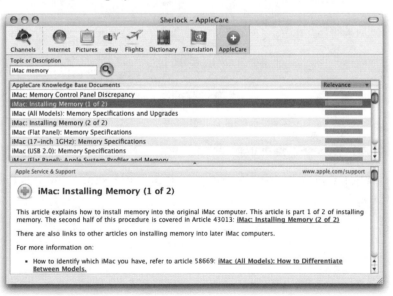

If you want to save this document to read later, you can print it by selecting File | Print.

Use Apple's Support Pages on the Web

Apple provides an extensive support section on its web site: it contains thousands of help documents, discussion forums, links to download updates, and much more. You can access this web site by typing **www.info.apple.com** in your web browser.

> NOTE   *You can also get specific help for Apple's .Mac service by going to www.mac.com and clicking the Support link.*

The main page of Apple's support site provides many links and search possibilities.

(This illustration represents Apple's support page at press time, but it is liable to change.)

Here are some of the sections available from this page:

■ **Support site sections**   At the top of the page, just beneath the Support tab, are clickable links to several sections of this site: Advanced Search (a page that guides you as you search for information), Downloads (links to updates and applications), Manuals (manuals for all Mac hardware), Specifications (detailed specifications of all Mac models), Discussions (technical support discussion forums), Training (information on Apple training and certification), and Products & Services.

■ **Search**   To get help on a specific subject, enter a question or a few keywords in this section. You can refine your search by choosing a part of the web site to search from the pop-up menu: Articles, Downloads, Manuals, or Discussions.

■ **What's New**   Some of the latest support information is highlighted here.

■ **Product Support**   You can choose a specific product from the pop-up menus to go to a support page for that product.

■ **Recent Software Updates**   This section always contains the latest system updates and application downloads for your Mac, with the newest downloads at the top of the list.

Follow any of the links to go to another part of the web site or to explore additional support options.

Apple offers AppleCare support contracts that extend your Mac's guarantee and support to three years. While Macs are well-built computers, your mileage may vary. I've bought AppleCare contracts for all my Macs in the past few years since I moved to a village hours away from any Mac dealer. I've had problems, and AppleCare has been very responsive in repairing them, both onsite and after shipping a portable Mac to the service center. Check the conditions to see whether AppleCare offers onsite service where you live.

Useful Mac Web Sites

With the amount of computer information available on the Internet, it should come as no surprise that there are hundreds of web sites that focus on the Macintosh. The problem with finding information about the Mac is one of quality, not quantity. Macintosh web sites range from amateur weblogs to huge commercial or advertising-supported sites, with every possibility in between. The following sites represent the best of the Macintosh Web and are sites that I use regularly.

General Macintosh Information and News

If there were just one Mac web site to recommend, it would have to be TidBITS (www.tidbits.com). This free weekly publication, available on the Web or by e-mail, is one of the most venerable Macintosh publications, with its first issue dating back to April 1990. (See Figure 20-5.)

I discovered TidBITS shortly after I bought my first Mac in 1991. At the time, the text version of this weekly publication was distributed on floppy disks included

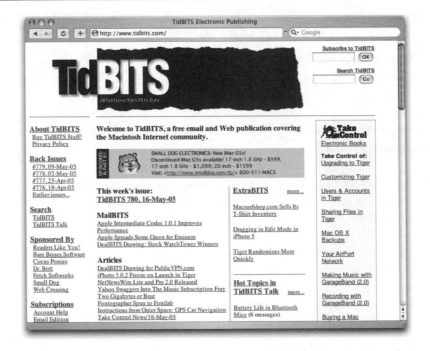

FIGURE 20-5   The TidBITS web site showing the May 16, 2005 issue

with a Mac magazine. I have been reading it ever since and am proud to be a regular contributor to this excellent publication.

TidBITS issues generally have a few news briefs and two or three longer articles covering such subjects as software reviews, tutorials, book reviews and articles on the Internet, Macintosh hardware, and much more. TidBITS publisher, Adam Engst, is regularly voted one of the most influential people in the Macintosh world thanks to the breadth and seriousness of TidBITS.

You can view TidBITS on the Web, or you can go to the TidBITS web site and subscribe to the free e-mail edition. You won't regret it.

Macintosh Magazines

Several Macintosh magazines have web sites that offer additional and complementary content to their print versions. Full of news and reviews, these magazine sites offer archives that allow you to search for articles about specific applications or hardware, and help you make comparisons when you are shopping for software or accessories for your Mac.

- ■ *Macworld* (**www.macworld.com**)   This is the oldest Mac magazine of them all, and its web site is chock full of reviews and tests. You can search these archives and read articles taken from the print edition, as well as read news available only on the web site. I'm a regular contributor to *Macworld* magazine.

- ■ *MacAddict* (**www.macaddict.com**)   *MacAddict* is a more iconoclastic magazine, with an in-your-face style. You can read all the magazine's reviews online and search its past reviews. Its home page also features the latest Mac news.

- ■ *MacHome* (**www.machome.com**)   Designed for home Mac users, this print magazine focuses more on the type of hardware and software that these users need, devoting a lot of coverage to games and other home-oriented products.

- ■ **About This Particular Macintosh (www.atpm.com)**   This e-zine is a monthly web-only magazine, available both on the Web and as a downloadable PDF file. Written by Mac users for Mac users, it offers a fine range of articles about software, hardware, and books.

Macintosh Troubleshooting Sites

In addition to using Apple's support web site (see earlier in this chapter), you can take advantage of many web sites dedicated to Macintosh troubleshooting. Most of these sites offer general troubleshooting information and forums where users can ask questions and share their experiences.

- **MacOSXHints (www.macosxhints.com)** This site is full of hints and tips for going the distance with your Mac. While it is geared more toward power users, there are many useful hints for beginners as well. The site also has excellent forums where users can ask questions and share their experiences.

- **MacInTouch (www.macintouch.com)** Created in 1994, MacInTouch is one of the premier troubleshooting sites for Mac. With timely information about Mac OS X problems, and information about new and updated software and hardware, this site provides invaluable resources for Mac users in a jam. It invites reader feedback and publishes long threads of comments on a wide variety of Mac troubleshooting issues. It is one of the first to react to problems caused by updates or new products.

- **MacFixit (www.macfixit.com)** MacFixit provides thorough coverage of all Mac hardware and software issues and offers in-depth articles and information on new and updated software and hardware. Part commercial and part free, MacFixit also has a forum section—one of the best for Mac troubleshooting—where you can ask questions and offer help.

Other Web Sites

I can't complete this chapter without a couple of shameless plugs: one about a web site I write for regularly, and another for my own site.

- **iLounge (www.ilounge.com)** If you have an iPod and want to learn all about the iPod and iTunes, discover iPod accessories, or get in touch with other iPod users, iLounge (formerly iPodlounge) is the site to visit. It is the most complete site about the iPod and has reviews of just about every new iPod accessory. I'm a contributing editor at iLounge.

- **Kirkville (www.mcelhearn.com)** My web site, Kirkville, contains information on Macs, iPods, music, books, and more. I opine about a variety of subjects and provide information about my books, among other things.

Macintosh Software Sites

In Chapter 19, I told you how important it is to keep both your Mac OS X software and your applications up-to-date. There are a few important web sites to check to find if updates are available for your software.

While it's best to use the Mac OS X Software Update function (see Chapter 19), you can also check Apple's web site to find the latest updates. Check the Downloads section at www.apple.com/software/ for the latest updates and new applications for Mac OS X.

You can find other software at www.apple.com/downloads/macosx/. The page is easily accessed by selecting the Apple Menu | Mac OS X Software, which opens a new web page at this address in your browser.

This page contains downloads of free software, shareware, demo versions of commercial software, and updates. You can click any of the category links in the Categories section to see what's new, and you can search by entering keywords in the Search Downloads field. You'll find special links for Dashboard widgets, Automator actions, and Spotlight plug-ins.

Other sites for finding Mac software include

■ **MacUpdate (www.macupdate.com)**   This site lists dozens of updates each day to commercial, shareware, and freeware programs. If you sign up as a member (for free), you can create your own watch list for programs you use, and the site will send you e-mail whenever these programs are updated. They also offer free newsletters listing new and updated programs.

■ **VersionTracker (www.versiontracker.com)**   VersionTracker is similar to MacUpdate, with lists of new and updated software, newsletters, and more. Access to the site is free, but a commercial version offers additional features.

Macintosh Mailing Lists

Mailing lists are discussion groups that work by e-mail. Each subscriber receives all the messages posted to the list and can send and receive questions and comments. While mailing lists are invaluable in the amount of information they provide and the number of users who offer solutions to problems, they can flood your Inbox. If you're hesitant about getting a lot of e-mail, you are better off avoiding them. However, mailing lists create a community of users who share their experiences with others in a true spirit of altruism.

There are many mailing lists dedicated to the Mac, and especially Mac OS X, and one site features a couple of dozen lists covering a variety of subjects: The Macintosh Guy (www.themacintoshguy.com/lists). Some lists are for specific applications and uses (iTunes, audio, business), and others are more general, such as the half-dozen lists dedicated to Mac OS X (lists for newbies and users, and lists about applications, Unix on Mac OS X, and so on).

Finally, the TidBITS-Talk mailing list, run by TidBITS publisher Adam Engst (www.tidbits.com), is a moderated mailing list that offers discussions about articles published in TidBITS as well as other general issues about the Mac.

Index

Know How

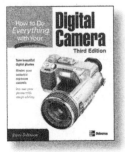

How to Do Everything with Your Digital Camera
Third Edition
ISBN: 0-07-223081-9

How to Do Everything with Adobe Acrobat 7.0
ISBN: 0-07-225788-1

How to Do Everything with Photoshop CS
ISBN: 0-07-223143-2
4-color

How to Do Everything with Windows XP
Third Edition
ISBN: 0-07-225953-1

How to Do Everything with eBay
ISBN: 0-07-225426-2

How to Do Everything with Your eBay Business
Second Edition
0-07-226164-1

How to Do Everything with Your Palm Handheld
Fifth Edition
ISBN: 0-07-225870-5

How to Do Everything with Your iPod & iPod mini
Second Edition
ISBN: 0-07-225452-1

How to Do Everything with Your iMac
4th Edition
ISBN: 0-07-223188-2

How to Do Everything with Your iPAQ Pocket PC
Second Edition
ISBN: 0-07-222950-0

O S B O R N E   D E L I V E R S   R E S U L T S !

McGraw Hill **Osborne**
www.osborne.com